Household Food Consumption, Women's Asset and Food Policy in Indonesia

DEVELOPMENT ECONOMICS AND POLICY

Series edited by Franz Heidhues, Joachim von Braun and Manfred Zeller

Vol. 69

Household Food Consumption, Women's Asset and Food Policy in Indonesia

Evita Hanie Pangaribowo

LIBRARY OF CONGRESS
WITHDRAWN
ADDITIONAL
SERVICE COPY

Bibliographic Information published by the Deutsche Nationalbibliothek
The Deutsche Nationalbibliothek lists this publication in the Deutsche Nationalbibliografie; detailed bibliographic data is available in the internet at http://dnb.d-nb.de.

Zugl.: Bonn, Univ., Diss., 2012

Printed with financial support of the German Academic Exchange Service (DAAD)

Picture on the cover with kind permission of Djaka Dwiandi

Library of Congress Cataloging-in-Publication Data

Pangaribowo, Evita Hanie, 1979- author.
  Household food consumption, women's asset and food policy in Indonesia / Evita Hanie Pangaribowo.
    pages cm
  Summary in German.
  Originally presented as the author's thesis (doctoral)—Universität Bonn, 2012.
  Includes bibliographical references.
  Summary: „Addresses the issue of household food consumption, its relation to gender and to food policy in Indonesia. Using econometric analyses of the Indonesian Family Life Survey, the study reveals that food expenditure patterns, particularly those of the poor households, warrant food policy attention. The poor households spent more on alcohol and tobacco goods when their income increased. The impact evaluation of the ‚Rice for the Poor' program reveals that the program enabled beneficiaries to increase expenditures on nutrient-rich, animal source foods; however, unintended program impacts also exist. The analysis of gender roles indicates that resource distribution and power relations within households are important considerations in the development of food policy"— Provided by publisher.
  ISBN 978-3-631-64004-3
  1. Food consumption—Indonesia. 2. Nutrition surveys—Indonesia. 3. Women—Nutrition—Indonesia. 4. Nutrition policy—Indonesia. I. Title.
  TX360.I5P36 2013
  338.1'91598—dc23
                                                                            2013007561

D 5
ISSN 0948-1338
ISBN 978-3-631-64004-3
© Peter Lang GmbH
Internationaler Verlag der Wissenschaften
Frankfurt am Main 2013
All rights reserved.
PL Academic Research is an Imprint of Peter Lang GmbH

All parts of this publication are protected by copyright. Any utilisation outside the strict limits of the copyright law, without the permission of the publisher, is forbidden and liable to prosecution. This applies in particular to reproductions, translations, microfilming, and storage and processing in electronic retrieval systems.

www.peterlang.de

Acknowledgments

Alhamdulillahirabbil'alamin. All praise and thanks are due purely to Allah, the Most Merciful, the Most Gracious who has granted me opportunity to complete this dissertation and made all of these things happen.

This dissertation is the product of joint efforts by many individuals to whom I owe my sincere gratitude. First I would like to thank my supervisor, Professor Joachim von Braun, who provided very kind support and guidance throughout my research. I have been very fortunate to be one of his students, through which I have learned about scholarly work and most importantly that research requires patience with others who support the research process. I would also like to thank my second supervisor, Professor Michael-Burkhard Piorkowsky, for his useful comments and suggestions. I sincerely acknowledge the scholarship from German Academic Exchange Service (DAAD) that has made my PhD study possible.

I am also indebted to my colleagues at ZEF, especially batch 2008, for their counsel and companionship during my PhD study. Among them I would like to personally thank Juliet Akello, Grace Villamor, Chiachi Wu, Erna Macusi and Liu Dan, from whom I received well rounded support during my academic life. I owe many thanks to the administrative services and support I received from Mrs. Rosemarie Zabel. Dr. Guenther Manske also provided considerable support, particularly in facilitating funding from the Dr. Hermann Eiselen Doctoral Program of the Foundation fiat panis for my conference travel grants. I also thank Volker Merx of the ZEF Library for being the best references support, and Ludger Hammer and Anja Köhler for their prompt responses on IT matters during my time at ZEF. I am greatly indebted to Dr. Brian Poi from StataCorp for answering my numerous questions about NLSURQUAIDS and the programming of Stata. Many of the IFLS users have contributed substantially to this study, especially Dr. Elan Satriawan and Dr. Firman Witoelar. Their input regarding the handling of IFLS data and econometrics techniques were very essential. I am also grateful for Dr. Elan Satriawan, my former undergraduate supervisor who continues to be my informal supervisor. The Center for Population and Policy Studies at Gadjah Mada University (CPPS-GMU) and Survey Meter, in collaboration with RAND Corporation, undertook the survey that I relied upon and I acknowledge the invaluable experience of being involved in the IFLS. I also thank my tutor, Dr. Daniel Tsegai for the attentive reading of this study and suggestions on methodological components. Dr. Seid Nuru Ali provided valuable comments at the initial stage of research development. I also thank Dr.

Degnet Abebaw who provided a prompt response on the Stata code in a particular section of one of my chapters. I am highly indebted to Dr. Guido Lütcher for all the support and discussion on statistics and econometrics, and many other topics during the course of my research. I would also like to thank Professor Rudolfo Nayga for the valuable comments on the first empirical chapter when I presented the results at the 5th ICSRC 2011. The second empirical chapter also benefited from input provided at the AAEA 2011 Annual Meeting in Pittsburgh and the FAO Symposium 2012 in Rome. I acknowledge the contribution of Erick Baur with English usage and Alina Paetz and Mikko Bayer for their kind help translating my abstract into German. My gratitude also goes to the Indonesian and Malaysian Moslem Community here in Bonn. They have become my extended family in Bonn. Tante Amina, Galura's second mother here, and her family have helped us solve our daycare needs before we finally managed to get to Kindergarten.

Now it is time to express my very special gratitude to my family and my colleagues back home. I do believe that the continuous support, bottomless love, and prayers from my family were the most essential nourishment that enabled me to finish this study. Bapak and Ibu, to whom I express my sincere gratitude for all those things that I can never ever pay them back for. May Allah grant you with much better ones and have mercy on you in this world and afterlife. To my brother, Umar Pangaribowo, thank you very much for your sincere love and support from home. To my mother-in-law, Mama, I would like to express my gratefulness for all the support and prayer in every phone call, which lifted my motivation when I felt very weak. To all of my extended family, Pakdhe, Budhe, Bulik, Om, cousins and nephews of Projo Soewarno and Harjo Idris, thank you very much for all of your attention and encouragement from home. I am also indebted to my colleagues at the Department of Environmental Geography at Gadjah Mada University. Among them I would like to mention Professor Suratman who serves as the Dean of Faculty of Geography, Drs. Sukamdi, M. Sc, Dr. Aris Marfai, Professor Junun Sartohadi, and many other colleagues whom I cannot mention individually.

At last, none of this would be possible without the support from my husband and daughter. Experiencing this journey with them is indeed life-altering, memorable, and meaningful. My most highest and humble appreciation goes to my husband, Deden Dinar Iskandar. Deden always played a supportive role both at home and at school with his enduring love and bottomless patience. My daughter, Galura, has boosted my spirit and motivated me to finish this PhD. Galura, you are indeed an extraordinary little girl who knows how to cheer up your ever-busy parent. Indeed, this dissertation is not only my achievement, it is theirs too.

Executive Summary

This dissertation examines the nexus between prices and income, the current food security program, intra-household power, and the distribution of household food expenditures in Indonesia, based on econometric analyses of a rich longitudinal dataset provided by the Indonesian Family Life Survey. Food demand behavior of Indonesian households was analyzed using the QUAIDS model which elaborates household characteristics and geographical aspects. The results showed a consistent pattern of expenditure and price elasticity as predicted by demand theory. Indonesian households were price and expenditure responsive, and food expenditure patterns varied across demographic and regional aspects. For the pooled sample, categories such as staple foods, oils, and other food items were necessities whereas vegetables, meat and fish, dairy products, and adult goods categories were all luxuries. Disaggregating by income group, the results show that poorest households demonstrated the highest expenditure elasticity on adult goods, which warrants policy attention. Noneconomic variables such as household size, education, gender, and geographical factors were relevant to household food demand. Education appears to play a key role in human capital development through improved consumption patterns, based on the fact that households with higher education levels exhibited relatively higher expenditures on nutritious food items.

Secondly I evaluated the impacts of an almost universal food security component of the Indonesian Social Safety Net Program that was implemented in response to the economic crisis of the 1990s. The food security effort has provided access to rice at highly subsidized prices for poor households. The matching method combined with difference in difference was used to describe aid recipient households, which were characterized by low quality housing, less education, and location in rural areas and on Java. The program was found to have performance issues related to recipient targeting, such as the fact that some higher income households received benefits from the program. Geographical biases were also evident in the program implementation. Despite concerns about the food security program's performance, it had positive impacts on selected food and nonfood expenditures. In particular, the program enabled beneficiaries to increase expenditures on nutrient-rich, animal origin foods. The program also had a positive impact on health expenditures. Aid-fungibility, or unintended aid impact, was also evident. Extra income resulting from the program appears to have increased expenditures on adult goods (alcohol and tobacco). The relationship between participation in the food security program and subjective well-being was also evaluated. Controlling for income, education, and regional characteristics, program recipients tended to perceive themselves as poorer than nonrecipient households.

The third emphasis of this research was how the role of women was related to the distribution of household expenditures. Resource distribution and decision making within households were found to be important for the direction of policy intervention, particularly in terms of program targeting. A women's share of household assets was used as an indicator of women's autonomy in the household, and was found to have a positive and substantial association with expenditures on richer nutrients foods such as meat, fish, and dairy products. Education expenditures were also positively associated with the women's share of household assets. I also examined the effect of women's social capital on household expenditure distribution. Participation in community-based activities improved women's understanding and the deliberate allocation of household budget resources according to their concerns, and reduced expenditures on items associated with adult male entertainment. This finding highlights the importance of women's roles in the household particularly in determining the distribution of expenditures to improve household welfare. It was found that the design of food subsidy efforts without consideration of household consumption behavior might lead to unintended or detrimental effects. In order to maximize the nutritional benefits of food subsidy programs, companion interventions such as nutrition education should be considered. Program conditionality and specific targeting to women might reduce performance errors and improve nutritional outcomes.

Zusammenfassung

In dieser Dissertation wird der Zusammenhang zwischen Preisen und Einkommen, dem aktuellen Programm für Ernährungssicherheit, der Machtverhältnisse innerhalb der Haushalte sowie der Verteilung der Haushaltsausgaben für Lebensmittel in Indonesien untersucht, basierend auf ökonometrischen Analysen eines umfangreichen Längsschnitt-Datensatzes, der durch die indonesische Familienuntersuchung (Indonesian Family Life Survey) zu Verfügung gestellt wurde. Das Lebensmittelnachfrageverhalten der indonesischen Haushalte wurde mit Hilfe des QUAIDS-Modells analysiert, welches Haushaltseigenschaften und geografische Merkmale berücksichtigt. Die Ergebnisse zeigen ein konsistentes Muster aus Ausgaben- und Preiselastizitäten, das den Vorhersagen gemäß der Nachfragetheorie entspricht. Indonesische Haushalte reagieren sensibel auf Änderungen von Preisen und Ausgaben, während die Ausgaben für Lebensmittel in Abhängigkeit von demografischen und regionalen Merkmalen variieren. Für die Stichprobe wurden beispielsweise Grundnahrungsmittel, Öle und bestimmte andere Nahrungsmittel als lebensnotwendige Güter; Gemüse, Fleisch und Fisch sowie Milchprodukte und Genussmittel wie Tabak und Alkohol hingegen als Luxusgüter betrachtet. Aufgeschlüsselt nach Einkommensgruppen weisen die ärmsten Haushalte die höchsten Ausgabenelastizitätswerte für Genussmittel auf, was in der Ausgestaltung eines entsprechenden Programms dringend berücksichtigt werden sollte. Nichtökonomische Variablen wie Haushaltsgröße, Bildung, Geschlecht und geografische Faktoren haben ebenfalls Einfluss auf die Lebensmittelnachfrage der Haushalte. Bildung erscheint durch ihren positiven Einfluss auf die Konsummuster als entscheidender Faktor für die Schaffung von Humankapital, da Haushalte mit höherem Bildungsniveau tendenziell höhere Ausgaben für nahrhaftere Lebensmittel aufweisen.

Weiterhin wurden die Auswirkungen eines während der Wirtschaftskrise in den 90er Jahren flächendeckend angewandten Instruments der Ernährungssicherheit als Teil des indonesischen Programms für soziale Sicherheit beurteilt. Im Rahmen dieser Maßnahmen wurde Haushalten mit niedrigem Einkommen Zugang zu stark subventioniertem Reis ermöglicht. Mit Hilfe der Matching-Methode in Verbindung mit der „Difference-in-Difference"-Schätzung wurden Haushalte beschrieben, die Beihilfen empfingen und durch niedrige Wohnstandards und Bildungsniveaus sowie ihren Wohnort in ländlichen Gegenden und auf Java charakterisiert sind. Das Programm hatte jedoch mit Problemen hinsichtlich der korrekten Identifizierung der tatsächlich bedürftigen Beihilfenempfänger zu kämpfen, was sich unter anderem darin äußerte, dass auch Haushalte mit höheren Einkommen in den Genuss von Leistungen kamen. Auch zeigten sich geografische Verzerrungen bei der Umsetzung des Programms.

Trotz solcher Bedenken hinsichtlich der Leistungsfähigkeit des Programms zeigten sich positive Auswirkungen auf die Ausgaben für bestimmte Nahrungsmittel und andere Produkte. Insbesondere ermöglichte das Programm den Beihilfeempfängern höhere Ausgaben für nährstoffreichere Lebensmittel tierischen Ursprungs. Ebenso ergaben sich positive Auswirkungen auf die Gesundheitsausgaben, aber auch unbeabsichtigte Nebeneffekte. So scheint das zusätzliche Haushaltseinkommen durch das Programm zu höheren Ausgaben für Alkohol und Tabak geführt zu haben. Weiterhin wurde der Zusammenhang zwischen der Teilnahme in dem Ernährungssicherheitsprogramm und dem subjektiven Wohlbefinden untersucht. Unter Konstanthaltung von Einkommen, Bildung und regionalen Merkmalen zeigte sich eine ärmere subjektive Selbstwahrnehmung der teilnehmenden im Vergleich zu nicht teilnehmenden Haushalten.

Ein dritter Forschungsschwerpunkt dieser Dissertation lag auf der Rolle der Frauen und ihrem Einfluss auf die Verteilung der Haushaltsausgaben. Die Verteilung von Ressourcen und Entscheidungsgewalt innerhalb der Haushalte erwiesen sich als wichtige Faktoren für die Ausgestaltung des Politikinstruments, insbesondere hinsichtlich seiner Zielgruppe. Der Anteil der Frauen am Haushaltsvermögen als Indikator für die Autonomie der Frauen innerhalb der Haushalte zeigte einen starken Zusammenhang mit den Ausgaben für nährstoffreichere Lebensmittel wie Fleisch, Fisch und Milchprodukte. Bildungsausgaben zeigten ebenfalls einen positiven Zusammenhang mit dem Anteil der Frauen am Haushaltsvermögen. Außerdem wurden die Auswirkungen des sozialen Kapitals von Frauen auf die Verteilung der Haushaltsausgaben untersucht. Die Teilnahme an Aktivitäten innerhalb der Gemeinschaft führte zu einer zweckmäßigeren Allokation des Haushaltsbudgets und geringeren Ausgaben für vorwiegend von erwachsenen Männern konsumierten Genussmitteln. Dieses Ergebnis unterstreicht die Rolle der Frauen im Haushalt, insbesondere was die Optimierung der Haushaltsausgaben angeht. Die Ausgestaltung der Nahrungssubventionsinstrumente ohne Berücksichtigung des Konsumverhaltens der Haushalte kann erwiesenermaßen zu unbeabsichtigten oder sogar schädlichen Folgen führen. Um die Ernährung mit Hilfe von Subventionsprogrammen gezielt zu verbessern, bedarf es zusätzlicher Maßnahmen wie z.B. einer Verbesserung der Erziehung im Hinblick auf das Ernährungsverhalten. Strengere Bedingungen für die Teilnahme an solchen

Programmen und eine gezielte Ausrichtung auf Frauen könnten die Schwächen solcher Programme beheben und die Ernährungssitutation entscheidend verbessern.

Table of Content

Acknowledgments V
Executive Summary VII
Zusammenfassung IX
Table of Content XIII
List of Tables XVI
List of Figures XIX
Abbreviations and Acronyms XX
Chapter 1. Introduction 1
1.1. Background 1
1.2. Objectives 4
1.3. Expected Contribution 5
1.4. Structure of Dissertation 6
Chapter 2. Analysis of the Food Demand of Indonesian Household 9
2.1. Introduction 9
2.2. Literature Review 12
2.3. Demand System Models in Empirical Studies 14
    2.3.1. The Linear Expenditure System 14
    2.3.2. Rotterdam Model 15
    2.3.3. The Indirect Translog Model 16
    2.3.4. Almost Ideal Demand System 16
    2.3.5. Quadratic Almost Ideal Demand System 17
    2.3.6. Choice of a Specific Demand System Model for the Estimation Strategy 17
2.4. Empirical Model: Quadratic Almost Ideal Demand System with Demographic Variables 18
2.5. Data and Household Expenditure on Food 20
    2.5.1. Data 20
    2.5.2. Indonesian Household Expenditure on Food 22

2.6. Results and Discussion.. 27
2.6.1. Household Responsiveness to Expenditure and Price Changes 28
2.6.2. The Effect of Domestic Production 34
2.6.3. Household Demographic Characteristics 35
2.6.4. Food Consumption Behavior of the Poorest................................ 37
2.7. The Projection of Food Demand.. 38
2.8. Limitations of the Study.. 40
2.9. Conclusion... 40
Chapter 3 Impact Evaluation of the Food Security Program in Indonesia: Household Level Analysis 43
3.1. Introduction 43
3.2. Brief Overview of Indonesian Food Policy 45
3.3. Rice for the Poor: The Food Security Program in Indonesia............... 47
3.4. Review of Existing Literature on Program Evaluation......................... 49
3.5. Data and Variables 54
3.5.1. Data 54
3.5.2. Dependent Variables.. 55
3.5.3. Explanatory Variables.. 57
3.6. Estimation Strategy 60
3.6.1. Evaluation of Observational Studies 60
3.6.2. Propensity Score Matching.. 62
3.7. Results and Discussion.. 64
3.7.1. Implementation of SSN and The Food Security Program 64
3.7.2. Matching Results 70
3.7.3. Impact on Food and Nonfood Expenditures................................ 72
3.7.4. Program Heterogeneity 74
3.7.5. The Food Security Program and Subjective Well-being............. 78
3.8. Conclusion.. 83

Chapter 4. The Role of Women's Assets and Social Capital on Food and Nonfood Expenditure 85
4.1. Introduction 85
4.2. Theory and Empirical Specification 87
 4.1.1. Unitary Model 87
 4.1.2. Collective Model 88
 4.1.3. Theoretical Framework 88
 4.1.4. Empirical Model Specification 90
4.2. Previous Empirical Studies 91
4.3. Data and Measures of Women's Power 93
 4.3.1. Data and Variables 94
 4.3.2. Operational Definition of Other Control 95
 4.3.3. Women's Asset Ownership 95
 4.3.4. Women's Social Capital 97
4.4. Estimation Results 100
 4.4.1. Characteristics of Households by Asset Type 100
 4.4.2. Household Characteristics and Participation in Local Organization by Women 102
 4.4.3. The Effects of Women's Assets and Social on Household Expenditures 103
4.5. Limitations of the Study 108
4.6. Conclusion 109

Chapter 5. Conclusion and Policy Implications 111

Reference 115

Appendix 135

XV

List of Tables

Table 2.1: Composition of Food Aggregation 23
Table 2.2: Selected Household Characteristics (figures represent mean values) 25
Table 2.3: Share of Food Expenditure across Commodity Groups, by Income Group and Year 27
Table 2.4: Expenditure Elasticity Estimates across Income Groups 29
Table 2.5: Own Price Elasticity Estimates 33
Table 2.6: Marshallian and Hicksian Own Price Elasticity Estimates across Surveys 35
Table 2.7: Expenditure Elasticity of the Poorest Households across Surveys 38
Table 3.1: Household Food Consumption of Post Exposure Year based on IFLS 2000 (in log term) 56
Table 3.2: Difference in Difference of Consumption 57
Table 3.3: Summary Statistics of Household Characteristics in Pre Exposure Year 59
Table 3.4: Distribution of the Food Security Program Based on IFLS Samples 68
Table 3.5: Food Security Targeting Performance by Income and Region 69
Table 3.6: Average Treatment Effect on Food and Nonfood Consumption 74
Table 3.7: Heterogeneous Impact of The Food Security Program 76
Table 3.8: Subjective Well-being by Income Quintiles 79
Table 3.9: Ordered Logit Models of Subjective Well-being 82
Table 4.1: Household Asset Ownership (percentage of total sample) 96
Table 4.2: Reported Household Asset Shares (in percentages) 97
Table 4.3: Women's Participation in Community Organizations 99
Table 4.4: Household Characteristics Based on Asset Types 101

Table 4.5: Household Characteristics According to Women's Participation in Local Activities 103

Table 4.6: The Effects of Women's Asset Shares on Selected Nutrient-Rich Foods, Alcohol and Tobacco Goods, and Nonfood Expenditures 105

Table 4.7: The Effects of Women's Social Capital on Selected Nutrient-Rich Foods, Alcohol and Tobacco Goods, and Nonfood Expenditures 107

Table A2.1: Prices across Surveys 135

Table A2.2: Parameter Estimates for QUAIDS Model (Pooled Sample) 136

Table A2.3: Marshallian Own and Cross-Price Elasticity Estimates 139

Table A2.4: Hicksian Own and Cross Price Elasticity Estimates 140

Table A2.5: Expenditure Elasticity Estimates of Food-Producing and Non-Food-Producing Households 141

Table A2.6: Own Price Elasticity Estimates of Food-Producing and Non-Food-Producing Households 142

Table A2.7: Parameter Estimates for QUAIDS model (Poorest Households) 143

Table A2.8: Marshallian Own and Cross-Price Elasticity Estimates of the Poorest Households 146

Table A2.9: Hicksian Own and Cross-Price Elasticity Estimates of the Poorest Households 147

Table A2.10: Demographic Characteristics 148

Table A3.1: Summary Statistics of Household Characteristics in the Post Exposure Year 152

Table A3.2: Results of the Matching Estimator 154

Table A3.3: Perception on Subjective Well-being (percentages) 156

Table A3.4: Perception on Selected Quality of Life (percentages) 156

Table A3.5: Ordered Logit Models of Food Consumption Perception 157

Table A3.6: Ordered Logit Models of Children Food Consumption Perception 158

Table A4.1: Household Expenditures Based on Women's Social Capital ... 159

Table A4.2: The Effects of Women's Assets on Budget Share of Vegetables, Meat and Fish, Dairy Products, and Alcohol and Tobacco Goods Expenditures ... 160

Table A4.3: The Effects of Women's Assets on Budget Share of Education, Medical, and Nonfood Expenditures ... 162

Table A4.4: The Effects of Women's Shares of Savings on Budget Share of Vegetables, Dairy Products, Alcohol and Tobacco Goods, and Nonfood Expenditures ... 164

Table A4.5: The Effects of Women's Shares of Jewelry on Budget Share of Vegetables, Dairy Products, Alcohol and Tobacco Goods, and Nonfood Expenditures ... 166

Table A4.6: The Effects of Women's Shares of Nonagricultural Land on Budget Share of Vegetables, Dairy Products, Alcohol and Tobacco Goods, and Nonfood Expenditures ... 168

Table A4.7: The Effects of Women's Shares of Livestock on Budget Share of Vegetables, Dairy Products, Alcohol and Tobacco Goods, and Nonfood Expenditures ... 170

Table A4.8: The Effects of Women's Shares of the House on Budget Share of Vegetables, Dairy Products, Alcohol and Tobacco Goods, and Nonfood Expenditures ... 172

Table A4.9: The Effects of Women's Participation in Community Meetings on Budget Share of Vegetables, Dairy Products, Alcohol and Tobacco Goods, and Nonfood Expenditures ... 174

Table A4.10: The Effects of Women's Participation in the PKK on Budget Share of Vegetables, Dairy Products, Alcohol and Tobacco Goods, and Nonfood Expenditures ... 176

Table A4.11: The Effects of Women's Participation in POSYANDU on Budget Share of Vegetables, Dairy Products, Alcohol and Tobacco Goods, and Nonfood Expenditures ... 178

List of Figures

Figure 2.1: Projected Domestic Demand of Selected Food Groups in Indonesia 39

Figure 3.1: Village Participation in Food and Health Card Program 65

Figure 3.2: Village Participation in Community Empowerment and Job Creation Program.. 65

Figure 3.3: Distribution of Food Security, Job Creation, and Community Empowerment Program 66

Figure 3.4: Distribution of Food Security, Health Card, and Village Midwife Program 66

Figure A3.1: Average Rice Distribution of the Food Security Program (in kg) per Household by Province 149

Figure A3.2: Estimated Propensity Score 150

Figure A3.3: Estimated Propensity Score without Health Card Program in the Participation Model 150

Figure A3.4: Distribution of Food Expenditure Change between Health Card Program Participants and Nonparticipants 151

Figure A3.5: Distribution of Non-Food-Expenditure Change between Health Card Program Participants and Nonparticipants 151

Abbreviations and Acronyms

AIDS	Almost Ideal Demand System
ATT	Average Treatment Effect on the Treated
Bappenas	*Badan Perencanaan Pembangunan Nasional* –National Development Planning Agency
BKKBN	*Badan Koordinasi Keluarga Berencana Nasional* – National Family Planning Agency
BULOG	*Badan Urusan Logistik* – National Food Logistic Agency
CCT	Conditional Cash Transfer
DiD	Difference in Difference
EA	Enumeration Area
FAO	Food and Agriculture Organization
GDP	Gross Domestic Products
IFLS	Indonesia Family Life Survey
ITS	Indirect Translog System
KS1	*Keluarga Sejahtera 1* – Prosperous Family 1
KS2	*Keluarga Sejahtera 2* – Prosperous Family 2
KS3	*Keluarga Sejahtera 3* – Prosperous Family 3
LES	Linear Expenditure System
OPK-Beras	*Operasi Pasa Khusus Beras* –Rice Open Market Operation
ORBA	Orde Baru – New Order
PKK	*Pemberdayaan Kesejahteraan Keluarga* – Family Welfare Empowerment Movement
POSYANDU	*Pos Pelayanan Terpadu* – Integrated Community Health Post
PSM	Propensity Score Matching
QUAIDS	Quadratic Almost Ideal Demand System
RASKIN	*Beras Miskin* – Rice for the Poor
SSN	Social Safety Net

SUR	Seemingly Unrelated Regression
SUSENAS	*Survei Sosial Ekonomi Nasional* – National Socio-Economic Household Survey
WHO	World Health Organization

Chapter 1. Introduction

1.1. Background

Food is a basic and fundamental need for everyone in every nation. The human right to food is declared in the UN Universal Declaration of Human Rights which states that "everyone has the rights to a standard of living adequate for the health and well-being of himself and his family, including food" (UN General Assembly 1948). The Universal Declaration on the Eradication of Hunger and malnutrition, adopted in 1974 by the World Food Conference and endorsed by the General resolution 3348 (XXIX) proclaimed that "every man, woman, and child has the inalienable right to be free from hunger and malnutrition in order to develop fully and maintain their physical and mental faculties"[1]. Based on this mandate, the right to food should be ascribed as a primary national agenda. At the global level, the first Millennium Development Goals to halve poverty and hunger are parallel with the mandate. To assure the right to food for everyone, each country should achieve food security. Food security exists when all people at all times have physical and economic access to sufficient food to meet their dietary needs for a productive and healthy life (FAO 1983, Timmer 2000, FAO 2003). Accordingly, food security has become one of the main national agendas in most developing countries (Maxwell 1990, von Braun et al. 1992, Maxwell 1996). It has been widely seen that developing countries have vast food problems ranging from production to distribution (Siamwalla and Valdes 1980). Even when sufficient food is globally available, it does not guarantee that everyone will be free from hunger (Sen 1981). The failure to resolve modern hunger is primarily due to the inability to resolve the way food is distributed among the world's inhabitants (Banerjee and Duflo 2011). The same idea has been previously discussed in Sen's (1981) renowned work, *Poverty and Famine*, which found that food related problems such as undernourishment, hunger, and famine are influenced not only by food production and agricultural activities, but also by entire economies and societies. Sen further mentioned that food problems have been caused not only by scarcity but by institutional failures that lead to poor food distribution.

As in many other developing countries, food is considered one of the most important issues in the economy as well as socio-political debate in Indonesia. Furthermore, food consumption patterns are considered one of the most im-

---

[1] http://www2.ohchr.org/english/law/malnutrition.htm

portant indicators of economic development in a country. The government of Indonesia, through the Food Security Council, has been devoted to large endeavors that address food insecurity. Since the independence of Indonesia, particularly in the 1960s and 1970s, its economy has been characterized by expansion and agricultural development. Aside from boosting production, food security was also pursued through government intervention in the domestic food market. Food self-sufficiency was achieved in the mid 1980s as a result of expansion in food production, price intervention, and trickle-down effects from economic expansion. The country's economic profile since the 1990s, though nuanced by several global economic crises, indicates that Indonesia should have met basic public needs including food security. Yet, the recent soaring food and fuel prices of the last decade have dampened people's ability to get food, indicating that access to food is related to economic stability (Timmer et al. 1983, Timmer; 2000, 2003).

Food consumption is a fundamental indicator of food security (Maxwell 1990, Hodinott and Yohanes 2002). Economic variables such as prices and income are among the main variables built into demand theory (Deaton and Muellbauer 1980a). Hence, households' consumption responses to changes in price and income are key considerations in food policy. Other noneconomic variables such as demographic characteristics of households might also influence taste and preference (Chung 2001, Turell et al. 2002). Substantial literature has described the microeconomic foundations (e.g., Deaton and Muellbauer 1980b, Banks et al. 1997) and demographic aspects (Byrton 1984, Pollak and Wales 1992, Blundel et al. 1993) of demand theory. How households respond to the changes of prices and income should determine food policy direction, such as whether to emphasize income, prices, or mixed policies (Rodgers 1986, Sadoulet and de Janvry 1995). Policy to improve household food security should therefore be grounded on sound knowledge of household response to these key determinants of food consumption. Other socio-economic variables such as household size, head-of-household characteristics, education, and regional aspects are also important factors that might affect food consumption (Deaton and Muellbauer 1980a, Pollak and Wales 1992). Investment in education and the redistribution of economic growth are also key ways of improving food consumption and avoiding food insecurity (Alderman 1993, Abdulai et al. 1999).

Socioeconomic aspects such as gender inequality also hinder the achievement of food security (Pitt et al. 1990). Research has revealed the effects of intra-household bias on food distribution(Haddad et al. 1996). Pro-male and pro-adult biases have been found to effect food intake (Senauer et al. 1988, Quisumbing and Mallucio 2003). Quisumbing and Mallucio (2003) further mentioned that in many households women and children do not receive enough food despite the fact that household calorie intake is well above normal. The inequality of resource distribution within households, among genders and age groups, has significant socio-economic consequences (Pitt et al. 1990, Kabeer 1991, Bhattacharya et al. 2004). The inequitable distribution of resources is also associated with certain countries and cultures (Quisumbing and McClafferty 2006). Some cultures with matriarchal systems give more autonomy within households to women (Blackwood 1997, Quisumbing and Otsuka 2001). Concerning women's autonomy in the household, studies have proven that control of resources by women increases household welfare with respect to nutrition and education, relative to control of resources by men (Garcia 1991, Hodinott and Haddad 1995, Haddad 1999). The distinct gender effect of resource control shows that households do not always act with consensus. Without considering gender-based inequality within households, policies to enhance household welfare or nutritional status might be highly inefficient and inappropriate. Gender issues are regarded as an important element of household consumption and prerequisite to improving household nutrition, therefore integrating gender aspects into the understanding of household food consumption provides a clearer picture of household food consumption patterns. Determining the effects of internal household characteristics is an alternative paradigm which could contribute to effective food policy formulation.

The Indonesian government also provides food subsidies to poor households for the purpose of maintaining access to basic food items. In fact, food subsidies have wide ranging socio-economic effects. According to Pinstrup-Andersen (1988), food subsidies can have a substantial effect on food prices if the size of subsidies are large enough and change considerably overtime. The immediate and feasible effect of food subsidies is on household incomes. The effect on household income is determined by the scheme of the subsidy, the targeting mechanism and the subsidized commodity. Food subsidy programs may be important as income transfer to beneficiaries. These income transfers through below average market food prices strengthen the purchasing power of low-income households (Pinstrup-Andersen and Alderman 1988, von Braun 1988). Furthermore, food subsidies may contribute to the formation of human capital of the poor by freeing financial resources for the purchase of health and education services and improving nutritional status. At the same time, it is known that the inability of the poor to feed themselves properly is one of the sources of the poverty trap (Banerjee and Duflo 2011). Policy action to improve food consumption and nutrition is needed to break the vicious circle of poverty and deprivation. There have been several successful experiences of government intervention through safety nets such as; conditional cash transfer (CCT) programs, school meal subsidies, food for education, and food for work schemes world-wide[2]. Many studies have documented successful programs for improving household per capita expenditure, nutritional status, and other human capital outcomes. Indonesia has the food security program RASKIN, which is an abbreviation of *beras miskin,* literally meaning "rice for the poor". Historically the program was part of the Social Safety Net program introduced by the government in 1998[3]. Another Indonesian social protection program based on unconditional cash transfers was reported to lead an increase of male-dominated expenditures such as cigarettes (Kompas 2009). To prevent unintended effects of government intervention to improve household food consumption, comprehensive information on household food consumption behavior is needed. Providing the poor with more money or subsidized food will not lead to better nutrition if the interventions are not based on information on the social returns of investing in nutrition. The success story of PROGRESA in Mexico, where cash money transfers are accompanied by instructional meetings on nutrition issues, is a model of government intervention that has desirable effects and benefits for the program recipients (Adato and Hodinott 2009).

Improving household food consumption involves a multitude of issues (von Braun et al. 1992). Without prudently taking into account household behavior and responsiveness, any food security policy will remain inefficient. Household consumption also has a gender dimension. The fact that extra resources from cash transfer are often used to purchase nonnutritional goods for consumption by adult males such as cigarettes, is another example that indicates that government intervention to improve household food consumption should consider the gender dimensions. The aim of this study was to address these issues, and in particular to examine the nexus between the fundamental economic variables of prices and income, as well as the Indonesian food security program, intrahousehold power, and the distribution of household food consumption.

1.2. Objectives

This study describes household food consumption behavior because information on household responses to changes in prices, income, and preference is a pre-

---

[2] PROGRESA in Mexico, food for education in Bangladesh, integrated food security and food for work in Ethiopia are examples of successful food programs.

[3] RASKIN was previously named OPK-Beras (Special Market Operation for Rice). The program's name was changed in 2002 because the program's function was expanded from an emergency program to part of the social protection programs (BULOG 2010).

condition for designing sound food policy. Despite massive governmental food intervention in Indonesia, approximately 32 percent of households remain food insecure, consuming less than dietary recommendations (Rusastra et al. 2008). Without comprehensive understanding of consumption behavior patterns and how these patterns change over time, it will be difficult to design policies that effectively improve food security. Simply evaluating the impact of food security programs at the level of program scope might mask the true impacts of any program. Motivated by the general situation of food consumption in Indonesia, this study attempts to analyze the responsiveness of Indonesian households to changes in food prices, income, and other socioeconomic factors. Based on current Indonesian food policies, this study also examines how Indonesian households respond to government interventions and whether household food consumption improved by actually improving spending higher nutrient foods. Furthermore this study investigates consumption preferences within household. The specific research objectives are outlined as follows:

- to estimate household food demand in Indonesia accounting for demographic and socioeconomic characteristics and to describe price and expenditure elasticity from this model
- to investigate the impact of the food security program on household food and nonfood consumption
- to examine the role of women's role and power on the distribution of household expenditures

1.3. Expected Contribution

This study is expected to make three main contributions. First, this is the only study based on panel data on food demand in Indonesia to date. Several studies on food consumption have been conducted, but they used either cross-sectional data (Chernichovsky and Meesook 1984, Pitt and Rosenzweig 1985, Pitt and Rosenzweig 1986, Ravallion 1990, Jensen and Manrique 1998, Skoufias 2003, Widodo 2006) or ignored the impacts of demographic factors (with the exception of Jensen and Manrique 1998). Those studies did not capture how changing policies affect household profiles and subsequently their consumption patterns. Second, this study evaluates the impact of the "rice for the poor" program at the microeconomic level. So far, evaluations have been conducted at the aggregate level and limited to program implementation (Tabor and Sawit 2005, Hastuti 2008). Accurate evaluation is important to clearly understand whether rice for the poor programs enable Indonesian households to eat enough and eat well. Third, the issues of intra-household resource allocation, particularly the role of women's assets to household food security in Indonesia are still few. Most previous studies of household welfare topics, particularly on poverty, were focused on aspects of female human capital such as education (Cameron and Worswick 2001, Quisumbing and Mallucio 2003). There is a lack of empirical studies that examine women's bargaining power influenced by women's asset and social capital on the distribution of household expenditures, particularly on nutrient-rich food expenditures. The results of this analysis of women's bargaining power on the distribution of household expenditures will be a complement to redesigning government intervention on household food consumption.

1.4. Structure of Dissertation

This dissertation consists of three empirical chapters unified by the element of food security in Indonesia, specifically household consumption. This dissertation examines the nexus between prices and income, the current Indonesian food security program, intra-household power, and the distribution of household food expenditures. Food consumption pattern is considered one of the most important indicators of economic development on the country level. Therefore, it is important for public policy to understand how household expenditures on food respond to changes in price and income, government intervention, and the bargaining power of women in the household. Each chapter applies appropriate econometric techniques to analyze rich longitudinal data derived from the Indonesian Family Life Survey (RAND 2010). IFLS is a longitudinal socioeconomic and health survey that has been conducted in 1993, 1997, 2000, and 2007 (RAND, 2010). The IFLS collects data on individual respondents, their families, the communities in which they live, and the health and education facilities they use.

Chapter two presents an analysis of the food demand behavior of Indonesian households in response to changes in food price and income, and other socioeconomic factors. The underlying assumption of the analysis is that inadequate information on household food expenditure patterns, which vary by income groups and regions, is likely to contribute to the persistence of food insecurity. The Indonesian Family Life Survey data was analyzed using a Quadratic Almost Ideal Demand System (QUAIDS) model including demographic and regional factors. In the case of Indonesia, this study is the first food demand analysis using the QUAIDS model, which elaborates household characteristics and geographical aspects. Compared to other demand system models, QUAIDS is more appropriate for analyzing food demand behavior since it has the ability to capture the curvature of Engel's law. The use of QUAIDS therefore provides a better position than other demand models to accurately portray household food demand behavior in Indonesia. In addition, the longitudinal data analyzed in this study offer the advantage of being able to level the dynamic behavior of food consumption over time.

Chapter three evaluates the impact of the current food security program, which is an almost universal program of the Indonesian Social Safety Net Program specifically for times of economic crisis. The food security program was aimed to protect poor households from the negative effects of the economic crisis by subsidizing rice prices. To assess the impact of the program, this study utilized a matching estimator approach combined with the difference in difference method. The rich longitudinal dataset used in this study enabled the matching estimator and difference in difference approaches to provide an accurate estimate of the program's impact on its beneficiaries. The impact evaluation of food security program at the household level investigates whether the program in fact supports households, particularly in terms of food security. In addition, the program's impact was evaluated on selected food expenditures that improve household nutritional well-being.

Chapter four investigates the role of women's power in the distribution of household expenditures. Current debates on intra-household resource allocation and decision making highlight how these factors affect household welfare. It is assumed that resources might be allocated differently depending on household demand for commodities, nutrition, and health depending on the individuals controlling the resources. Resource distribution and household decision making processes are important for guiding policy intervention, particularly in terms of program targeting. Using the Indonesian context with its cultural complexity on the variability of household decision making, this chapter examines the role of women in the distribution of household expenditures. Rather than measuring the relative importance of women based on variables such as nonlabor income or assets that have been widely used in other studies, this research used women's social capital as a proxy of women relative importance in the household. Women's social capital is described by variables that reflect participation in village and community level organizations. Specifically we measured women's participation in the three leading civic activities in their village; community meetings, *Pemberdayaan Kesejahteraan Keluarga* (PKK or Family Welfare Empowerment Movement) or women's association activities, and *Pos Pelayanan Terpadu* (POSYANDU), an integrated community health post. Women's social capital is assumed to reveal more about relative influence than simply assets because it not only represents women's decision making authority but it also has multiplier effects in terms of empowering women. Chapter 5 provides direction for future policy as well as recommendations for future research on household food consumption.

Chapter 2. Analysis of the Food Demand of Indonesian Household

2.1. Introduction

Food security is an essential issue in a developing country like Indonesia. Food is even considered as a political issue since the policies related to food not only have impacts on economic aspects such as food consumption and production, but are also closely associated with political issues. During the regime of Soekarno[4], food was used as a tool to engage in the international political arena which resulted in international food aid disbursement to Indonesia and also to increased international involvement (Sidik 2004). During the administration of Soeharto[5], achieving food self-sufficiency, in particular rice production, was made the ultimate goal of food policy.

The most fundamental food-related issues in Indonesia are aspects of production, consumption, and distribution. More importantly, food production is strongly linked to structural changes in Indonesia. In the 1960s, the agricultural sector was a major contributor to the national GDP (Hill 2000), however, the manufacturing and services sectors overtook agriculture in the early 1970s. The increased share of the manufacturing sector was due to the rise of mining operations, particularly oil production increases motivated by the oil price boom (Piggot et al. 1993). The agricultural sector's contribution to the national GDP decreased sharply, from 55 percent in the 1960s to just above 10 percent in 2000. In addition, structural changes in the economy from agricultural to nonagricultural sectors also altered the allocation of input factors, in particular the labor force has largely been absorbed into nonagricultural sectors. Despite the declining percentage contribution of the agricultural sector to the national economy, agricultural production has increased slightly during the last decade. However, the growth rate of agricultural production has not kept up with the rate of population growth (ADB 2008).

---

4   Soekarno was the first president of Indonesia. He is a prominent figure in Indonesian history due to his leadership in the struggle for independence from the Netherlands. He was elected president for the first 20 years after gaining independence (Hill 2000).

5   Soeharto was the second president of Indonesia. He ruled from 1967 to 1998 (Schwarz 2000). He stepped down in 1998 after large demonstrations and requests from the Indonesian people. The Soeharto administration was notorious for corruption, collusion, and nepotism.

Consumption patterns are also considered to be among the most important indicators of economic development in a country. In theory, changes in consumption patterns are determined by price and income changes as well as changes in tastes. As is evident in most developing countries, food typically constitutes the largest household expenditure and staple foods dominate this consumption category (Indonesian Bureau of Statistics 2009). In early 2000, the share of household budget spent on food was 58 percent in Indonesia, which decreased to around 50 percent in 2009, whereas nonfood consumption increased from 40 percent to 50 percent during this period (Indonesian Bureau of Statistics 2009). The most recent report from the Indonesian Ministry of Agriculture (2007) stated that average calorie availability and consumption[6] were 3,035 kcal per capita and 2,015 kcal per capita, respectively. These levels are above the recommended energy availability and consumption levels of 2,200 kcal per capita and 2,000 kcal per capita respectively. These figures indicate that Indonesia should successfully meet the food needs of its population. Aggregate income per capita, which stood at around 3,500 USD in 2006 also indicates that Indonesia should have achieved food security for at least for all staple foods (ADB 2008).

National-level data might not represent micro-level evidence. Despite food security policies pursued by Indonesian government through improving aggregate production and supply, this achievement has not transferred to the household level. There are still approximately 32 percent of households that consume less than the recommended diet (Rusastra et al. 2008). In addition, about 30 percent of Indonesian children suffer from inadequate nutritional status as revealed by the high incidence of underweight and stunted children (Schmidt 2002). This evidence indicates that food insecurity in Indonesia is not a problem of aggregate (national) food availability (Tabor et al. 1999). Food insecurity is a problem availability of food and access to food (von Braun et al. 1992). Food security exists when all people at all times have physical and economic access to sufficient food to meet their dietary needs for a productive and healthy life (FAO 1983, Timmer 2000, FAO 2003). Managing food security requires, therefore, not only understanding of how policies influence the availability of food and income but also how households can have sustainable access to food, and cope with insecurity and income shocks. According to Hartmanshenn et al. (2002), national food security focuses on addressing food availability, where at the household level, food access and utilization are the most pressing issues. Food

---

[6] Calorie availability measures per capita per day availability of food (food expenditure) while calorie consumption refers to food consumption converted into calories (Bouis 1995).

security much depends on the distribution of economic resources (Timmer; 1997, 2004).

To achieve food security at the household level, the Indonesian government has established the Food Security Council through Presidential Decree No. 132/2001 and generated several ambitious programs such as local food development and empowerment of "food security areas" [7](Rusastra et al. 2008). Since 1999, the government has provided food aid for poor households through subsidized rice prices, nevertheless, food insecurity remains. Other policies[8] aimed at reducing food insecurity have failed so far. These failures might have to do with the inadequacy of government knowledge of household food expenditure patterns including differences among income groups and regions. Designing remedial policy measures without comprehensive understanding of the household demand behavior has proved ineffective. Hence, it is vital to gain a thorough knowledge of the factors underlying consumption behavior patterns for future food policy direction.

It is important for public policy to consider how consumers change their expenditure on goods in response to changes of prices and income. This paper intends to improve understanding of the heterogeneous pattern of food consumption behavior in Indonesia. Following Banks et al. (1997), this study employed a QUAIDS analysis with demographic effects added to the model. This study specifically examined food expenditure patterns across income groups and regions. The main contribution of this effort is the unique combination of household longitudinal data with QUAIDS analysis methods. To our knowledge, there are no previous studies on food demand based on longitudinal data and QUAIDS, particularly in Indonesia. Compared to other demand system models, the QUAIDS model is more appropriate for analyzing food demand behavior since it has the ability to capture the curvature of Engel's law. The use of QUAIDS therefore, provides a more accurate picture of households' food demand behavior in Indonesia than other analytic methods.

---

7   In cooperation with the World Food Program, Indonesia developed a food security atlas, which identified areas with and without food security in 265 rural districts of 30 provinces.

8   These programs include people's food barn development, delayed selling system development, local food development, home yard utilization, and participatory integrated development in rain fed areas that were formulated by the Indonesian Food Security Council.

2.2. Literature Review

A number of empirical studies have identified that food and calorie demands are income and price responsive (Alderman and von Braun 1983, von Braun and de Haen 1986, Deaton 1990, Garcia 1990, Michalek and Keyzer 1992, Molina 1994, Fan et al. 1995, Moro and Sckokai 2000, Abdulai 2002, Gould and Villareal 2006, Ecker and Qaim 2008). Notwithstanding, price elasticity and food consumption patterns vary across countries. In the context of developed countries food demand is price and income inelastic and food has been found to be a necessity good (Michalek 1992, Abdulai 2002, Chern et al. 2003). This situation might be strikingly different in the case of developing countries. Alderman and Garcia (1993) pointed out that changes in food prices affected household welfare directly through real income and altered nutritional status over the long term. In Malawi, Ecker and Qaim (2008) found that price elasticity was high with regard to food demand and low for nutrient consumption. They also found that price subsidies on staple foods to promote food and nutrition security can result in undesirable effects and that income related and direct nutrient intervention was a better means to improve overall nutritional status.

Several previous studies have examined food demand in Indonesia (Kakwani 1977, Timmer and Alderman 1979, Dixon 1982, Deaton 1990, Jensen and Manrique 1998, Skoufias 2003, Fabiosa et al. 2005, Widodo 2006). These studies assessed food consumption patterns of Indonesian households using data from the national expenditure survey conducted by the Indonesian Bureau of Statistics and focused on cross-sectional data. A classic food demand analysis was conducted by Kakwani (1977) using 1969 Indonesian National Socio-Economic Household Survey (*Survei Sosial Ekonomi Nasional* [SUSENAS]) data. That study estimated expenditure elasticity of eight food groups and non-food consumption, then compared elasticity across several forms of Engel functions, including: semilog, linear, double log, hyperbolic, semilog inverse, double log inverse, and log inverse. It was found that expenditure elasticity varied across different forms of the Engel curve, although the differences were not substantial. The study also evaluated price and income elasticity across different income groups. In all models, expenditures for cereals, cassava, and vegetables were inelastic. Within food groups, expenditures for eggs, milk, and meat were the most elastic.

Timmer and Alderman (1979) and Dixon (1982) also found similar results on the expenditure and price elasticity for selected food crop commodities. Deaton (1990) estimated food demand function in Indonesia with a focus on unit value and embraced that it was a valid proxy of price. That study also found that the use of unit value accounted for price and income elasticity of quality. Eleven food commodities were evaluated and it was found that staple food prices were inelastic. Compared to Timmer and Alderman (1979), cross price elasticity of cassava with rice in Deaton's study were significantly different. In Timmer and Alderman the cross price elasticity of cassava to rice prices was 0.77, whereas Deaton calculated 0.15, perhaps due to unit value specification. Jensen and Manrique (1998) estimated food demand for eight commodity groups among Indonesian urban households that were classified by income. That study employed the Almost Ideal Demand System (AIDS) model and also incorporated demographic variables, and found that for high-income households, rice was the least price responsive commodity and all food demand had expenditure elasticity less than unity. Low-income urban households were found to be much more sensitive to changes in rice and fish prices. The demographic variables were only significant for high-income households.

In the last decade, studies on food demand have taken into account how economic crises might influence consumption. Skoufias (2003) examined the effect of price and income on food and calorie demand. Using SUSENAS data from 1996 and 1999, this study described the behavioral changes in consumption in the aftermath of an economic crisis. Nonparametric methods were implemented to observe the different elasticity estimates between poor and rich households. The empirical findings revealed that income elasticity for calorie demand was slightly higher in 1999 (post-crisis period) compared to that of in 1996 (pre-crisis period). This finding indicates that the calorie-income elasticity was insensitive to price changes even though prices were very volatile during the crisis. Households smoothened their consumption during the time of crisis through the increase of calorie-income elasticity for cereals whereas the calorie-income elasticity for other food decreased.

Recent studies of food demand in Indonesia were conducted by Widodo (2006) and Fabiosa et al. (2005). Widodo (2006) estimated food demand function of Indonesian households based on seven years of Survey of Living Cost Indonesia (1980, 1981, 1984, 1987, 1990, 1993, and 1996). Using the Linear Expenditure System (LES), it found that Indonesian households had the highest responsiveness of expenditure change on meat (0.367) and the lowest on fruit (0.03). This finding showed that when there was an increase in income, the biggest proportion of extra income was spent on meat and the smallest proportion on fruit. Fabiosa et al. (2005) estimated elasticity for nine food groups based on 1996 SUSENAS data using an incomplete demand system (LinQuad). In the case of cereals and vegetables, it was found that Indonesian households mostly responded to changes in income through changes in the quantity demanded. Fruit and eggs-milk showed very low price elasticity while the highest price elasticity among the nine food groups was for meat and fish.

The previous empirical studies on food demand in Indonesia limited their focus on cross-sectional or pooled data which do not capture how consumption behavior may change over time. The existing studies also lack noneconomic variables such as household size and composition that could affect consumption. Even though previous studies have revealed food demand behavior, the empirical strategies used in the studies refer to expenditure share Engel functions that are linear in the logarithm of total expenditure. However, in developing country settings like Indonesia, incomes vary highly across households and regions. The income effect among various income groups should be fully captured in a demand model in order to forecast how households respond to changes in economic policies. Capturing the income effect with the extension of demographic variables will add value to the growing body of literature on food demand behavior in developing countries.

2.3. Demand System Models in Empirical Studies

The application of demand system models enables the modeling of allocation of total expenditures among commodities given a certain budget set. To apply demand theory in the real world, an empirical model of demand system is needed. This section outlines selected demand systems including LES, the Rotterdam model, the Indirect Translog System (ITS), AIDS, and QUAIDS. Those models were chosen according to the most commonly used models and the development of state-of the-art consumer modeling.

2.3.1. The Linear Expenditure System

The LES is one of the most widely used models in demand system analysis. It was introduced by Stone in 1954 and used to analyze Britain expenditure survey data. LES is derived from the Stone-Geary utility function which is formulated as follows (Sadoulet and de Janvry 1995):

$$\bar{u} = \prod (q_k - \gamma_k)^{\beta_k} \tag{2.1}$$

where u refers to utility, q is consumption of good, and γ and β are parameters. The function can be transformed to its monotone form as:

$$\ln \bar{u} = \sum_{k=1}^{n} \beta_k \ln(q_k - \gamma_k) \tag{2.2}$$

Following the adding up property in demand theory, the parameter is restricted as:

$$\sum_{k=1}^{n} \beta_k = 1 \quad 0 < \beta_k < 1$$

The coefficient β represents marginal budget share which shows how expenditure on goods changes with income. Since β should be greater than zero, LES does not allow for an inferior good classification. The demand function derived from maximizing utility subject to budget constrain in LES is:

$$p_i q_i = p_i \gamma_i + \beta_i (x - \sum_{k=1}^{n} p_k \gamma_k) \qquad (2.3)$$

The second part of the LES demand function is comprised from subsistence expenditure ($\Sigma p_k \gamma_k$) and supernumerary expenditure ($x - \Sigma p_k \gamma_k$) which is spent between commodities in fixed proportion β. Another feature of LES is that all commodities are gross complements due to a strongly separable utility function. Therefore, the LES model is more applicable to large categories of expenditure instead of individual commodities. LES also has an important caveat with regard to the linearity of Engel function such that the model is only suitable with a short variation of income (Sadoulet and de Janvry 1995).

2.3.2. Rotterdam Model

The Rotterdam model was developed by Barten (1964) and Theil (1965). The model provides many features not available in prior consumer modeling such as LES and works in terms of a differential approach instead of a logarithm level (Barnett and Serletis 2008). This approach lets p_i, q_i, and x represent price, quantity, and total expenditure respectively and uses w_i as the expenditure share on commodity i. Taking differentials of the expenditure share, the demand function of the Rotterdam model is the following (Byron 1984):

$$w_i d\ln q_i = (p_i \partial q_i / \partial x) d\ln x + \sum_{j=1}^{n} (p_i p_j / x)(s_{ij} - q_j \partial q_i / \partial x) d\ln p_j \qquad (2.4)$$

where s_{ij} are the symmetric Slutsky coefficients.

$$s_{ij} = \partial q_i / \partial p_j + q_j \partial q_i / \partial x \qquad (2.5)$$

Equation (2.4) then yields

$$w_i d\ln q_i = \beta_i \left(d\ln x - \sum_{j=1}^{n} w_j d\ln p_j \right) + \sum_{j=1}^{n} \pi_{ij} d\ln p_j \qquad (2.6)$$

where $\beta_{it} = p_i (\partial q_i / \partial x)$ and $\pi_{ij} = (p_i p_j / x) s_{ij}$

Equation (2.6) can be applied to real data with the introduction of the error term. The Rotterdam model also satisfies the properties of demand theory: adding up, homogeneity, symmetry, and negativity. Unlike LES, the Rotterdam model has the ability to examine complementary or substitutive relationships across commodities, however, the model is not based on an explicit utility or cost function.

2.3.3. The Indirect Translog Model

The ITS model was developed by Christensen et al. (1975). The model is derived from a flexible indirect utility function that is quadratic in the logarithms of prices ratios to total expenditure. It is approached by taking a logarithmic second-order Taylor series approximation. The form of translog utility function is presented as follows (Christensen et al. 1975):

$$\ln v = \alpha_0 + \sum_{i=1}^{n} \ln\left(\frac{p_i}{x}\right) + \frac{1}{2}\sum_{i=1}^{n}\sum_{j=1}^{n} \ln\left(\frac{p_i}{x}\right)\ln\left(\frac{p_j}{x}\right) \quad (2.7)$$

where α_0, γ_i and β_{ij} are the parameters to be estimated. The translog utility demand function satisfies the properties of demand function and also has the ability to depict complementary or substitutive relations between commodities. This model is complex and involves a large number of independent parameters. Analyzing fewer goods in the model might reduce the complexity of empirical estimations.

2.3.4. Almost Ideal Demand System

The AIDS model was introduced by Deaton and Muellbauer (1980). AIDS has become popular in empirical studies because it is derived from a flexible expenditure function. The model also satisfies demand theory properties. The demand functions in AIDS are specified as follows (Sadoulet and de Janvry 1995):

$$w_i = \alpha_i + \sum_i \gamma_{ij} \ln p_j + \beta_i \ln(x/P) \quad (2.8)$$

where w_i is the budget share of commodity i, p_j is prices of commodity j, x is the total expenditure, and α_i, β_i, and γ_{ij} are the parameters to be estimated. The parameters are subject to some restrictions to hold the properties of demand. P is the aggregate price index defined as:

$$\ln P = \alpha_0 + \sum_{i=1}^{n} \alpha_i\, p_i + \frac{1}{2}\sum_{i=1}^{n}\sum_{j=1}^{n} \gamma_{ij} \ln p_i \ln p_j \quad (2.9)$$

To simplify the nonlinear relationship between the price index and commodity prices, Deaton and Muellbauer (1980) suggest approximating the price index (P) with Stone's price index (P*):

$$\ln P^* = \sum_j w_j \ln p_j \quad (2.10)$$

The parameter β_i of the AIDS model depicts the effect of a change in expenditure on the budget share of good i and indicates the type of the good, whether it is a luxury, a necessity, or an inferior good. When β_i is greater than zero and the expenditure elasticity is larger than unity, the good is classified as a luxury and the budget share of good i increases as total expenditure rises. In contrast, a commodity is classified as an inferior good if β_i is negative and the expenditure elasticity is smaller than zero. A commodity is a normal good if β_i is negative and the expenditure elasticity ranges from zero to one.

2.3.5. Quadratic Almost Ideal Demand System

The QUAIDS model was developed by Banks et al. (1997). Based on nonparametric analysis of consumer expenditure patterns, it was shown that Engel curves require a higher order of logarithm of expenditure. Furthermore, Banks et al. (1997) stated that models that fail to account for Engel curvature generate distortion in welfare losses when demand functions were estimated. Previous models such as AIDS did not consider this issue and linearized the logarithm of total expenditure in the model. QUAIDS extends the AIDS model with a quadratic logarithm of expenditure. Banks et al. (1997) applied the model to capture the curvature of the Engel curve using UK Family Expenditure Survey data. Basically QUAIDS is a nested model of AIDS that also satisfies the properties of demand function.

2.3.6. Choice of a Specific Demand System Model for the Estimation Strategy

Based on features of each model, LES has a problem in describing demand behavior based on Engel's law. As income increases, a good might change from normal to inferior good which is implausible to examine in LES. The Rotterdam system is consistent with demand theory and has the ability to examine relationships across commodities, however, since it is not derived from specific utility or cost function, the model is inconsistent with utility maximizing behavior. The translog model is favorable in terms of its flexibility of functional form but has a major problem in the estimation due to the relatively large number of independent parameters. The AIDS model demand function satisfies the principles in demand theory and its estimation is less complicated than other models.

Based on nonparametric analysis of consumer expenditure patterns, it was shown that Engel curves require a higher order of logarithm of expenditure. Previous models such as AIDS did not consider this issue and linearized the logarithm of total expenditure in the model. The QUAIDS model extends the AIDS model with a quadratic logarithm of expenditure. The QUAIDS model has similar features to AIDS and is able to capture the Engel curvature. Therefore, QUAIDS was chosen as the demand model for the empirical strategy of estimation. Furthermore, this study extended the QUAIDS model with demographic variables to investigate the role of noneconomic variables in food demand behavior. In the setting of developing countries there are only a few studies that have applied the QUAIDS model. Hence this study contributes to a small but growing body of literature on food demand behavior in developing countries.

2.4. Empirical Model: Quadratic Almost Ideal Demand System with Demographic Variables

In econometric studies of food demand, partial and complete demand systems are used to model consumer behavior (Chern et al. 2003). However, most studies have employed complete demand systems because they model consumer demand in a way that allows systems to specify the allocation of total expenditures for all goods in the budget. Accordingly, the models generate expenditure and price elasticity. The complete demand system employed in this study is the QUAIDS model (Banks, et al. 1997), which is an extension of the AIDS model that includes a higher order of expenditure term to capture the nonlinearity of the Engel curve. The QUAIDS model assumes that household preferences follow a quadratic logarithm of household expenditure functions as follows:

$$\ln c(u, p) = \ln a(p) + \frac{ub(p)}{1 - \lambda(p)b(p)u} \qquad (2.11)$$

where u is utility, p is a set of prices, a(p) is a function that is homogenous of degree one in prices, and b(p) and $\lambda(p)$ are functions that are homogenous for degree zero in prices. The household cost function in QUAIDS is similar to AIDS if λ is set to zero. The indirect utility function accordingly is as follows:

$$\ln V = \left\{ \left[\frac{\ln m - \ln a(p)}{b(p)} \right]^{-1} + \lambda(p) \right\}^{-1} \qquad (2.12)$$

where m is the total expenditure, and ln a(p) and b (p) are the translog and Cobb-Douglas functions of prices as in the AIDS model formulation:

$$\ln P(p) = \alpha_0 + \sum_{i=1}^{K} \alpha_i \ln p_i + \frac{1}{2} \sum_{i=1}^{K} \sum_{j=1}^{K} \gamma_{ij} \ln p_i \ln p_j \qquad (2.13)$$

$$b(p) = \prod_i^n p_i^\beta \qquad (2.14)$$

The $\lambda(p)$ in QUAIDS is defined as:

$$\lambda(p) = \sum_{i=1}^{K} \lambda_i \ln p_i \quad \text{where} \sum_{i=1}^{K} \lambda_i = 0 \qquad (2.15)$$

The subscript $i = 1, \ldots, K$ in the model denotes the number of goods in the demand systems. Applying Shephard's lemma to the cost function (2.1) or Roy's identity to the indirect utility function (2.2), the QUAIDS model expenditure shares are given as the following:

$$w_i = \alpha_i + \sum_{j=1}^{K} \gamma_{ij} \ln p_j + \beta_i \ln\left\{\frac{m}{P(p)}\right\} + \frac{\lambda_i}{b(p)}\left[\ln\left\{\frac{m}{P(p)}\right\}\right]^2 \quad (2.16)$$

where, w_i is the food budget share of eight commodities and α, γ, β, and λ are parameters. Therefore, there will be eight equations in the demand system. When λ is equal to zero, the equation (2.16) represents the AIDS model. The presence of higher order expenditure does not imply that QUAIDS is better compared to other AIDS models (Gould and Villareal 2006). The quadratic term provides a benefit to evaluate the higher order of Engel curves while maintaining the utility maximization behavior assumption. Banks et al. (1997) mentioned that the influence of demographic and other household characteristics can be integrated into the model. The QUAIDS model with household characteristics is represented as follows:

$$w_i = \alpha_i + \sum_{j=1}^{K} \gamma_{ij} \ln p_j + \beta_i \ln\left\{\frac{m}{P(p)}\right\} + \frac{\lambda_i}{b(p)}\left[\ln\left\{\frac{m}{P(p)}\right\}\right]^2 + \sum_{s=1}^{s} \vartheta_{is} D_{st}^h + u_{it}^h \quad (2.17)$$

where D is a set of household characteristics including household size, urban or rural setting, gender, education, and community-level variables, where s refers to food groups and t refers to the survey year.

In terms of theoretical aspects, the QUAIDS model also satisfies the properties of demand function; adding-up, homogeneity, and symmetry. The adding up restriction requires that the total budget share is equal to one, meaning that the household does not spend more than the total budget (Deaton 1997). Using non-linear seemingly unrelated regression, these restrictions will be maintained during estimation.

From the QUAIDS model provided in equation (2.6), expenditure and price elasticity can be derived by differentiating equation (2.6) with respect to $\ln m$ and $\ln p_j$, respectively. The derivation results are:

$$\mu_i \equiv \frac{\partial w_i}{\partial \ln m} = \beta_i + \frac{2\lambda_i}{b(p)}\left\{\ln\left[\frac{m}{a(p)}\right]\right\} \quad (2.18)$$

$$\mu_{ij} \equiv \frac{\partial w_i}{\partial \ln p_j} = \gamma_{ij} - \mu_i\left(\alpha_j + \sum_k \gamma_{jk} \ln p_l\right) - \frac{\lambda_i \beta_j}{b(p)}\left\{\ln\left[\frac{x}{a(p)}\right]\right\}^2 \quad (2.19)$$

The parameter α_i in equation (2.6) is the share of an item in the budget of a subsistence household, while $\beta_i + 2(\lambda_i/b(p))[\ln(x/a(p))]^2$ measures the effect of a 1 percent increase of real expenditure on budget share of good i. Unlike AIDS, the

QUAIDS[9] model allows variability of a commodity depending on the expenditure range. For instance, with a positive β and negative λ, a commodity is categorized as a normal good at low level of total expenditure but becomes inferior at a high level of total expenditure. The expenditure elasticity can be calculated by:

$$e_i = \frac{\mu_i}{w_i} + 1 \qquad (2.20)$$

From μ_{ij}, Marshallian uncompensated price elasticity can be calculated as:

$$e_{ij}^u = \frac{\mu_{ij}}{w_i} - \delta_{ij} \qquad (2.21)$$

where δ_{ij} is equal to one if i=j, and equal to zero if i≠j. From the Slutsky equation, Hicksian or compensated price elasticity is calculated as follows:

$$e_{ij}^c = e_{ij}^u + w_j e_i \qquad (2.22)$$

2.5. Data and Household Expenditure on Food

This section describes the IFLS data. Methodological issues such as missing data and commodity grouping are also discussed. The descriptive results of household food expenditure patterns show that staple foods constitute the largest expenditure share (24 percent) followed by meat and fish (17 percent). Dairy products expenditure remains low (5 percent of the total expenditure).

2.5.1. Data

The data used in this research is from the Indonesian Family Life Survey (IFLS). IFLS is a longitudinal socioeconomic and health survey that has been conducted in 1993, 1997, 2000, and 2007 (RAND, 2010). IFLS collects data on individual respondents, their families, the communities in which they live, and the health and education facilities they use. The first IFLS effort in 1993 included interviews of 7,224 households. The second IFLS effort sought to re-interview the same respondents in 1997. The third IFLS effort was administered to the full sample interviewed in 2000. The latest IFLS effort was carried out in 2007. Like earlier efforts, the final IFLS re-interviewed all target households as well

---

9 This model does not capture the quality effect of income as does the model developed by Deaton (1990). In addition, the QUAIDS model does not specifically address the issue of inter-temporal consumption, but Banks et al. (1994) handled this issue by using time series, cohort-level data.

new split-off households that contained at least one target respondent from previous efforts. IFLS is the only longitudinal data in Indonesia with a very high follow-up rate. The second IFLS effort was able to re-interview 94.4 percent of the households included in the first survey. In the third IFLS the follow-up rate was 95.3 percent of the first IFLS households. In the final IFLS the follow-up rate was 93.6 percent which was lower than previous IFLS efforts due to the longer time lag[10]. The IFLS sample represented approximately 83 percent of the Indonesian population living in 13 provinces. Within these 13 provinces, enumeration areas (EA) were randomly chosen based on a SUSENAS sampling frame. There were a total of 321 EAs and within each EA, households were randomly chosen based on 1993 SUSENAS listings. Twenty households were selected for each urban EA and 30 households were chosen for each rural EA (Strauss et al. 2009). This study only used IFLS data from the second, third, and final efforts. Data from the first IFLS was not used in the analysis because the expenditure module is not comparable to the other rounds of IFLS, particularly concerning items of prepared food away from home.

The IFLS provides a rich dataset of household expenditures on both food and nonfood items. The food expenditures comprise 38 items[11] and the recall period of these food expenditures is one week. For the purpose of this study, expenditure for food items was used since IFLS does not provide quantity consumed by household. In addition to food expenditures, prices are also key variables in modeling demand. Fortunately, IFLS also provides detailed information on the communities in which IFLS households are located and from the facilities that were used by participating households. The community level information includes price data in each EA. With the absence of quantity data for consumption, price data from community questionnaire were used (Deaton and Zaidi 2002). The IFLS collected price data from two sources: traders or markets near the corresponding village office and the *Pos Pelayanan Terpadu* (POSYANDU), or community health post[12]. There were 31 price items collected

---

10 The time lag between IFLS1, IFLS2, and IFLS3 is 3 years whereas the time lag between IFLS3 and IFLS4 is 7 years.
11 There might be issues of product quality differences among these items particularly when the commodities are aggregated. Quality will be reflected in the price of commodity, particularly in the aspect of unit value (Deaton 1990). The quality of commodities might affect utility, which becomes a crucial issue in the aggregation (Lewbel 1996). It is assumed that quality choice is a function of household income, household characteristics, and also price and this study has involved those variables in the model. Detailed discussion on the commodity aggregation is presented in section 2.5.2.
12 POSYANDU is one of the public health facilities used by Indonesian households. It provides health services, particularly for women and children. The services provided by

which were in line with the commodities in the expenditure module. In this study, prices were the average values from the two sources.

The use of longitudinal data provides an opportunity to understand the dynamic behavior of households. For the purpose of this study, only panel households[13] were analyzed and the split-off households were excluded owing to the fact that split-off households might have different characteristics compared to their status in the original households. Moreover, price data are also not available for the split-off household, most of which do not reside in the original survey EA. The total number of observations in this study included 16,836 panel households with approximately 5,600 households for each survey.

2.5.2. Indonesian Household Expenditure on Food

As mentioned in the previous section, the IFLS collected data on expenditure for 38 food items. Those data were collected by asking if households had purchased a particular food item during the week prior to the interview. To simplify the analysis and estimation in the demand systems, those food items were aggregated into eight food groups: staple foods, vegetables and fruit, meat and fish, oils, dairy products, alcohol and tobacco goods, snacks and dried foods, and other foods (Table 1). The aggregation is also important to detect whether households were consuming the same basic food items or higher nutrient foods. The food items were aggregated based on the substitutions of each food item and are placed in groups along with close substitutes. Lewbel (1996) proposed commodity aggregation to relax the assumption of perfect correlation among group prices. In a micro data study setting, there is still limited empirical study of the prices and commodity grouping (Blundell et al. 1993). Following Bopape (2006), price data in this study were generated based on close substitutes in each commodity aggregation.

Some data were missing from the dataset used in this study. To handle this issue, imputation-based methods were used to replace the missing data (Levy and Lemeshow 1999). In particular, the method of imputation in this study was based on substitution of the mean. If the price of a certain commodity was missing in an EA, the missing price was substituted by the average price at the vil-

---

POSYANDU include the registration of pregnant women, basic observations of pregnant women and children, family planning, nutrition counseling, and the provision of vitamins, food supplements, and contraceptives. Since the cadres were also involved in food supplement provision their information on prices is assumed to be valid.

13 Panel households in this study are defined as the original households interviewed in the first IFLS survey that were followed and interviewed in all subsequent IFLS efforts.

lage level. In addition, the imputation also captured seasonality issues by basing substituted prices on interviews conducted during the same month. Normally, the community data were collected in EAs which are close to each other and in the same month. The imputation procedure was employed as follows: If there was missing data for the price of rice in an EA, the imputed price was the average rice prices of another village belonging to the same EA during the same interview month. When these data were also missing, the imputed price was based on kecamatan (sub-district) level prices where the village is located. The detailed price information is presented in Table A2.1 in the Appendix to this chapter. The food groups are presented in Table 2.1.

Table 2.1: Composition of Food Aggregation

Food Groups	Food items
Staple Foods	Rice, corn, sago/flour, cassava, tapioca, dried cassava, sweet potatoes, potatoes, yams
Meat and Fish	Fresh meat (beef, mutton, water buffalo, chicken, duck, etc), fish (fresh fish, oysters, shrimp, squid etc), preserved meat (jerky, shredded beef, canned meat, sardines etc), tofu, and tempeh
Vegetables and Fruit	Vegetables (kangkoong, cucumber, spinach, mustard greens, tomatoes, cabbage, katuk, green beans, string beans etc), other beans (mung-beans, peanuts, soya-beans etc), fruit (papaya, mango, banana etc)
Oils	Butter and cooking oils (coconut, peanut, corn, palm etc)
Dairy Products	Eggs, fresh milk, canned milk, powdered milk etc
Alcohol and Tobacco	Alcohol, tobacco
Snacks and Dried Foods	Noodles, cookies, dried food, snacks, prepared foods eaten away from home etc
Other Foods	Spices, sugar, beverages

Source: Aggregation based on IFLS data

Table 2.2 presents descriptive figures of household characteristics. In this study, income groups were derived from household per capita expenditures where the poorest households include the bottom 20 percent of the income range and the richest households include the top 20 percent of the income range. The mean household size shows a typical nuclear family consisting of a couple with two children. The poorest households tended to have a larger household size.

Interestingly, urban households had a slightly larger size than their rural counterparts. Though this is beyond the scope of the analysis, internal migration to urban areas may partly explain this difference. The mean income per capita each month was 294,658 rupiahs14 ($32 USD) and the average level of education of the household head was primary school15. It is shown that there was a wide income and education gap across income groups and region. The difference in the level of education of the head-of-household was almost double between urban versus rural households and richest versus poorest households. The average head of the poorest households had not completed elementary school. Most of poorest and rural households were engaged in agriculture. The income gap per capita between the poorest and the richest was wide. The disparity of income and other socio-economic characteristics is likely to have an influence on household consumption behavior (Becker et al. 1986, Lalluka et al. 2006).

---

14 One US dollar was equal to 9,000 Indonesian currency (rupiah) in February 2011.
15 The average exchange rate (rupiahs per US dollar) between 2000 and 2007 was based on selected key indicators provided by the Asian Development Bank (ADB 2008).

Table 2.2: Selected Household Characteristics (figures represent mean values)

Variables	Pooled	Poorest	Richest	Rural	Urban
Household size	4.37	5.38	3.49	4.22	4.56
Education of Household Head (in years)	6.34	3.73	10.12	4.86	8.04
Age of Household Head	51.12	51.38	51.33	51.09	51.15
Proportion of Male Household Heads	0.80	0.83	0.77	0.81	0.79
Proportion with Agricultural based income	0.40	0.56	0.20	0.62	0.15
Household income per capita (in thousands of rupiah per month)	295	70	1050	226	377

Source: Author calculation based on IFLS data

The budget shares of each food group are presented in Table 2.3. It is shown that staple foods were the dominant food expenditure for Indonesian households in all IFLS efforts, accounting for almost a quarter of total food expenditure. A high share of expenditure on staple foods is typical for developing countries (Bouis 1999). The share of staple foods decreased in 2000 but increased again slightly in 2007. Households might have shifted their consumption to cheaper calorie sources in this period. This suggestion is supported by declines in the shares of vegetables-fruit and meat-fish expenditures. Meat and fish, the most expensive calorie source, formed the second largest share of food expenditure in all surveys. It was also shown that the consumption of dairy products was low, accounting for only 5 percent of the total food expenditure. The figures also indicate that expenditures for snacks and dried foods increased, revealing that Indonesian households started to shift to fast and processed foods. Increased snack and dried food consumption is likely to have health consequences in the future (St-Onge et al. 2003). The tradeoff between home production and market production, particularly due to women entering the labor market, drove households to consume increased quantities of processed food or food prepared away from home, a phenomenon which is already evident in developed countries (Yen 1992, Nayga 1996).

Disaggregated by income groups, it is evident that the poorest households' dominant expenditure was staple foods and that they were less likely to consume dairy products. The secondary expenditure share among the poorest households was meat and fish. The expenditure share of alcohol and tobacco goods was higher than for dairy products. The Indonesian Consumer Foundation reported that 70 percent of smokers in Indonesia are poor, signifying that the poor are the main contributor to government revenue from tobacco (Suara Media 2010). The predominance of smoking behavior among the poor might be related to addiction and a lack of knowledge on the health risks of smoking. Table 2.3 presents data that indicate that the dominant share of expenditures of the richest households belonged to snacks and dried foods, followed by meat and fish. Although the richest group also spent some of their budget on alcohol and tobacco goods, their expenditure share on better diet items such as vegetables and fruit, meat and fish, and dairy products were much larger than the share of alcohol and tobacco goods. In terms of geographical aspects, urban households consumed more snacks and dried foods, and dairy products, whereas rural households consumed more staple foods. Interestingly, the expenditure share of vegetables and fruit, meat and fish, oils, and alcohol and tobacco goods were almost uniform.

Table 2.3: Share of Food Expenditure across Commodity Groups, by Income Group and Year

Food Group	All	Poorest	Richest	Urban	Rural	1997	2000	2007
Staple Foods	0.24	0.36	0.14	0.20	0.27	0.25	0.23	0.24
Vegetables and Fruit	0.11	0.10	0.12	0.12	0.11	0.12	0.12	0.10
Meat and Fish	0.17	0.14	0.19	0.18	0.17	0.17	0.18	0.16
Dairy Products	0.05	0.03	0.07	0.06	0.04	0.05	0.05	0.05
Oils	0.04	0.05	0.04	0.04	0.05	0.04	0.04	0.05
Alcohol and Tobacco Goods	0.08	0.08	0.07	0.08	0.09	0.07	0.09	0.09
Snacks and Dried Foods	0.15	0.09	0.24	0.18	0.12	0.13	0.15	0.16
Other Foods	0.15	0.16	0.13	0.14	0.16	0.15	0.15	0.14
N	16,836	1,675	1,675	7,692	9,144	6,593	5,119	5,124

Source: Author calculation based on IFLS data

2.6. Results and Discussion

This section presents the behavior of household food consumption and the results obtained from the QUAIDS model analysis of the Indonesia Family Life Survey data. The first part of this section explains expenditure and price elasticity estimates generated from the QUAIDS model that are important for policy. The second part of this section shows how demographic variables are relevant to household food consumption. The last part of this section discusses food demand behavior of the poorest households.

2.6.1. Household Responsiveness to Expenditure and Price Changes

Based on the IFLS data the QUAIDS model revealed that the quadratic term of food expenditure for all food groups was significant (Table A2.2 in the Appendix). This result implies the nonlinearity of the Engel curve with respect to total food expenditure for all food groups. Furthermore, the QUAIDS model allows the possibility of normal commodities changing to luxury ones or luxury goods becoming normal as depicted by the parameters. When a commodity has a positive sign of expenditure and a negative sign of higher order of expenditure term, this commodity is considered a luxury good at low levels of expenditure and a necessity at high levels (Banks et al. 1997). Meat and fish followed this pattern while dairy products remained a luxury in all expenditure ranges. The QUAIDS model was applied to each survey dataset and income group. In such subsamples, the higher order of expenditure was not necessarily different from zero because the subsamples presented a more homogenous expenditure pattern. The detailed subsample estimation results are reported in Table A2.5 and Table A2.6 in the Appendix. In terms of policy purpose, how the households responded to price and income changes is explained from the expenditure and price elasticity.

The expenditure elasticity estimates are reported in Table 2.4. In the column labeled "All Samples", most food groups were found to be elastic except for staple foods, oils, and other foods which were found to be inelastic and thus necessities. Expenditure on necessities increased with income, but more slowly in the percentage of magnitude. Dairy products had the highest expenditure elasticity followed by meat and fish. For meat and fish, a 10 percent increase in total food expenditure lead to an 11.5 percent share increase in consumption. This finding reveals that the increase of income shifted consumption patterns from staple foods to more meat and fish, and dairy products. Even though this pattern is a good sign for Indonesia, where more people consumed high nutrient foods, health problems as a consequence of this dietary change should also be anticipated (Walker et al. 2005). Staple foods and oils were necessities for all income groups, a 1 percent change in total food expenditures resulted in the change of consumption of staple foods and oils less than proportionately. Interestingly, expenditures on alcohol and tobacco goods were found to be elastic, meaning that a 10 percent increase of total expenditures lead to a 10.6 percent increase in consumption. Compared to previous studies on alcohol and tobacco goods consumption (Erwidodo et al. 2002, Adioetomo et al. 2005), the expenditure elasticity in this study was relatively high, although very similar to findings of Witoelar et al. (2005). As adult expenditures comprised of tobacco and alcohol goods increased over the last decade and the elastic nature of alcohol and tobacco goods expenditures, caution should be taken due to the possible crowding-out effect of alcohol and tobacco goods expenditures on more nutritious food items.

Table 2.4: Expenditure Elasticity Estimates across Income Groups

Food Groups	All Samples	Poorest	Middle	Richest	Urban	Rural
Staple Foods	0.7564	1.0152	0.8798	0.8623	0.7866	0.7566
	(0.0083)	(0.0424)	(0.0201)	(0.0356)	(0.0135)	(0.0104)
Vegetables and Fruit	1.0532	0.9967	0.9754	0.8380	1.0362	1.0659
	(0.0094)	(0.0639)	(0.0259)	(0.0288)	(0.0164)	(0.0130)
Meat and Fish	1.1475	1.0358	1.1318	1.0494	1.0876	1.1771
	(0.0079)	(0.0549)	(0.0227)	(0.0228)	(0.0142)	(0.0109)
Dairy Products	1.3025	1.2800	1.3793	1.1246	1.2017	1.4078
	(0.0140)	(0.1240)	(0.0453)	(0.0377)	(0.0779)	(0.0208)
Oils	0.8879	0.7960	0.7484	1.0744	0.9292	0.8625
	(0.0115)	(0.0712)	(0.0296)	(0.0511)	(0.0220)	(0.0151)
Alcohol and Tobacco Goods	1.0667	1.3568	1.2806	0.9849	1.0378	1.1030
	(0.0159)	(0.1327)	(0.0442)	(0.0560)	(0.1326)	(0.0205)
Snacks and Dried Foods	1.1586	0.9091	1.0203	1.0876	1.1163	1.1097
	(0.0125)	(0.1021)	(0.0373)	(0.0311)	(0.1015)	(0.0177)
Other Foods	0.9131	0.9138	0.8963	1.0143	0.9160	0.9065
	(0.0070)	(0.0465)	(0.0189)	(0.0241)	(0.0118)	(0.0094)

Source: Author calculation based on IFLS data

Note: Standard errors are shown in parentheses

The results also showed that expenditure elasticity estimates varied across income groups. This evidence reassures the importance of disaggregated analyses of consumption patterns by income groups in a developing country with wide income gaps like Indonesia. Expenditure elasticity for staple foods was elastic for the poorest group. Interestingly, expenditure elasticity for alcohol and tobacco goods among the poorest households was the highest. This fact indicates that income changes of the poorest households corresponded most to alcohol and tobacco goods expenditures. The Indonesian Consumer Foundation reported that there was a misuse of direct cash aid from government. Instead of supporting expenditures that lead to human capital development, more than 50 percent of the direct cash aid was spent on tobacco (Kompas 2009). On the other hand, dairy products and snacks and dried foods were luxury items for the richest households, whereas staple foods, vegetable and fruits, and alcohol and tobacco goods were necessities. Comparing urban to rural areas, the expenditure elasticity for staple foods was slightly higher in urban areas. One explanation for this might be related to the characteristic of rural households acting as both consumers and producers of staple foods simultaneously. Both urban and rural households were expenditure elastic for meat and fish, dairy products, alcohol and tobacco goods, and snacks and dried foods. Rural households were more elastic for meat and fish, and for dairy products, whereas urban households were more elastic for snacks and dried foods.

Table 2.5 presents estimates of compensated and uncompensated price elasticity. The results showed that the signs of own price elasticity values were as expected. Based on Marshallian price elasticity estimates, only meat and fish were found to be unitary price elastic for all samples. This means that a 10 percent increase in the price of meat and fish lead to a decrease of around 10 percent in the consumption of meat and fish. Nevertheless, meat and fish became less price elastic when only substitution effects were considered as shown by the inelastic compensated (Hicksian) price elasticity estimates. Comparing expenditure and price elasticity is important for policy direction considerations. For all commodities, it is pointed out that expenditure elasticity outweighs price elasticity. It was indicated that income policies for food consumption seemed to be more efficient compared to price policies as the expenditure elasticity estimates for all food groups surpassed the price elasticity estimates.

For price elasticity estimates, disaggregation based on income group revealed an interesting finding. The magnitude of price elasticity between the poorest and the richest households did not vary significantly. These two groups were price elastic on meat and fish, dairy products, and alcohol and tobacco goods, however, the price elasticity of staple foods for the poorest households was nearly close to unity. For the poorest households, when income effects were not considered, it was found that only dairy products and alcohol and tobacco goods remained price elastic. Based on geographical aspects, urban households were price inelastic for all food groups, while rural households were price elastic for vegetables and fruit, meat and fish, and alcohol and tobacco goods.

It is interesting to investigate the relationships among these food groups. Table A2.3 in the appendix reports the cross-price elasticity estimates of the eight food groups. Forty out of 56 cross-price elasticity estimates were found to be different from zero and showed a mixture of complementary and substitution relationships. Compared to own price elasticity, cross-price elasticity in this study was much lower, which implies that consumers were more responsive to changes in own prices. All cross-price elasticity estimates were found to be inelastic. The relationship between vegetables and fruit demand and meat and fish demand showed the largest substitution effects. The largest complementary effect was shown in the relationship between the demand for dairy products prices and staple foods. Even though the size of elasticity estimates were pretty small, staple foods, vegetables and fruit, and meat and fish appeared to be complementary to snacks and dried foods.

Another striking substitution effect, though inelastic, was found in the relationship between the demand for alcohol and tobacco goods and meat and fish. The vegetables and fruit prices to meat and fish demand elasticity was 0.17, while the alcohol and tobacco goods price and meat and fish quantity elasticity was 0.11. The increase of vegetables and fruit prices was responded to by increased consumption of meat and fish. Comparing vegetables and fruit to meat and fish, Indonesian households diversified their diet in terms of more vegetables and fruit. However, the increase of prices for vegetables and fruit lead households to shift to greater meat and fish consumption, which is more expensive but more nutritious. The result of a substitutive relationship between alcohol and tobacco goods and meat and fish is also challenging for national food policy. Indonesian households seemed to give up meat and fish consumption when the prices of alcohol and tobacco goods increased so that they are able to maintain that expenditure. The large expenditure share of adult goods, particularly for tobacco consumption, has been traded for richer nutrient foods such as egg, meat, dairy products, and also nonfood expenditures such as education and medical expenses (Bappenas 2006, Mukherjee 2006). Given this situation, the loss in terms of improved nutrition through meat and fish consumption would have been considerable.

The longitudinal data used in this study allowed observation of the dynamic behavior of household response over time. Table 2.6 presents price elasticity estimates over time, which changed for all food groups from 1997 to 2007. Among the eight food groups, only the price elasticity of staple foods and alcohol and tobacco goods were very volatile, even considering the substitution effects. The World Bank (2008) reported that domestic wholesale rice prices increased sharply from 2004 to 2007 from less than 3,000 rupiahs to almost 5,000 rupiahs. In the 2000s, the Indonesian government pursued several critical food policies. In 1998, the monopolistic power over imports of major agricultural products of the National Food Logistic Agency (*Badan Urusan Logististik* [BULOG]), was abolished. From 2000 onwards, private imports of rice were subject to a specific tariff of up to 25 percent of the import price. The tariff and nontariff barriers contributed to increased rice prices. To stabilize the food market, BULOG and local governments regularly intervene in the market through special market operations for specific commodities such as rice, cooking oil, sugar, and meat. The market operations are normally administered during specific holidays, particularly during *Idul Fitri - Idul Adha*[16] and Christmas. Market operations are also conducted when there is a sign of scarcity or increases in commodity prices. These policies might explain the variation of expenditures and price elasticity over time. More strikingly, prices of alcohol and tobacco goods in 2007 were very elastic compared to 1997. This behavior might be associated with tobacco and cigarettes policy in Indonesia. In fact, Indonesia was categorized among the top five countries in terms of tobacco consumption and has lower tobacco taxes compared to other Asian countries (Barber et al. 2008). In the case of the price elasticity of alcohol and tobacco goods, the increase of tobacco retail prices might explain this phenomenon. The retail prices for cigarettes almost doubled from 2000 to 2007 (Barber et al. 2008).

---

16   Idul Fitri and Idul Adha are the two main Muslim holiday celebrations in Indonesia.

Table 2.5: Own Price Elasticity Estimates

Food Groups	All Samples	Poorest	Middle	Richest	Urban	Rural
Marshallian Own Price Elasticity Estimates						
Staple Foods	-0.7706 (0.0324)	-0.9473 (0.1081)	-0.7457 (0.0440)	-0.8080 (0.1460)	-0.6827 (0.0642)	-0.8380 (0.0391)
Vegetables and Fruit	-0.9580 (0.0160)	-1.0703 (0.0654)	-0.9848 (0.0266)	-0.7772 (0.0488)	-0.8483 (0.0228)	-1.0297 (0.0231)
Meat and Fish	-1.0032 (0.0331)	-1.1402 (0.1510)	-0.9741 (0.0553)	-1.1228 (0.0979)	-0.9202 (0.0496)	-1.0532 (0.0454)
Dairy Products	-0.9771 (0.0367)	-1.2391 (0.1786)	-0.8917 (0.0660)	-1.0179 (0.0986)	-0.9419 (0.0542)	-0.9961 (0.0535)
Oils	-0.7367 (0.0292)	-0.7757 (0.0981)	-0.7380 (0.0421)	-0.6215 (0.1221)	-0.7981 (0.0454)	-0.6891 (0.0390)
Alcohol and Tobacco Goods	-0.9451 (0.0438)	-1.2450 (0.1868)	-0.9617 (0.0696)	-1.1954 (0.1439)	-0.7940 (0.1268)	-1.0255 (0.0526)
Snacks and Dried Foods	-0.9374 (0.0181)	-0.7680 (0.0954)	-0.9321 (0.0313)	-0.9453 (0.0419)	-0.9649 (0.0411)	-0.9043 (0.0287)
Other Foods	-0.9495 (0.0230)	-0.7258 (0.0874)	-0.9146 (0.0356)	-0.8961 (0.0740)	-0.9037 (0.0357)	-0.9676 (0.0305)
Hicksian Own Price Elasticity Estimates						
Staple Foods	-0.5899 (0.0324)	-0.6194 (0.1074)	-0.5022 (0.0437)	-0.6796 (0.1460)	-0.5276 (0.0643)	-0.6305 (0.0390)
Vegetables and Fruit	-0.8391 (0.0158)	-0.9666 (0.0643)	-0.8799 (0.0253)	-0.6698 (0.0488)	-0.7265 (0.0226)	-0.9135 (0.0229)
Meat and Fish	-0.8071 (0.0330)	-0.9988 (0.1505)	-0.7963 (0.0549)	-0.9073 (0.0974)	-0.7289 (0.0495)	-0.8571 (0.0451)
Dairy Products	-0.9077 (0.0367)	-1.2085 (0.1783)	-0.8319 (0.0660)	-0.9307 (0.0986)	-0.8639 (0.0554)	-0.9348 (0.0536)
Oils	-0.6978 (0.0292)	-0.7343 (0.0980)	-0.7038 (0.0420)	-0.5798 (0.1221)	-0.7601 (0.0453)	-0.6493 (0.0390)

Alcohol and Tobacco Goods	-0.8556 (0.0438)	-1.1651 (0.1863)	-0.8525 (0.0696)	-1.1282 (0.1433)	-0.7101 (0.1192)	-0.9301 (0.0526)
Snacks and Dried Foods	-0.7678 (0.0183)	-0.6550 (0.0956)	-0.8021 (0.0314)	-0.7252 (0.0427)	-0.7627 (0.0291)	-0.7626 (0.0288)
Other Foods	-0.8126 (0.0229)	-0.5639 (0.0867)	-0.7742 (0.0352)	-0.7637 (0.0737)	-0.7739 (0.0354)	-0.8255 (0.0304)

Source: Author calculation based on IFLS data

Note: Standard errors are shown in parentheses

2.6.2. The Effect of Domestic Production

This study also examined for effects of household food production on consumption patterns. The sample was regrouped into food-producing households and non-food-producing households. Based on IFLS data, 72 percent of the households engaged in the production of at least one food commodity. Most rural households (83 percent) engaged in food production compared to 60 percent among their urban counterparts. Forty five percent of food-producing households produced staple foods and vegetables. The expenditure elasticity estimates for both non-food-producing and food-producing households were almost uniform and also had similar expenditure elasticity estimates to the pooled sample. Interestingly, households that engaged in food production had slightly higher price elasticity of staple foods compared to non-food-producing households. This finding is consistent with the price elasticity of meat and fish. For food-producing households a 10 percent increase in staple food prices reduced consumption by 9 percent but was only reduced by 7 percent for non-food-producing households. This finding is consistent with Timmer (2004) which found that Indonesian farm households were net consumers of food. Dairy products were price elastic for non-food-producing households and inelastic for food-producing households. The detailed results are presented in Table A2.5 and Table A2.6 in the Appendix.

Table 2.6: Marshallian and Hicksian Own Price Elasticity Estimates across Surveys

Food Groups	1997	2000	2007	1997	2000	2007
	\multicolumn{3}{c}{Marshallian Price Elasticity Estimates}	\multicolumn{3}{c}{Hicksian Price Elasticity Estimates}		
Staple Foods	-0.8642	-0.6178	-1.1332	-0.6795	-0.4407	-0.9490
	(0.0633)	(0.0749)	(0.0690)	(0.0633)	(0.0748)	(0.0689)
Vegetables and Fruit	-0.9992	-0.9935	-1.0193	-0.8658	-0.8750	-0.9239
	(0.0359)	(0.0325)	(0.0267)	(0.0358)	(0.0320)	(0.0272)
Meat and Fish	-0.9732	-1.2496	-1.0003	-0.7769	-1.0438	-0.8147
	(0.0536)	(0.0693)	(0.0801)	(0.0533)	(0.0692)	(0.0798)
Dairy Products	-1.0459	-0.9585	-0.8497	-0.9766	-0.8905	-0.7794
	(0.0558)	(0.0637)	(0.0951)	(0.0558)	(0.0637)	(0.0951)
Oils	-0.8134	-0.9057	-1.1044	-0.7726	-0.8748	-1.0604
	(0.0641)	(0.0805)	(0.0775)	(0.0641)	(0.0805)	(0.0775)
Alcohol and Tobacco Goods	-1.2331	-0.7574	-1.6259	-1.1580	-0.6613	-1.5212
	(0.0657)	(0.0893)	(0.1526)	(0.0657)	(0.0892)	(0.1526)
Snacks and Dried Foods	-0.9439	-1.0030	-1.1064	-0.7858	-0.8349	-0.9257
	(0.0427)	(0.0306)	(0.0962)	(0.0429)	(0.0307)	(0.0964)
Other Foods	-1.0689	-0.7908	-0.9365	-0.9266	-0.6550	-0.8016
	(0.0448)	(0.0590)	(0.0577)	(0.0447)	(0.0590)	(0.0577)

Source: Author calculation based on IFLS data

Note: Standard errors are shown in parentheses

2.6.3. Household Demographic Characteristics

In this study, household demographic characteristics were also introduced into the QUAIDS model to capture the effects of noneconomic variables on household food consumption. The variables were household size, a regional dummy indicating either urban or Java[17], and education level and gender of the household head. The regional dummy was included to capture regional variation in food consumption patterns. The level of development in Indonesia was found to be imbalanced, leading to internal migration, particularly from rural to urban, as well as to Java from the rest of the country (Hill 1992, Akita 2003).

In terms of household characteristics, household size had a positive effect on the expenditure share of staple foods but negatively affected the expenditure share of meat and fish, and dairy products. This finding indicates that larger households tended to choose cheaper calorie sources rather than more expensive sources such as meat and fish or dairy products. The regional dummy variable for Java was significant but varied in direction for all food commodities. Households in Java were more likely to consume vegetables and fruit, dairy products, and snacks and dried foods, whereas households in the rest of the country consumed more staple foods, fish and meat, oils, and alcohol and tobacco goods.

Gender of the household head was also associated with the consumption behavior. Male-headed households had significantly lower consumption of vegetables and fruit, meat and fish, dairy products, and snacks and dried foods and significantly higher alcohol and tobacco goods consumption. These findings imply that male household heads exhibit typically gender-based consumption preferences. The education level of the household head had a significant and positive influence on the consumption of vegetables and fruit, meat and fish, dairy products, snacks and dried foods, and other foods which implies that more education contributes to the consumption of more nutritious foods. In contrast, household head education had a negative effect on the consumption of staple foods and alcohol and tobacco goods, implying that households with less educated heads were more likely to consume alcohol and tobacco goods.

Existing literature associates better education with higher income (Psacharopoulos and Patrinos 2004, Heckman et al. 2006). In terms of food consumption behavior, there is evidence that education level correlates with better understanding of the importance of a healthy diet and nutritional status (Garett and Ruel 1999). The results of this study show that one extra year of education of the household head increased expenditures on vegetables and fruit, meat and fish, and dairy products by 0.04 percent, 0.16 percent, and 0.20 percent respectively and reduced expenditures on alcohol and tobacco goods by 0.12 percent. Therefore, policies that promote nutritional education are consistent with im-

---

17   Java is one of the main islands of Indonesia and the most densely populated. It is where the capital city is located and is also the economic and governmental center of the country.

proving food consumption and household nutritional status. Providing information on nutrition and healthy diet through extension work or informal community meetings might be an appropriate strategy.

2.6.4. Food Consumption Behavior of the Poorest

The behavior of poor households should be policy interest for governments (von Braun et al. 2009). This section focuses on interpreting the results pertaining to the poorest households. Table 2.7 presents the expenditure elasticity estimates for the poorest households. The mean income percapita each month of these households was around 120,000 rupiahs ($13 USD). In 1997, staple foods were expenditure elastic for the poorest households, but became less elastic in the following periods. This finding is consistent with Bennet's law which states that households switch from cheaper to more expensive calorie consumption as income rises (Timmer et al. 1983, Fuglie 2004). Dairy products remained expenditure elastic for over a decade. As mentioned earlier, the poorest households were expenditure elastic on alcohol and tobacco goods and this elasticity increased during the course of the decade.

This study found that lower income households consumed more alcohol and tobacco goods when they had increased income. Although alcohol and tobacco consumption, particularly tobacco consumption in developed countries has decreased over the last decade (World Bank 2000), it is becoming a luxury good for poor households in Indonesia. Table A2.5 in the Appendix presents the expenditures and higher order estimates of expenditures for the sub-sample of the poorest households. The sign of both parameter estimates were positive and significant and according to Banks et al. (1999) indicate that alcohol and tobacco goods were luxury items for the poorest households.

It is also important to note the results of the cross-price elasticity estimates (Table A2.6 in the Appendix). The largest substitution relationship was found for alcohol and tobacco goods price and the demand for meat and fish. The cross-price elasticity of these two goods was 0.40 in absolute value, which means that a 10 percent increase in alcohol and tobacco goods prices reduced demand for meat and fish by 4 percent. On the other hand, the largest complementary relationship was found in dairy products and staple foods. The results show that a 10 percent increase in dairy products prices reduced the demand for staple foods by 6 percent. The price of dairy products were relatively more expensive compared to other food commodities which may have affected consumption by poor households.

Table 2.7: Expenditure Elasticity of the Poorest Households across Surveys

Food Groups	1997	2000	2007
Staple Foods	1.1232 (0.0601)	0.9129 (0.0714)	0.9677 (0.4189)
Vegetables and Fruit	0.9089 (0.0983)	1.0640 (0.1061)	0.9804 (0.3990)
Meat and Fish	0.9333 (0.0844)	1.1085 (0.0855)	1.2387 (0.6125)
Dairy Products	1.4963 (0.2005)	1.0663 (0.1948)	1.2389 (0.2612)
Oils	0.7757 (0.1044)	0.8645 (0.1264)	0.7814 (0.1671)
Alcohol and Tobacco Goods	1.1909 (0.2168)	1.5788 (0.1669)	1.4227 (1.2463)
Snacks and Dried Foods	0.8115 (0.1743)	0.9752 (0.1595)	0.6652 (0.2463)
Other Foods	0.9118 (0.0646)	0.8666 (0.0779)	1.0573 (0.2760)

Source: Author calculation based on IFLS data

Note: Standard errors are shown in parentheses

2.7. The Projection of Food Demand

The findings of the food demand behavior and the elasticity estimates for different food groups in the earlier section provide a useful foundation to the projections of food demand in Indonesia in the future. In estimating the projections of selected food demand, IFPRI's IMPACT Model offers a methodology for analyzing the alternative scenario for global food demand, supply and trade (Rosegrant et al. 2001).Nevertheless, due to the limited data on the indirect demand of seed, feed, industrial use and wastage, supply and trade of each commodity, the projected food demand in this study only accounts for the direct demand (human demand). The projected demand method is adopted from Mittal

(2006) in the case of Indian food demand projection. It is assumed that the future food demand is influenced by the income and population growth as well as expenditure elasticity of a specific commodity. Demand for staple foods, vegetables and fruit, meat and fish and dairy products have been estimated for the years 2015 and 2020. The base of per capita demand for staple foods, vegetables and fruit, meat and fish and dairy products are drawn from the per capita consumption derived from SUSENAS as given by Ariani (2010). The estimates of population and economic growth, (6 percent and 1.2 percent respectively) are obtained from the ADB Key Indicators for Asia and the Pacific (ADB 2008). The demand elasticity estimates as derived from the QUAIDS model are utilized in the projection.

The projections of the domestic food demand are presented in Figure 2.1. The results indicate that staple foods are expected to be the dominant source of energy through 2020. In 2020 the projected domestic demand for staple foods is more than 35 million metric tonnes or 137 kg per capita. The projected demand for meat and fish and dairy products remain stagnant which might be primarily due the low intake of those food groups as these food groups are considered as high-cost.

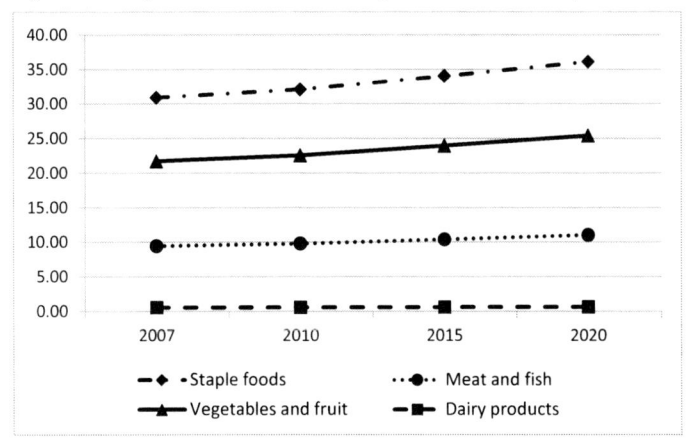

Figure 2.1: Projected Domestic Demand of Selected Food Groups in Indonesia

Note: Domestic demand in the base year (2007) as given by Ariani (2010); projected demands are in million metric tonnes

2.8. Limitations of the Study

Many factors could have affected consumption behavior over the period represented by the dataset. Study efforts focused on consumption behavior changes as a result of price and income (expenditure was used as a proxy of income) changes between 1997 and 2007. The quality of food likely changed during the decade represented by the dataset but unfortunately any quality differences could not be considered in the model. The availability of substitutable food items, and consumer preferences might have also changed over that period. We used the same set of food items in the analyses from 1997 and 2007, assuming that preferences remained constant, which in reality may not be the case. Another issue that has not been taken into account in this study is a life-cycle consumption model that would capture inter-temporal consumption aspects. It is important to incorporate inter-temporal consumption in demand analyses because these factors might affect household welfare, particularly when certain policies are introduced. Though beyond the purpose of this study, aspects such as food preparation and provision also deserve consideration for policy development regarding healthy food consumption behavior particularly for urban and wealthier households. We suggest that future studies of this kind take steps to incorporate these important issues which may vary over time in the QUAIDS model specifications.

2.9. Conclusion

In the case of Indonesia, this study is the first food demand analysis using the QUAIDS model that incorporates household characteristics and geographical aspects. In addition, the longitudinal dataset analyzed in this study was an unprecedented opportunity to observe the dynamic behavior of household food consumption over time. The results show that Indonesian households were price and expenditure responsive and that food expenditure patterns varied over several demographic and regional contexts.

All food groups exhibited positive expenditure elasticity values but the magnitude of those values differed among food categories. Consistent with demand theory, all own price elasticity estimates were negative. Results also show that price and expenditure elasticity changed over time from 1997 to 2007. Own price elasticity estimates increased for most food items, implying that households have become more responsive to changes in prices. In contrast, expenditure elasticity declined for most food items (except for alcohol and tobacco goods) which implies welfare improvement since the 1997 crisis. For the pooled sample, staple foods, oils, and other foods were necessities, whereas vegetables and fruits, meat and fish, dairy products, and alcohol and tobacco goods were luxuries. Expenditure on alcohol and tobacco goods was very elastic for the poorest households while the richest households were expenditure elastic on dairy products. As expenditure elasticity for all food commodities surpassed the own price elasticity, policy tools for enhancing income generating activities might be more effective relative to policies that affect price. In order to improve household food consumption with regard to consumption of higher nutrient foods, income oriented policies will provide support for such efforts.

Results also show that the poorest households demonstrated the highest expenditure elasticity on alcohol and tobacco goods which should warrant policy attention. Income policies could have unintended effects rather than supporting food security or increased consumption of higher nutrient foods. This finding explains the failure of government intervention in the case of food security programs through which the poorest households spent their governmental assistance on luxury goods. There is potential to raise the nutritional status of poor households, because they were also expenditure elastic on meat and fish, and dairy products.

This study also found that noneconomic variables such as household size, education, gender, and geographical factors were relevant to food demand. Education appears to improve human capital through increased consumption of healthier food commodities because more educated households consumed more nutritious food items. One extra year of household head education increased expenditures on vegetables and fruit, meat and fish, and dairy products by 0.04 percent, 0.16 percent, and 0.20 percent respectively. Each additional year of schooling reduced expenditures on alcohol and tobacco goods, and staple foods by 0.12 percent and 0.5 percent respectively. Regional dimensions also affected food consumption. Java residents and urban households were more likely to consume higher nutrient food items than their counterparts. This finding confirms that regional level development considerations are essential to improving consumption behavior.

In conclusion, these findings show that in a developing country with wide income disparity and a rural versus urban population gap like Indonesia, a comprehensive analysis of food demand which accounts for those differences is essential to get a better understanding of household demand behavior and to determine effective food policy. The resulting patterns of expenditure elasticity across income groups and commodities point to the potential for underestimation or overestimation of the effectiveness of government intervention when these behaviors are not considered. Knowledge of household food consumption behavior is a basic foundation to evaluate the impact of government food intervention in order to improve household nutrition.

Chapter 3 Impact Evaluation of the Food Security Program in Indonesia: Household Level Analysis

3.1. Introduction

Indonesia's economic performance has seen ups and downs in the past few decades and is regarded as one of the emerging economies in Southeast Asia. From 1965 until the mid 1990s, Indonesia recorded around 7 percent annual per capita income growth (ADB 2007). That period was labeled as the "New Order Era" (*Orde Baru* [ORBA]) under the Soeharto regime. During that period, the success of economic growth was accompanied by equitable income distribution and declining poverty rates (World Bank 1993). There was also latent political turbulence and uncertainty during the Soeharto period even though it did not affect major economic indicators (Hill 2000). Capital inflows and exchange rates remained stable until mid 1997.

As the Asian financial crisis spread throughout Southeast Asia in 1997, the Indonesian economy was also affected. It is reported that the crisis raised the poverty rate to 40 percent from around 12 percent just before the crisis (Solomon 1998, Thoenes 1998). Indonesia recorded the highest inflation in recent history with the exchange rate of around 15 thousand rupiahs to one US dollar. Many experts claimed that the collapse of the Indonesian economy was not merely due to the regional financial crisis, but rather due to failed economic policies developed under ORBA. During the Soeharto administration, the Indonesian economy was characterized by imprudence and poorly monitored domestic financial systems, high levels of corruption, and nepotism or patrimonial relations between governments and business (Krugman 1998, Pincus and Ramli 1998, Stiglitz 1998). The crisis indeed dampened the national economy and deteriorated the living standards of Indonesian households.

Before the crisis, government anti-poverty programs were focused on social services spending such as education, health and family planning, and development programs featuring infrastructure. Consequently, anti-poverty programs intended to protect the chronic poor and the newly impoverished due to the economic crisis were almost absent before the crisis period. In order to protect Indonesian households from the economic crisis, the national government launched social safety net (SSN) programs in 1998. The SSN effort consisted of five major programs: food security (*Operasi Pasar Khusus* [OPK]), employment creation (*Padat Karya*), education scholarship, health programs, and community empowerment.

Each of the SSN programs had a specific purpose. The food security program provided poor households with highly subsidized rice while the education program provided poor households with children in school monthly cash transfers to support education expenditures. The health programs supported medical services to poor households such as free family planning, midwives, and health services in community health centers. The health programs also provided nutrition supplements to children and pregnant women through community health posts. The financial crisis forced poor households to streamline their consumption and prioritize basic needs. Health and education expenditures were some of the sacrifices made by poor households[18]. Education and health support from the government were important for the poor in order to sustain their consumption, particularly for nonfood expenditures. While the food security, health, and education programs addressed household consumption sustainability, the employment creation and community empowerment programs were intended to sustain economic activity and employment. The community empowerment program provided grants to communities which managed that assistance communally according to their need. During the implementation stage of this program, communities utilized the grants primarily for infrastructure and micro credit. The employment creation program provided work opportunities for unemployed or laid-off workers on government projects in coordination with the community empowerment program. The SSN has used up a large amount of resources. Sumarto et al. (2000) mentioned that SSN's financial cost amounted to 5.62 percent of the government budget in 1998-1999 fiscal year alone.

Because the SSN program was nonexistent before the crisis, it had institutional problems associated with program design and targeting[19]. The financial crisis needed an immediate response and there was no well-designed program established prior to the crisis. In the three decades before the crisis, Indonesia was controlled with by a strict centralized government. As a consequence, SSN was designed by the central government and provided only limited ability to adapt to local contexts. Since the program was designed in a hasty way, it result-

---

18 Frankenberg et al. (1999) reported that the use of health services for children dropped substantially between 1997 and 1999. The percentage of children under three years of age receiving vitamin A supplements also decreased substantially during that period. Strauss et al. (1999) pointed out that the unenrollment rate increased between 1997 and 2000 and that children of poor and rural households were less likely to be enrolled in school.

19 The general poverty programs were in the forms of social services spending such as health, education, family planning and subsidized credit (Sumarto et al. 2002).

ed in mistargeting beneficiaries and program inefficiencies. There were large numbers of poor or needy groups that were not covered by the SSN programs, and at the same time there was substantial program support provided to households that were not poor. Huge amounts of government resources have been dispersed to mitigate the worst impacts of the financial crisis. Consequently, impacts of the program need to be assessed to determine whether government policies have been able to mitigate the worst consequences of the crisis.

This chapter examines the economic impact of the food security component of the SSN programs. The food security program was chosen because it was an almost universal program and had the largest coverage of the SSN programs. The food security program also absorbed a more sizeable share of the government budget compared to the other SSN programs. The impact evaluation conducted in this study specifically assessed the impact of the "rice for the poor" program at the micro level. Previous efforts have evaluated this project at the aggregate level and were limited to program implementation (Tabor and Sawit 2005, Hastuti 2008). Evaluating the impact of the food security program only at the program implementation stage might fail to capture the real impact of the program. Moreover, given the government's limited resources, a credible impact evaluation is needed to determine whether the resources were used effectively. Accurate evaluation is important to clearly understand whether the "rice for the poor" program has helped Indonesian households in an efficient manner. Therefore, the findings of this study shall provide feedback to the government and a basis to propose appropriate strategies for future food policy.

3.2. Brief Overview of Indonesian Food Policy

Indonesia has been pursuing food policy efforts since independence and were formally documented in the first Five Year Development Plan from 1969 to 1974. During this stage, food policy was yet not formulated as specific policy, rather it was part of broader agricultural policies. In terms of strengthening the institutional capacity to deliver food policy in an active way, the Indonesian government established BULOG, Indonesia's National Food Logistic Agency, in 1967. In the first phase of development, the stability of food availability was one of the main goals of agricultural policy and it was established through efforts to achieve self-sufficiency in rice production. In line with agricultural sector development, pursuing food security through rice production self-sufficiency was on top of the Indonesian government's agenda. To achieve rice self-sufficiency, the government introduced a "production driven" program that provided access to subsidized credit and production input subsidies. In addition,

BULOG imposed a floor price for rice as a tool to stabilize prices in the early 1970s. At the second phase of the national 5-year development plan, food policies in Indonesia were driven by pro-poor economic growth and a Green Revolution program featuring high-yield rice varieties, investment in rural infrastructure, and support for irrigation and fertilizer (Timmer 2004). Timmer (2004) also mentioned that by 1984 Indonesia was self-sufficient in rice production despite severe rural poverty due to the unstable macroeconomic conditions of oil prices and results of the "Dutch Disease" phenomenon.

Although rice production self-sufficiency was achieved, there had been some major challenges in food security including high procurement and storage costs and the less successful floor price policy. The benefits from rice price stabilization decreased overtime. To address high costs, BULOG used a low-interest credit system through the Indonesian Central Bank. BULOG, which had exclusive control of the food sector in Indonesia, encountered serious financial viability, management, and accountability problems. With the economic crisis and an El Nino related drought in 1997, BULOG was forced to introduce institutional reforms and finally in 2003, was formally changed into a public corporation (Yonekura 2005). These facts suggest that Indonesian food policy cannot be disentangled from macroeconomic policy goals such as stable growth, political aspects, and institutional changes in the management of national food security. In the macroeconomic context, food policies should ensure that food is accessible for every Indonesian household. Adequate access to food includes maintaining purchasing power which is highly associated with a stable and sound macroeconomic profile as well as stable food supplies at national, regional, and local markets. Stable prices managed by the government accommodated the interests of both consumers and producers (Timmer 2004).

Indonesian food policies also address microeconomic perspectives through promoting individual nutritional well-being, which embraces the importance of nutrition in human and economic development. The promotion of nutrition outcome has been introduced sin 1950's with the "Healthy Four Perfect Five" *(Empat Sehat Lima Sempurna)* program which aimed to promore diet diversification (Soekirman 2011). Compared to neighboring Southeast Asian countries such as the Philippines, Malaysia, and Vietnam, Indonesia was a pioneer in nationwide micronutrient policy. In the early 1980s Indonesia developed policy and launched programs addressing micronutrient issues such as iron and vitamin dietary supplements and iodized salt. Other programs focused on children's nutrition and health, and pregnant and lactating mothers were launched later. The Indonesian government also formulated the Food and Nutrition Plan of Action (FNPA) in 1998 and presented nutrition indicators and targets to be achieved during the five-year development plan. In this program, the government collaborated with international agencies such as the World Food Program, FAO, WHO, and Helen Keller International. Vitamin A supplementation was distributed twice a year for infants aged 6 to 12 months. The program was also supported through local health practitioners such as village midwives and community-level health service providers. The implementation of nutrition policies has also been integrated at the village-level and involves community participation such as food supplementation for children through POSYANDU integrated community health post activities.

This study also evaluates the targeted food subsidies program, which is a direct intervention to make food more accessible to poor households. Initially, the program was part of the SSN packages and later it became a regular government program. The program provides food subsidies to poor households, but there were implementation problems related to institutional issues such as program beneficiary targeting and inefficiency (program details are presented in the following section).

3.3. Rice for the Poor: The Food Security Program in Indonesia

From a historical point of view, the Indonesian government has set food security high on agenda since the beginning of the New Order Era (1965-1990). The government defined food security as the national ability to have adequate rice supplies at an affordable price (Tabor and Sawit 2001), even though this condition might not guarantee food security at household level. Because a large number of poor households were engaged in agriculture and rice production in particular, food security strategy focused on production was in accordance with the poverty reduction strategy. In the 1980s under the Soeharto regime, Indonesia became a food self-sufficient country. Nevertheless, the government failed to stabilize rice prices in 1996. The financial crisis forced households to adjust their consumption behavior due to soaring food prices. The dramatic price increase of most commodities, particularly foods with rich micronutrient content such as meat, dairy products, and vegetables and fruit brought negative consequences for the nutritional welfare of Indonesian households. Therefore the Indonesian government introduced the food security program as part of the SSN package to prevent more severe nutritional effects from financial crisis.

Food security intervention became the main component of the SSN program. Officially, the food security program was named *Operasi Pasar Khusus Beras* (OPK) or "rice special market operation". The purpose of this program was to ensure that poor households were able to access basic food at affordable prices (Sumarto 2006). Eligible households were selected based on *Badan Koordinasi Keluarga Berencana Nasional* (BKKBN), or the National Family Planning Agency in Indonesia. Tabor and Sawit (2001) mentioned that the program authorities were aware that BKKBN welfare criteria were not designed to identify food insecure households. BKKBN evaluated households based on the following indicators: whether all household members had at least two meals a day, whether household members had different set of clothes for each type of activity (home, work, school, and public), whether houses had dirt-floors, whether households were able to bring their children to health centers to receive medical treatment when they were sick, whether the households used family planning methods, and whether household members were able to practice their religious duties[20]. BKKBN involved volunteers and family planning cadres and placed them in village health posts. The cadres collected and updated household data along with family planning monitoring. BKKBN welfare criteria received many criticisms regarding data accuracy. Nevertheless, BKKBN welfare criteria were the only available option at that time and the government needed to immediately ease the impact of the financial crisis.

The food security program was managed by BULOG . The program provided highly subsidized rice at a price of Rp 1,000 per kg compared to average market prices of Rp 3,000 per kg. The amount which could be purchased by beneficiary households was originally 20 kg per month, but was reduced to between 10 and 20 kg in 2000 (Tabor and Sawit 2005, Hastuti 2008). During the first twelve months of the food security program, around Rp 3.3 trillion were spent on more than 9 million beneficiary households, making the program a sort of income transfer to the households.

The food security program was centrally designed but there were design modifications added during the implementation, particularly in an attempt to accommodate local issues. The list of beneficiaries was determined by BKKBN welfare criteria, whereas village authorities were responsible for the distribution of benefits at the village-level (Olken et al. 2001). In some communities, the subsidized rice was well-targeted to poor families, but in other villages the subsidized rice was simply divided equally among recipients (Tabor and Sawit 2001, Olken et al. 2001). In more drastic cases, any household was allowed to purchase the subsidized rice. This situation was facilitated by the rice distribu-

---

[20] BKKN classified households into four categories: keluarga pra-KS (pre-prosperous households), KS 1 (prosperous 1), KS 2 (prosperous 2) and KS 3 (prosperous 3). Eligible households for food security program were pre prosperous and prosperous 1.

tion methods, which were administered on a cash-and-carry basis. As poorest households often did not have cash to purchase the subsidized rice were unable to do so, this could result in an excess of rice in some villages. Villages had to pay for all of the rice received and fulfill governmental reporting requirements. Therefore, any excess rice was sold to noneligible households in order to meet these administrative requirements. The deliveries of subsidized rice were terminated if villages could not account for the previous deliveries according to a designated schedule.

Another food security program problem was the price of subsidized rice at the point of distribution. According to national guidelines the rice was to be sold at Rp 1,000 per kg. However, the administration of the program varied across regions and recipients were required to pay higher prices in some cases (Hastuti 2008, Olken 2001, Olken et al. 2001). Some of the price increases were intended to cover transportation costs and other costs associated with rice distribution such as plastic bags or sacks and labor costs, which were not covered by the food security program. Therefore, the final price of subsidized rice was highly correlated with the remoteness of the villages. Village governments that were aware of this problem often solicited additional funding from *kecamatan* (sub-district) or *kabupaten* (district) governments to cover the distribution costs instead of putting the burden on the recipients. Hastuti (2008) mentioned that some districts anticipated this extra cost and allocated part of their regional budget, therefore, local politics also played a role on the food security program administration.

3.4. Review of Existing Literature on Program Evaluation

It is likely for the government to favor policies that protect poor households from higher food prices. One common response is to institute food price subsidies. The policies have been widely introduced and became favorable in developing countries. The general goal of providing food price subsidies is to achieve household food security through reducing uncertainty at the household level regarding the ability to access a certain minimum of food staples (von Braun et al. 1992). Food subsidies have wide ranging socio-economic effects. According to Pinstrup-Andersen (1988), food subsidies can have a substantial effect on food prices if the size of subsidies is large enough and change considerably overtime. The immediate and feasible effect of food subsidies is on household incomes. The effect on household income is determined by the scheme of the subsidy, the targeting mechanism and the subsidized commodity. Food subsidies generally increase household food consumption (Pinstrup-Andersen 1988, von Braun et al. 1992). In addition, food price subsidies also alter intrahousehold food distribution and individual consumption. Further, von Braun et al. (1992) pointed out that food subsidy programs had a positive and significant impact on the food consumption of younger household members. However, there might be program leakage to other household members and the program might shift food consumption to adult household member engaged in income activity. To assess food subsidy scheme on income food consumption, some studies relied on observational studies (Jensen and Miller 2002, Kochar 2005) and field experiment through randomized design approach (Jensen and Miller 2008). Through appropriate techniques, observational studes might produce unbiased estimate (Ahmed et al. 2009). Prices variation drawn from survey data possibly contains endogenous variation in market prices which may confound causal relationship (Jensen and Miller 2008). To address this issue, Jensen and Miller (2008) conducted field experiment to maintain exogenous prices variation.

Previous literature on the evaluation of the impacts of anti-poverty programs, particularly programs that addressed household nutritional welfare, have in some cases shown encouraging results. Efforts to provide meals at schools in the Philippines had positive and significant impacts on children's nutrition even though it also created an intra-household "fly-paper"[21] effect (Jacoby 2002). The fly-paper effect was also evident in the case of a food supplementary program in Guatemala (Islam and Hodinott 2009). Hodinott and Skoufias (2004) found that PROGRESA, an anti-poverty program in Mexico, had no impact on food consumption at the stage of implementation but gradually had a significant impact on household calorie intake. Ruiz-Arranz et al. (2006) found that PROGRESA and another Mexican program PROCAMPO[22] had increased food consumption and calorie intake through different channels. PROGRESA boosted food consumption through income effect whereas PROCAMPO increased food consumption through investment in home food production. Rivera et al. (2004) found that infants of household beneficiaries of PROGRESA had improved growth rates.

Similar impacts have also been reported in Sub-Saharan Africa. Using the case of food aid and food-for-work programs in Ethiopia, Quisumbing (2003) found that these programs had a significant and positive impact on children's nutritional status that varied based on gender. In that study free food distribution

---

21 The "fly-paper" effect is a term from the public finance literature which refers to the phenomenon that grants stimulate higher local spending than an increase in local income (Hines and Thaler 1995, Jacoby 2002).
22 PROCAMPO was a cash transfer program in Mexico (Sadoulet et al. 2001).

was associated with better nutrition among girls, whereas food-for-work was associated with improved nutrition among boys. Evaluating the same program, Gilligan and Hodinott (2007) measured impact in terms of broader outcomes. They examined whether the emergency food aid had a short-term impact on food and nutrition security or if they served as insurance through asset accumulation. Free food distribution was found to have had a positive impact on food consumption but negatively affected food security, however, the food-for-work program had positive impacts on both food consumption and food security. The free food distribution program had no impact on the growth of household livestock, but the food-for-work program had a negative effect on livestock growth. These findings confirmed that food programs had heterogeneous impacts. More recently, Abebaw et al. (2010) evaluated the impact of an integrated food security program in Northwestern Ethiopia and found that it had a positive impact on calorie intake. Program beneficiaries had a 30 percent higher calorie intake compared to nonparticipants but the impact was heterogeneous depending on household size, land holding size, and gender of the household head. Ninno and Dorosh (2002) evaluated the impact of a food and cash transfer program on food consumption in Bangladesh and found that the marginal propensity to consume food out of food transfers was significantly higher than the effect of income. However, the impacts were heterogeneous depending on the size of in-kind transfer, smaller amounts of in-kind transfer had insignificant impacts on the marginal propensity to consume.

In the case of Indonesia various anti-poverty programs have been implemented, particularly in response to the financial crisis. Several social programs have also been introduced to promote public health. Johar (2009) measured the effectiveness of the health card program that was initiated in 1994 and targeted poor households. The program aimed at enhancing health care utilization among the poor and for its eligibility criteria it also followed the BKKBN welfare criteria. This study applied matching estimators and difference in difference methods to panel data of Indonesian households. The impact of the health card program was measured in terms of health care consumption and enrollment in a contraceptive program. It was found that the presence of a health card in the household had a significant and positive impact on the expenditure of curative treatment for younger household members but not for other household members. The health card program also had a significant effect on the enrollment of household women in contraceptive programs.

There have been a few evaluations of SSN programs. Cameron (2009) evaluated the impact of the SSN scholarship program on the drop-out rate from secondary level education. The purpose of the SSN scholarship program was to reduce drop-out rates during times of economic crisis. The Indonesian government imposed a mandatory goal of primary school education attainment but the the high drop-out rate from secondary education level remained high (Jones and Hagul 2001). Using 100 Village Survey data[23], this study employed an instrumental variable approach to evaluate the impact of the program. Cameron (2009) also examined the targeting design of the program and how effectively it reached the designated households. The results showed that the targeting performance of the program was effective and it was found that the probability that a household became a scholarship grantee decreased as household per capita rises. The latter result was promising since Indonesia had a poor track record of allocating funds to support large-scale aid projects during the Soeharto period (Simpson 1998). The study also identified program inefficiency as evidenced by a sizeable number of scholarship recipients (5.1 percent) who were from households in the upper quintiles of per capita expenditure. In the impact evaluation method, instrumental variables which affect the probability of receiving a scholarship but not the probability of dropping-out were involved in the model. The BKKBN poverty indicator criteria were chosen as instrumental variables. The probability of receiving a scholarship was indeed influenced by the BKKBN welfare criteria such as housing quality and asset holdings. Furthermore, this study showed that the program impact was substantial. The scholarship program reduced lower secondary education level drop-out rates by 3 percent. This means that cash aid distributed to households based on certain conditions, in this case education, can be beneficial by allowing poor households to keep children in school and discourage dropping-out. Nevertheless, improving targeting is still an area that requires improvement on behalf of the government.

As the financial and economic crisis affected mostly children's and maternal nutritional status (Block et al. 2004), Giles and Satriawan (2010) evaluated the effectiveness of the supplementary feeding program on the nutritional status of infants and young children affected by the economic crisis. Using Indonesian Family Life Survey data, this study accounted for the variations in the program exposure to assess the program impact. The supplementary feeding program was intended for poor children aged between 6 and 60 months and pregnant women. For infants, the supplementary food was in the form of soft meals and supplement breast milk while young children received prepared energy snacks (360-430 kcal) and protein (9-11 grams) for 90 consecutive days. The younger children (12-24 months) received supplements three to four times a day while the older children (24-60 months) were provided supplement once a week. Based on the IFLS sample, 95.4 percent of sampled communities participated in the pro-

---

[23] This survey covered 100 villages located in ten districts across eight provinces in Indonesia (Sumarto et al. 2005).

gram between 1998 and 2000 which means that the program was almost universally distributed, but program duration varied among sites. The outcome variable measured in this study was height-for-age. The results showed that community characteristics such as health, physical infrastructure, and geographical aspects affected the program placement and duration. Program duration was longer in more remote communities. The findings confirmed that the supplementary feeding program improved the nutritional status of children aged 12 to 24 months.

An alternative to economic and nutrition impact assessments are direct inquiries into change of subjective well-being. The issue of subjective well-being and economic growth firstly was embraced by Nordhaus and Tobin (1973). Nordhaus and Tobin (1973) raised a radical question whether the increased material wealth as an engine of well-being. Later, Easterlin (1974, 1995) also pointed out the similar issue on the paradox of real income growth. Subjective well-being has received enormous attention recently even though the measures of subjective well-being is still debatable (Stevenson and Wolfers 2008). Even if subjective well-being indicators cannot serve a good indicator, they still can be an important measure in their own way (Deaton 2011). In this sense, it is definitely better to perceive a standard of living more than adequate rather than less adequate. Subjective well-being therefore complements in capturing the multidimensional of economic development. The successful of economic development not only indicates numerical and monetary increases of capital accumulation, production and consumption, but also enlarges social, political and institutional progress (Clark and Senik 2011). Borrowing from Easterlin paradox (1974), this study examines the relationship of food security program participation and subjective well-being. In the case if subsidies received by the program recipients might not be accompanied by improvement in subjective well-being, it simply cannot be concluded that the program brings no impact. Nonetheless, the program might be deficient in engaging and empowering the poor of which this study attempts to explore. This study contributes to the growing literature of subjective well-being, particularly in seeking the effect of food security program participation on noneconomic and nutrition dimensions.

Literature on the association between subjective well-being and aid is still limited, particularly in the context of Indonesia. Subjective well-being is often associated with income or health. People who are richer tend to have a subjective well-being that is significantly higher than poor people (Cummins 2000). Kahneman and Krueger (2006) pointed out that individual responses to subjective well-being questions vary with circumstances and other factors. The relationship of aid and subjective well-being can be mixed. Aid may have positive effect if it affects household income and the income elevates subjective well-being. In contrast, aid might have a negative effect if it psychologically affects people sense of self-reliance and thus increase feelings of powerlessness and dependence. Oswald and Powdthavee (2005) found that the average life satisfaction decreased after the onset of a disability but fully recovered to the pre-disability level within two years. Based on previous research on the relationship between income and subjective well-being, mean incomes and expenditures are central determinants of subjective well-being, and community wealth ranking affects individual perceptions on subjective well-being.

As mentioned above, impact evaluations of the food security program in Indonesia were mostly conducted at the macro level. Therefore, the contribution of this study in the program evaluation literature is twofold. The first contribution is the description of the impact of a targeted food security program during a time of financial crisis in Indonesia. The impact of the food security program was evaluated based on estimations of household food and nonfood expenditures before and after the program. More specifically, the outcomes of food expenditures were classified into rice, other staple foods, meat and fish, dairy products, and adult goods. Outcomes of nonfood expenditures concerned education and health expenditures. Issues of aid-fungibility[24] and "fly-paper effects" are examined in this context. The second contribution of this study is the examination of the program impact across income groups. The evaluation examines the relationship between the food security program and subjective well-being and whether subjective well-being varies between program beneficiaries and nonbeneficiaries.

3.5. Data and Variables

3.5.1. Data

The data used in this study are from the 1997 and 2000 Indonesia Family Life Survey (IFLS) efforts which capture periods before and after the economic crisis and the period corresponding to the food security program[25]. The IFLS represents 13 out of 27 provinces in Indonesia during that period. The first round of IFLS interviewed 7,224 households and approximately 22,000 individuals. The follow up rate on the subsequent IFLS was high (95 percent).

---

24 Aid is displaced to unintended purposes desired by the donors (Pack and Pack 1990).
25 The IFLS 2 was fielded before the crisis hit the Indonesian economy. An IFLS 2+ was conducted in 1998 and aimed to describe the immediate effect of the economic crisis, but it only sampled around 25 percent of the total IFLS sample.

IFLS collected longitudinal data on household characteristics, the communities in which they live, and the health and education facilities they used. Further information on community characteristics was available from the food security program. The 2000 IFLS round included a particular section regarding the SSN program in community questionnaires. This provided enough information on the food security program to observe the program distribution. The sample was restricted to panel households because split off households might have different characteristics compared to their original status. The total sample used in this study was 7,178 panel households.

Questions regarding individual assessment of economic welfare were introduced in the third round of IFLS. The questions were aimed at identifying how individuals classified themselves and measured their personal welfare. The questions applied the Russia Longitudinal Monitoring Survey (RLMS) method, asking respondents to imagine their position within a six-step ladder, on which the poorest people are on the first step and the richest people are on the sixth step. Respondents are also asked about their past and future economic welfare perception. Other questions regarding subjective well-being were about personal satisfaction on food consumption, healthcare, children's standard of living, nonfood consumption, and education. Respondents were asked to assess whether these aspects of their lives were less than adequate, adequate, or more than adequate.

3.5.2. Dependent Variables

To assess the impact of the food security program, certain outcomes were measured. The outcomes examined were household food and nonfood expenditures. Specifically, food expenditures were broken down into rice, other staple foods, meat and fish, dairy products, and adult goods. Nonfood expenditures included medical and education expenses. Information on food and nonfood expenditures were derived from an expenditure module and were adjusted to 2000 prices so that real expenditure values between the two surveys were comparable[26].

Table 3.1 presents the selected outcomes of "the post-exposure period" between the food security program recipients and a control group of nonrecipients. Based on the IFLS samples, 2,729 households reported that they were beneficiaries of the program. The outcomes of the recipient group were higher than the control group for rice, other staple foods, adult goods, and meat expenditures. This means that program recipient households consumed cheaper calorie sources as indicated by higher expenditures on rice and other staple foods. Medical and

---

26 The detailed calculation of deflators is available in Strauss et al. (2004).

education expenditures were lower than food expenditures. The higher expenditure on basic food items is also a strong indication that the recipient households were less prosperous than control households. Nonfood expenditures of the program households were lower than adult goods expenditures.

Table 3.1: Household Food Consumption of Post Exposure Year based on IFLS 2000 (in log term)

Expenditures	Recipient		Control	
	Mean	Std. Deviation	Mean	Std. Deviation
Total Food Expenditure	12.96	0.70	13.27	0.75
Rice	10.30	3.36	9.32	4.65
Staple	11.01	2.30	10.71	3.05
Dairy Product	7.29	4.61	8.46	4.27
Meat	9.66	2.97	9.18	4.09
Fish	8.27	3.94	9.04	3.98
Adult Goods	7.70	4.85	7.08	5.35
Nonfood Expenditure	12.39	0.83	12.93	1.04
Medical	7.24	3.44	7.45	3.84
Education	6.81	5.22	7.78	5.31
N	2,729		4,449	

Source: Author calculation based on IFLS data

Before doing calculation of the food security program impact, table 3.2 presents the difference of expenditures between recipients and non-recipients households capturing the periode before and after program implementation. It is shown that the recipients and non-recipients households had a significant different on food and nonfood expenditure before and after program exposure, particularly in terms of staple and education expenditures.

Table 3.2: Difference in Difference of Consumption

Expenditures	DID	Std Error
Food Expenditure	0.048***	0.020
Rice	0.069	0.129
Staple	0.217***	0.089
Dairy Product	-0.107	0.128
Meat and Fish	0.004	0.103
Adult Goods	-0.137	0.134
Non-food Expenditure	0.119***	0.022
Medical	0.071	0.124
Education	0.249***	0.121

Source: Author calculation based on IFLS data

Note: *** Denotes statistical significance at 1% level.

3.5.3. Explanatory Variables

The explanatory variables were used to calculate the probability of receiving rice from the food security program in the matching estimator. Therefore, conditions that influence program eligibility will be used to calculate propensity score matching. As mentioned earlier, program eligibility criteria were based on BKKBN welfare criteria including household welfare conditions as indicated by housing characteristics and income. The covariates involved in propensity score estimators were household head and housing characteristics since these variables were observed and influenced program eligibility. In greater detail, housing characteristics included the type of walls and floors in the house, whether the house had piped water, and whether the occupants were renters or owners. Table 3.2 presents selected covariates based on the pre-exposure year. It is evident that household characteristics varied between recipient and control groups and that the controls had higher per capita expenditures and assets. The control groups were more educated and had younger household heads. The recipient households lived in lower quality houses. More than 20 percent of recipient households had dirt-floors and bamboo walls and only 15 percent had direct water access. Interestingly, there were more households in the control group who owned health cards, despite the fact the health card were intended for poor households and the eligibility conditions also followed BKKBN welfare criteria.

Village characteristics and provincial dummy variables were also included to control for regional heterogeneity. Village characteristics involved in the model included proxies of remoteness such as the distance to the nearest bus stop or terminal, and distance to the district capital. Table 3.2 reports that only 20 percent of recipient households resided in a village with a bus station. This means that most food security program recipients were located in areas with limited access by four-wheel-drive vehicles. This finding is closely related to the fact that most of the recipient households were located in rural areas (70 percent) and less than 2 percent of the recipient households were located in a district capital. To control for economic conditions in the community, major commodity prices such as rice and chicken prices, as well as average village per capita expenditures were entered into the matching estimator.

Table 3.3: Summary Statistics of Household Characteristics in Pre Exposure Year

	Recipient Mean	Recipient Std. Deviation	Control Mean	Control Std. Deviation
Household Head's Characteristics				
Age (in years)	49.281	14.310	47.333	13.948
Education (years of schooling)	4.068	3.703	6.693	4.808
Work (dummy, working=1)	0.792	0.406	0.774	0.419
Male household head (dummy, male=1)	0.800	0.400	0.848	0.359
Household characteristics				
Under 6 years	0.511	0.711	0.518	0.725
6 - 14 years	0.951	1.002	0.920	1.043
15 - 59 years (male)	1.188	0.918	1.306	0.979
15 - 59 years (female)	1.309	0.799	1.447	0.945
60 years and over (male)	0.204	0.405	0.166	0.376
60 years and over (female)	0.241	0.437	0.192	0.411
HH size	4.404	1.975	4.549	2.100
Ln PCE	11.165	0.712	11.550	0.848
Ln Asset	15.200	1.659	15.825	2.060
Fridge	0.027	0.162	0.167	0.373
Health Card	0.082	0.275	0.123	0.328
Urban	0.348	0.477	0.512	0.500
Java	0.754	0.430	0.497	0.500
Housing characteristics				
Owner	0.865	0.342	0.766	0.423
Ceramic floor	0.038	0.191	0.132	0.338
Tiles floor	0.217	0.412	0.234	0.423

Dirt Floor	0.304	0.460	0.085	0.278
Bamboo wall	0.236	0.425	0.079	0.270
Brick wall	0.518	0.500	0.625	0.484
Piped water	0.156	0.363	0.300	0.458
Community Remoteness				
Nearest bus stop in the village (dummy, yes=1)	0.195	0.396	0.228	0.420
District capital in the village (dummy, yes=1)	0.012	0.108	0.027	0.161
Average Prices at Village Level				
Rice price (per kg)	1,156.974	143.198	1,214.136	195.330
Chicken price (per kg)	4,424.294	844.967	4,657.458	1,106.642
N	2,729		4,449	

Source: Author calculation based on IFLS data

Note: Prices are in Indonesian rupiahs

3.6. Estimation Strategy

This section presents the econometric techniques employed in this part of the study. The beginning of this section discusses the methods of program evaluation in the nonexperimental settings. The advantages and shortcomings of the study are also described. The second part provides the specific model applied in this study.

3.6.1. Evaluation of Observational Studies

In the field of impact evaluation, an appropriate method is needed to assess program performance against the counterfactual situation of the program being absent (Ravallion 2009). There have been a number of studies of methods of program evaluation in the last two decades (Lechner 2002, Jalan and Ravallion 2003, Yanovitzky et al. 2005, Austin; 2008, 2011). These studies were driven by the need to evaluate social programs that were not conducted in an experimental setting. Innovation in social programs within experimental settings through randomization has been growing. Despite the advantages of getting valid estimates of program impacts, it also has some drawbacks such as high cost, external validation, ethical issues, and program compliance. Many anti-poverty programs are prompted by immediate needs and critical situations. In situations where randomized experiments are absent, more complex and careful methods are needed.

In the observational studies setting, program evaluations should consider the issue of nonrandom selection which might not be found in experimental studies. A major problem in program evaluation is to create a suitable image of the unobserved counterfactual setting. Measuring impact as the difference of outcomes between program recipients and nonrecipients may provide a biased estimate of the program's impact (Moffitt 1991, Gilligan and Hodinott 2006, Ravallion 2009). A bias is present if there are unobserved characteristics that influence program participation that are correlated with the outcomes. Gilligan and Hodinott (2006) mention that the selection bias often comes from unobserved characteristics of targeting program recipients and self-selection into programs.

In the nonexperimental setting, the appropriate method of impact evaluation depends on three factors: the type of information available, the underlying model, and the parameters of interest (Blundell and Dias 2000). Datasets that are longitudinal or repeated cross-sectional allow less restrictive estimators. According to Blundell and Dias (2000), instrumental variables and Heckman selection estimators are relevant for cross-sectional datasets while double differences can be applied in longitudinal or repeated cross-sectional datasets. Another approach that can be implemented in nonexperimental setting is the matching method. The method of matching is relevant both for cross-sectional and longitudinal data. Matching method works through constructing a comparison group of individuals with observable characteristics similar to those of program participants (Rubin and Thomas 1996, Rosenbaum 2002). It is conducted by modeling the probability of participation, estimating the propensity score for each individual, and then matching individuals with similar propensity scores. With various methods available, the main obstacle in implementing an observational impact evaluation study is choosing the most appropriate among the large variety of estimation methods.

3.6.2. Propensity Score Matching

This study employed propensity score matching (PSM). The large amount of information contained in the IFLS efforts allowed this study to mimic an experimental setting through PSM estimators. With sufficient data, PSM provides a useful econometric tool (Smith and Todd 2005). The underlying assumption of matching estimators is that the outcomes are independent of program participation and conditional on a set of observed covariates. PSM is not a silver bullet for the evaluation problem, but with sound data and ample knowledge of the program, PSM may produce reasonable results.

We let Y_i^1 be the outcome of the ith household if it participated in the program, and let Y_i^0 be the household's outcome if the household did not participate in the program. Thus, the program impact can be calculated as $\Delta = Y_i^1 - Y_i^0$. The program participation is represented by D, where D = 1 if the household is a program recipient and D = 0 if otherwise. Therefore:

$$E(\Delta \mid X, D=1) = E(Y^1 - Y^0 \mid X, D=1) = E(Y^1 \mid X, D=1) - E(Y^0 \mid X, D=1) \quad (3.1)$$

X in equation (3.1) is a vector of the control variables and subscripts have been excluded to simplify the model illustration. However, the counterfactual outcomes as indicated in $E(Y^0 \mid X, D = 1)$ is not observed. Fortunately, PSM constructs counterfactual outcomes for participants. The probability of participation in the program is formulated as:

$$P(X) = Pr(D = 1 \mid X) \quad (3.2)$$

Rosenbaum and Rubin (1983) created comparison groups through matching observations regarding program households to observations regarding nonprogram households with similar values of P(X). There two assumptions underlying this argument. The first assumption is known as conditional mean independence. This can be expressed as:

$$E(Y^0 \mid X, D=1) = E(Y^0 \mid X, D=0) \quad (3.3)$$

This assumption requires controlling for a vector of variables (X), that the mean outcomes of nonparticipants be identical to the program household outcomes if the households had not participated the program. This implies that program participation was based exclusively on the observed characteristics. The second assumption is common support or overlap condition (Khandker et al. 2009) which is expressed as follows:

$$0 < \Pr(D = 1 \mid X) < 1 \tag{3.4}$$

This condition means that recipient observations are comparable to control observations. If those two assumptions hold, PSM provides unbiased estimates of equation (3.1). Though in observational data it is not plausible to test those two assumptions, Heckman et al. (1998) found that PSM provided reliable and low-biased program impact estimates.

In choosing the covariates of matching estimators, there is no algorithm technique that automatically selects sets of variables X that satisfy the conditions. However, the covariates should include the key factors affecting program participation and outcomes. Therefore, a clear understanding of the institution which governs the program is important to avoid biased estimates of the matching estimators. In the implementation, a set of covariates which captures the BKKBN welfare criteria and geographical aspects which affect program placement were entered into the program participation model.

Employing panel data allowed this study to combine PSM and the difference in difference method (DiD). The use of panel data enabled comparison of the change of outcomes between program and nonprogram households before and after program implementation and also eliminates the unobserved time-invariant differences between program and nonprogram households. Hence, PSM and DiD were used to examine the average exposure effect on the program recipient (Johar 2009).

The food security program allowed households to save more resources, which enabled them to purchase nutritious but more expensive food such as meat, fish, vegetables, and dairy products. In addition, the extra resources might have been invested in nonfood consumption such as education and health. The changing pattern of household consumption, particularly from cheaper low-calorie to higher nutrient food, is an indication of welfare change. When the income effects do not improve human capital or condition, it is a strong sign of aid-fungibility. Another issue in the aid program is the fly-paper effect. More specifically, the impacts of the "rice for the poor" program were evaluated among seven food consumption groups: rice, other staples, meat, fish, vegetables and fruit, dairy products, and adult goods, and nonfood expenditures on education and medical needs. Aid-fungibility occurs when the "rice for the poor" program had a positive effect on the share of less nutritional food items, such as adult goods, whereas the fly-paper effect exists when the program increased expenditures on rice and other staple foods.

3.7. Results and Discussion

This section presents the results of the impact evaluation of the food security program in Indonesia during a time of economic crisis. It is revealed that the food security program almost covers the study area. However, the program is still subject to leakage. The matching estimators show that rural and less educated households are more likely to participate the program. Lower income households tended to participate in the program. The third and fourth part discusses the program impact and the particular impact is detailed in part four. The last part of this section relates food security program and subjective well-being.

3.7.1. Implementation of SSN and The Food Security Program

The SSN programs were intended to help the chronically and newly impoverished to cope with the severe impacts of the economic crisis. The SSN programs included programs on food security, employment creation, education, health, and community empowerment. While the food security, health, and education programs were specifically targeted to households, the employment creation and community empowerment are not independent programs but were attached to other ongoing activities (Sumarto et al. 2005). The employment creation program is a collection of public works that are attached to sectoral ministries. The community empowerment program provides a village block grant intended as a revolving fund for credit. In the implementation phase of the program, villages were given full authority to use the grant and most of villages opted to use the fund for physical infrastructure development to generate employment and for local credit schemes.

The IFLS community data revealed regional variation in participation in SSN programs. Most of the IFLS villages (98 percent) received food program assistance. Village participation in the health card and community empowerment programs was also high (80 percent and 73 percent respectively). The job creation program was less popular, with only 54 percent of the total IFLS villages participating the program. Since SSN programs are delivered via a packaged system, it was very likely that villages received benefits from multiple programs. Less than 40 percent of the villages received all SSN programs, and approximately 75 percent of the villages received food security program benefits also received community empowerment program benefits, and only 55 percent of the food security program villages also participated in the job creation program. Villages that did not participate in the food security program were also less likely to participate in either the job creation or community empowerment programs. Therefore, it is also very likely that the recipients participated in multiple programs. Unfortunately, the IFLS data only provided information on household participation in the healthcard program. The details of program participation across villages is presented in Figure 3.1 and Figure 3.2.

Figure 3.1: Village Participation in Food and Health Card Program

[Bar chart: Village had Food Program 98-00 — No: 2.6, Yes: 97.4. Village Had Healthcard Program — No: 19.6, Yes: 80.4. Source: IFLS 2000 Community Data]

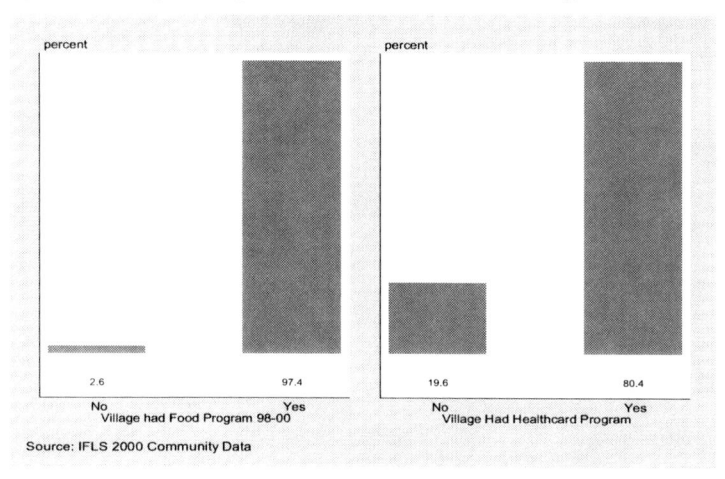

Figure 3.2: Village Participation in Community Empowerment and Job Creation Program

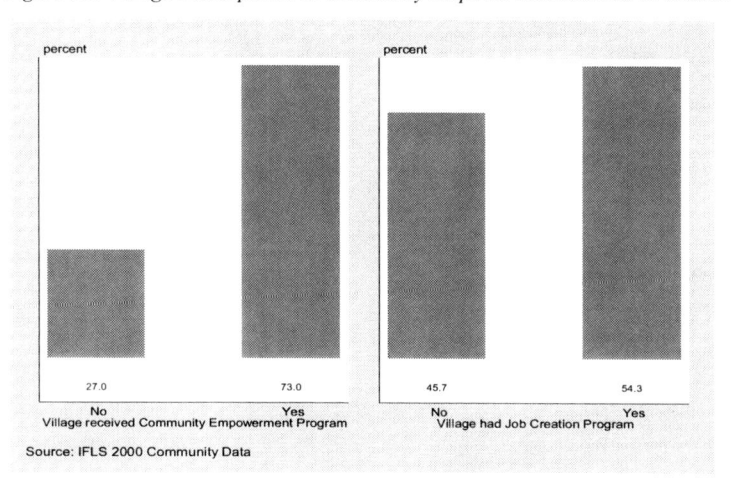

[Bar chart: Village received Community Empowerment Program — No: 27.0, Yes: 73.0. Village had Job Creation Program — No: 45.7, Yes: 54.3. Source: IFLS 2000 Community Data]

Figure 3.3: Distribution of Food Security, Job Creation, and Community Empowerment Program

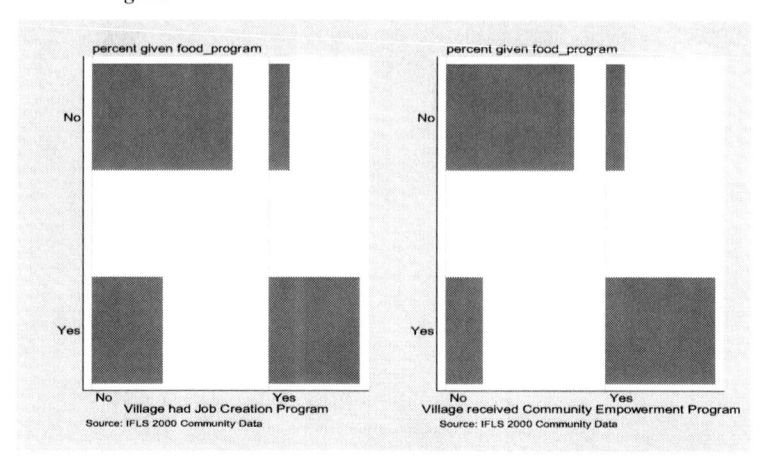

Figure 3.4: Distribution of Food Security, Health Card, and Village Midwife Program

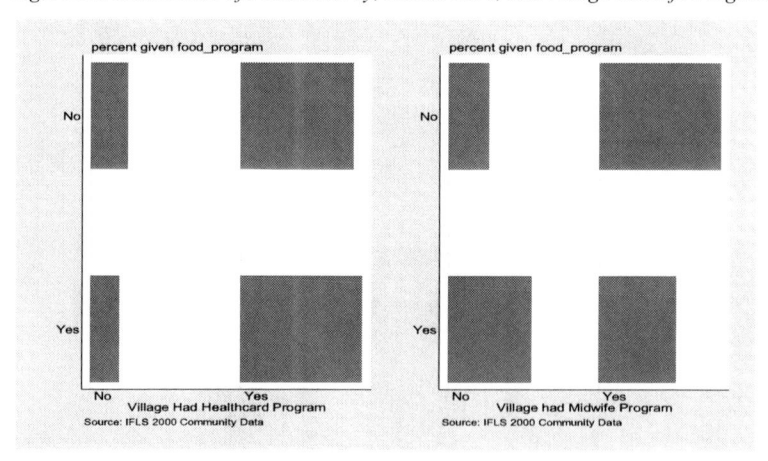

The overlapping participation of SSN programs such as the employment creation and community empowerment programs might confound the impact of food security program to be analyze in this study. Employment creation and community empowerment program also had income transfer to the households through different scheme. Both programs were based on placement on the village level and more in the scheme of village block grant. Especially for job creation, the income transfer of this program is sort of 'crash transfer'. If that was the case, the impacts of the food security program is biased by the effects of the other programs. Unfortunately, IFLS did not provide detailed information on whether the households were also participants in other SSN programs. Alternatively, removing all participants that participated in multiple programs could also bias the results. In fact, from the nature of program implementation, Figure 3.1 to Figure 3.3 depict a certain pattern that the distribution of job creation and community empowerment program follow a program placement. This pattern is different from the food security program where almost villages receive the program and show no indication of program placement.

Within the SSN program package, the food security program is the most critical program because it dealt with basic food needs that are most important during times of crisis. The program was almost universal and had the highest program coverage (Sumarto et al. 2003). The program was also subject to inefficiency. Olken et al. (2001) and Olken (2006) found that inefficiency was often associated with local contexts in which local elites affected benefit disbursements. Olken (2006) also mentioned that 18 percent of the rice in the food security program could not be accounted for, which may have related to the ethnically heterogeneous and sparsely populated nature of some beneficiary areas. Sumarto et al. (2003) mentioned that the food security program was also subject to bias based on location within or outside Java.

Table 3.4: Distribution of the Food Security Program Based on IFLS Samples

	Rural	Urban	Total
Community with The food security program (%)			
1998	80.92	76.67	78.46
1999	93.89	95.00	94.53
2000	85.50	89.44	87.78
Proportion of Recipient Households (%)			
1998	41.07	22.84	30.15
1999	41.78	25.49	32.01
2000	40.06	23.81	29.83

Source: Author calculation based on IFLS data

Table 3.4 presents the food security program distribution based on the IFLS efforts in 1998 and 2000. The program was launched in April 1998, but the timing of the program disbursement varied by community due to variable local capacity. Table 3.4 shows that the program coverage was lower in 1998 compared to the following years. Based on the IFLS sample, only 78.46 percent of the communities received food security program benefits and the program reached more rural communities in 1998. The program coverage expanded in 1999 when 95 percent of the IFLS communities received food security program assistance. Urban communities were more exposed to the program during the expansion period (1999 and 2000), although the difference is not high. Higher urban coverage might be associated with greater suffering due to the crisis in urban areas relative to rural areas (Suryahadi and Sumarto 2003). The program exposure and duration as presented in table 3.4 may also have affected this evaluation of the program impacts. The program was implemented in different stages and continues to operate. Defining meaningful spatial and temporal evaluation scales will be necessary steps in evaluating the sustainability and impacts of the program and to justify whether the food security program is an appropriate investment to improve food and nutrition security. Accordingly, appropriate econometrics techniques beyond propensity score matching and difference in difference become essential to address this issue.

Even though the food security program was administered in more urban communities, the number of recipient households was higher in rural areas (Table 3.4). The percentage of rural households participating in the program was almost double that of urban households. The number of program beneficiaries also increased in the second year of program. This might be associated with the expansion of the food security program, particularly after BKKBN relaxed the eligibility criteria of the food security program beneficiaries to include both pre-prosperous and prosperous I category households. The number of beneficiaries decreased in 2000 when most households had recovered from the economic crisis.

Table 3.5: Food Security Targeting Performance by Income and Region

Per capita expenditure quantile	Percentage of households		
	Java	Outside Java	All
1st (lowest)	28.58	32.59	29.56
2nd	25.33	26.91	25.71
3rd	19.99	21.52	20.37
4th	16.55	12.56	15.57
5th (highest)	9.56	6.43	8.79
Total	100	100	100

Source: Author calculation based on IFLS data

Table 3.5 presents the targeting performance of the food security program. The effectiveness of targeting of the food security program was assessed by looking at the income distribution patterns and regional dimension of the program participants. It is shown that the percentage of households receiving the program fell as household per capita expenditure rose in both Java and the rest of the country. Almost 30 percent of the food security program beneficiary households were among the poorest 20 percent and 55 percent were among the poorest 40 percent of all households. The targeting performance was slightly better in outside Java where almost 60 percent of the food security program beneficiaries were among the poorest 40 percent of households. Strikingly, almost 20 percent of the program beneficiaries were from the highest income quintile households even though the program was intended to help the poor. The misadministration of the program was also evident in Java where almost 10 percent of the richest households benefitted from the program. This indicates a failure of the food security program to provide oversight of the selection of beneficiaries. This result is consistent with the findings of Hastuti (2008) based on SUSENAS data that found more than 10 percent of the highest income quintile households were also beneficiaries of the food security program. This finding is also consistent with other evaluations of SSN programs that found that even rich households were benefiting from anti-poverty programs (Sumarto et al. 2002, Cameron 2009). The average amount of rice received by the households is reported in Figure A3.1 (in the Appendix). Again, geographical biases were also present and the rice that was unaccounted for is also evident. That figure presents that beneficiary households in all Indonesian provinces received less than what they were supposed to receive. Households were entitled to receive 20 kg per month, though in reality they received only 11 kg[27]. Outside Java households received a larger amount than Java households. This fact was associated with the tendency in Java of distributing rice to unintended households that reduced aid available to target households. Improved targeting would be an effective method for the Indonesian government to improve program benefits for the poor, but the costs and feasibility of more narrow targeting would need to be assessed in order to identify economically optimal targeting.

3.7.2. Matching Results

As previously mentioned, the matching method was used to estimate program participation and select a comparison group for each recipient household based on propensity score. Figure A3.6 in the Appendix presents the quality of matching based on IFLS samples. Besides propensity score, a balancing property test was also conducted. In this case, the balancing property test ended up with eight blocks of propensity score. The figure shows overlapping areas of support. The overlap regions of support are encouraging for propensity score matching. Considering the food security program is a targeted program, less significant area of overlap is common since the program selection was based on certain criteria. There was no household in the sample with either 0 or 1 as a propensity score. The histogram shows the control and recipient group skewness and there was a significant difference in propensity scores between the control and recipient groups. The mean propensity score of control and recipient groups were 0.26 and 0.59 respectively. This means that conditional on covariates, the control group had less probability of receiving benefits from the program. The distribu-

---

27 The wide gap in the average amount of rice received by households might be related to the later phase of food security program administration when the amount of rice distributed to households was reduced to 15 kg.

tion of propensity scores for the control group being frequently located on the left of the distribution for the treatment group for targeted social program, indicated effective targeting (Ahmed et al. 2009). The test of equality of mean values between the recipient and control groups could not reject the equality of all covariates. In some other cases, PSM did not yield identical means for all covariates unlike the case of covariate matching (Johar 2009). This result is not surprising because the food security program is a targeted program.

Covariates involved in program participation were based on the BKKBN eligibility criteria and geographical characteristics. The program selection was estimated using a Probit model. Based on the sample, about 38 percent of households were recipients of the food security program. There were big differences between program recipients and nonrecipients. More information on post-exposure figures is presented in Table A3.1 in the Appendix. The results of program participation are presented in Table A3.2 in the Appendix. It is revealed that the urban household dummy had negative and significant impacts on program participation. This finding confirms the descriptive statistics that found higher proportions of beneficiaries among rural households. The household income category also had a significant effect on program participation. The higher the income the less likely the household participated in the program. Low housing quality as indicated by dirt floors had a significant and positive effect on food security program participation. This result shows that on average, the program reached the targeted group. The regional factors as shown by the provincial dummy had a significant effect on program participation and provinces in Java were more likely to benefit from the program. Households in Lampung and West Nusa Tenggara were more likely to become program recipients. Those provinces are known as chronically food insecure provinces (Suyanto et al. 2007, Salim 2010). Community characteristics as measured by remoteness from public transportation (bus station) and district capital, average per capita expenditure, and rice price indicated a significant impact. The program tended to operate in relatively remote and poorer communities. The communities with higher rice prices also tended to receive food security program assistance. This finding is consistent with the result of a food supplementary feeding program evaluation by Giles and Satriawan (2010) which found that households residing in more remote areas were most likely to participate in the program.

Following Gilligan and Hodinott (2007), this study included a control variable of participation in other programs to observe the potential influence of other programs. Household participation in the health card program was one of covariates in the propensity score matching estimator. The propensity score results did not change significantly when health card program participation was dropped from the food security program participation model (Figure A3.3 in the Appendix). This supports the hypothesis that participation in the healthcard program did not influence the food security program impacts. The last robustness check was conducted by checking the distribution of selected expenditures between households receiving the food security program only and households receiving both the food security and health card programs. The expenditures of those two household categories were not significantly different (Figure A3.4 and A3.5 in the Appendix).

3.7.3. Impact on Food and Nonfood Expenditures

The measurable outcomes of the food security program were changes in food and nonfood expenditures. The food expenditure was broken down into rice, other staples, dairy products, meat and fish, and adult goods expenditure. Nonfood expenditure was focused on education and health spending. The food security program enabled households to have extra resources which allowed them to allocate those resources into human capital investment such as higher nutrient food, education, and health expenditures. Matching estimators and difference in difference were applied to examine the program effects.

The average treatment effects were evaluated based on cross-sectional data (IFLS 2000) which captured the post-exposure period only, as well as panel data which measured the change of consumption before and after the program. In conducting the average treatment effect, this study employed the Kernel method because bootstrapping of standard error procedures may not be appropriate for other matching method such as nearest neighbor matching due to nonsmoothness of the method (Abadie and Imbens 2006). The standard errors of the average treatment effects were given by bootstrapping with 150 replications. The results are presented in Table 3.6. The second column presents the average treatment effect based on post exposure data, only (IFLS 2000) the third column was derived from panel data. The results show that the food security program had no impact on total food and non-food consumption, but that it helped the program recipients in smoothing within food consumption, particularly by allowing them to afford meat, fish, and dairy products.

In a more detailed analysis, the food security program had a positive and large effect on rice and other staple foods expenditures based on the post-exposure data. This means that in the short run, the food security program did help the recipients to cover their basic food needs, though this is evidence of a fly-paper effect of the program. Borrowing from Okun's expression, it is found that the government program "sticks where it hits" (Hines and Thaler 1995). Extra resources from the food security program were not a perfect substitute for rice and other staple expenditures, but rather acted as a complement. The food security program indeed helped the program recipients, because the rice price from the program was much lower than the market price. The increase of rice expenditure as a result from the food security program should be explored to determine whether it was a shift in quality or quantity. In addition, households tended to smoothen their consumption and prioritize their primary consumption during the period of economic crisis. Based on post exposure data, it is also revealed that the food security program had positive and significant effects on meat and fish expenditures (column 2 of Table 3.6). The program also had a positive influence on medical expenditures, although the overall impact on nonfood expenditure was negative. The impact of the food security program was even greater than the health card impact. Johar (2009) revealed that the health card program had a very limited impact on the consumption of primary health care. There is a possible explanation for the negative impact of food security on nonfood expenditure. Recipients of the food security program had to increase their food expenditure to meet their basic needs and avoided nonfood expenditures.

The post exposure data shows that there were also unintended effects from the food security program. The extra resources available as a result of the food security program was also transferred into adult goods consumption and the effect was significant and even larger than increases in meat and fish expenditures. It has been a long-term debate on whether government support has led to aid-fungibililty in Indonesia. The Indonesian Consumer Foundation reported that there was a misuse of direct cash aid from government. Instead of improving human capital related expenditures, more than 50 percent of the direct cash aid was spent on tobacco consumption (Kompas 2009). In this case, the aid fungibility was evident.

From the panel data DiD and PSM estimations showed that food security had no impact on food and nonfood expenditures. In particular, the food security program also had no impact on education expenditures. Notwithstanding, it is consistently revealed that the food security program had a positive and substantial effect on meat and fish, and medical expenditures. In addition, based on the panel data there was a significant effect of the food security program on dairy product expenditures and the impact was slightly larger than the impact on meat and fish expenditure. This means that the food security program did support recipients and contributed to the income of poor households, enabling them to shift their consumption to more expensive nutrient sources. Accordingly, the program enabled beneficiaries to invest in improving human capital.

Table 3.6: Average Treatment Effect on Food and Nonfood Consumption

Outcomes	ATT (post exposure)	ATT (DiD and matching)
Total Food Expenditures	-0.010	0.037
	(0.027)	(0.026)
Rice	0.367**	0.036
	(0.141)	(0.168)
Staple	0.138*	-0.037
	(0.083)	(0.112)
Dairy Product	-0.004	0.383**
	(0.167)	(0.195)
Meat	0.308**	0.244*
	(0.120)	(0.142)
Fish	0.454**	0.344*
	(0.159)	(0.188)
Adult Goods	0.466**	0.262
	(0.178)	(0.193)
Nonfood Expenditure	-0.087**	0.027
	(0.029)	(0.037)
Medical	0.274**	0.387**
	(0.142)	(0.187)
Education	-0.139	0.008
	(0.195)	(0.188)

Source: Author calculation based on IFLS data

*Note: Standard errors are shown in parentheses, * Denotes statistical significance at 10% level, ** Denotes statistical significance at 5% level.*

3.7.4. Program Heterogeneity

This section discusses the program impact by consumption tercile. The average impact of the food security program may mask significant impacts of the program on certain types of households. To investigate the heterogeneity of the program impacts, the impacts were differentiated by tercile of real per capita expenditure. Program impact based on tercile categories showed considerable variation. The program heterogeneity was not only captured in the magnitude of difference of the impact across households, but also the diversity patterns of the impact. Heterogeneous impacts were estimated both with post exposure and panel data. For the lowest tercile households, the program had a significant and positive impact on meat expenditure. This means that the food security program enabled the bottom income households to spend more than half of their expenditure on more expensive nutrients. Interestingly, the food security program had positive but less conclusive effects on adult goods expenditure as has been found in the average program impact. This might be due to a homogeneous pattern of adult goods expenditure among the lowest income households. According to the PSM and DiD methods of panel data analysis, the food security program had no impact on any expenditures except on dairy products. The lower section of Table 3.7 represents the heterogenous program impact on the change of expenditures. The panel data shows that the program had been able to increase dairy product expenditure by about 90 percent for the poorest tercile. Nevertheless, this finding shows that the food security program only had a limited impact on the neediest group, as the richer second tercile household had been able to increase the expenditures on meat and fish by 40 percent and 60 percent respectively.

Table 3.7 also presents data that show that the program impact patterns were different for middle income households (second tercile) and more affluent households (third tercile). For the second tercile households, the food security program had significant impacts on total food expenditure even though the magnitude was small (around 3 percent). The significant parameter of 0.445 of the tercile 2 households indicates that the food security program increased the household expenditures on rice by 45 percent. The program had a substantial impact on rice and other staple food expenditures, and the largest impact on fish expenditure, indicating program fungibility. The results of the PSM and DiD methods were slightly different, indicating that the program only had a significant impact on meat and fish expenditures. The food security program also had a positive impact on rice, fish, and adult good expenditures. The positive impact of the food security program on rice expenditure of the affluent (third tercile) households is somewhat surprising. It may be that the extra resources received from the program were translated to better rice quality. The positive impact of the food security program indicates that aid-fungibility was due to the wealthy households and that the program was actually more beneficial to more affluent households than poor households.

Disaggregating the impact based on income groups, it was found that the poorest households only received limited benefits whereas the higher income households enjoyed greater gain from the program. Even though the program increased poorest household expenditures on meat and dairy products by 60 percent and 80 percent respectively, the program improved richer households' expenditures on more diverse consumption such as rice, meat-fish, and dairy products. This implies that the impact estimate based on the full sample overestimated the true impact of the food security program for the neediest households. This finding is challenging from the perspective of aid programs. As previously mentioned, the food security program seems to have had many loopholes. By design, the food security program provided generous support to the households that were suffering most from the crisis. The food security program was also expanded. Although it is found that the program reached intended households, the mistargeting is clear, which lead to unintended program effects.

Table 3.7: Heterogeneous Impact of The Food Security Program

Outcomes	Tercile 1	Tercile 2	Tercile 3
ATT			
Food Expenditure	0.008	0.035**	-0.035
	(0.032)	(0.019)	(0.031)
Rice	0.181	0.445***	0.615***
	(0.231)	(0.183)	(0.260)
Staple	0.097	0.214**	0.165
	(0.167)	(0.112)	(0.148)
Dairy Product	0.283	-0.020	-0.228
	(0.368)	(0.280)	(0.195)
Meat	0.649***	0.315*	-0.086
	(0.212)	(0.175)	(0.137)
Fish	0.298	0.607***	0.526***
	(0.292)	(0.264)	(0.213)
Adult Goods	0.475	0.487	0.583**
	(0.358)	(0.301)	(0.294)
Nonfood Expenditure	-0.003	-0.033	-0.198***
	(0.037)	(0.025)	(0.041)
Medical	0.269	0.489***	0.114

	(0.281)	(0.197)	(0.230)
Education	-0.272	0.303	-0.435
	(0.372)	(0.305)	(0.330)
ATT and DID			
Food Expenditure	0.029	0.077*	0.016
	(0.047)	(0.045)	(0.059)
Rice	0.055	0.112	-0.150
	(0.300)	(0.253)	(0.369)
Staple	-0.198	0.072	0.084
	(0.254)	(0.177)	(0.222)
Dairy Product	0.889***	0.042	0.055
	(0.388)	(0.042)	(0.332)
Meat	0.278	0.385***	0.004
	(0.220)	(0.191)	(0.184)
Fish	0.228	0.628***	0.029
	(0.320)	(0.298)	(0.299)
Adult Goods	0.204	0.555	-0.009
	(0.375)	(0.364)	(0.398)
Nonfood Expenditure	0.049	0.047	0.016
	(0.055)	(0.048)	(0.064)
Medical	0.532	0.434	0.124
	(0.362)	(0.299)	(0.303)
Education	-0.025	0.233	-0.290
	(0.353)	(0.309)	(0.312)

Source: Author calculation based on IFLS data

*Note: Standard errors are shown in parentheses, terciles are in ascending order, * Denotes statistical significance at 10% level, ** Denotes statistical significance at 5% level, *** Denotes statistical significance at 1% level.*

3.7.5. The Food Security Program and Subjective Well-being

This section presents details of the analysis on how the food security program beneficiaries subjectively evaluated their well-being. The welfare of households as evaluated by the program criteria for participation might have been associated with subjective well-being. Quality of the institutions and political process were vital to people's sense of subjective well-being. People's subjective well-being should be considered in the political process (Stutzer and Frey 2010). There were several measures of subjective well-being in the IFLS dataset used in this study, including the subjective well-being ladder and subjective satisfaction regarding food consumption. This study recognized that reported subjective well-being could not be disentangled from income, therefore, the descriptive relationship between subjective well-being and income is first discussed here.

Table 3.8 presents subjective well-being by income. In general, households tended to classify themselves in the moderate rank or third step of the ladder. The figures also depict that perception of well-being varied by income. The poorest households tended to perceive themselves belonging in the second (35.29 percent) and the third rank (47.65 percent), while the most affluent households assessed themselves primarily in the third (59.15 percent) or fourth level (26.42 percent). There were very few households (less than 1 percent) that considered themselves as belonging to the richest step of the ladder. An interesting figure is the subjective well-being of third quintile households. Even though most of them (58.44 percent) classified themselves in the moderate rank, 1.1 percent of the households placed themselves in the fifth ladder, and 0.39 percent in the highest rank, surpassing even the richest households.

Table 3.8: Subjective Well-being by Income Quintiles

Income Quintiles	1 (poorest)	2	3	4	5	6 (richest)
1st	9.27	35.29	47.65	7.02	0.52	0.26
2nd	6.77	29.12	52	11.28	0.71	0.13
3rd	4.51	22.49	58.44	13.08	1.1	0.39
4th	3.48	18.49	58.18	18.62	0.97	0.26
5th	2.19	9.99	59.15	26.42	1.8	0.45

Source: Author calculation based on IFLS data

Disaggregating by program recipients, table A3.3 in the Appendix shows a similar pattern between the two groups. In general, both the food security program recipients and their wealthier counterparts tended to place themselves in the moderate level (third ladder). Nonrecipient households considered themselves more prosperous. In contrast, the recipient households considered themselves on the left side of the ladder. Table A3.3 also shows that there was a strong tendency of households to put themselves in the same step of the ladder during each period. A slight sense of optimism was also evident in a small shift of approximately a quarter of the households that classified themselves in the fourth rung one year later. The subjective well-being in this case was also subject to a bias since both recipient and nonrecipient households were more likely to put themselves in the middle rungs.

Table A3.4 presents the head-of-households' perception of their general living standard and food consumption. Both recipients and nonrecipients primarily reported adequate standards of living (66.94 percent and 68.11 percent, respectively). Both household types were satisfied with their consumption, their children's standard of living, and children's food consumption. More recipient households perceived their standard of living and food consumption as less than adequate (21.36 percent and 12.66 percent) compared to nonrecipient households (15.93 percent and 17.68 percent). From the descriptive figures, it is clear that subjective well-being is associated with income, although more than half of households consider themselves in the moderate ladder. The richer households tended to place themselves in the higher rungs of the ladder compared to lower income households. Accordingly, the food security program recipients tended to put themselves in lower ladder rungs compared to the control group. Table 3.9

presents associations of subjective well-being, income, and food security program participation. The association between subjective well-being and the food security program participation can be identified using an ordered logit model. Other covariates entered into the model were household and regional characteristics. Based on the ordered logit regression of the IFLS sample shown in Table 3.9, it was evident that being a food security program recipient was associated with a negative perspective on subjective well-being. In contrast, income (as proxied by per capita expenditure) was associated with households indicating that that they felt richer. The level of education of the household head was a strong predictor for placement higher on the ladder. Households residing in Java tended to indicate higher subjective well-being than households in the rest of the country. However, households in Java province and the rest of the country were indifferent on food consumption perception. The marginal effect of food security program participation on subjective well-being shrank when income was controlled in the model. The food security program also had a negative effect on food consumption perception but was insignificant on the perception of children's food consumption when income was controlled (Table A3.5 and Table A3.6). This finding is consistent with the findings of previous studies on subjective well-being in Indonesia linking subjective well-being with income (Cummins 2000, Diener and Biswas-Diener 2002). Being a food security program recipient was associated with the household feeling poorer and indicating a less than adequate living standard.

The findings have several policy implications. Despite evidence that the food security program lead to significantly increased expenditures on nutrient-rich, animal sourced foods, it also displayed problems related to the distribution of benefits. As mentioned earlier, some villages distributed subsidized rice equally among villagers. Despite the program's positive impacts, the costs of the 18 percent of the rice that was unaccounted for (Olken 2006) might potentially outweigh the welfare benefits from the program. The food security program had little bottom-up process in the implementation, particularly the households' involvement as the ultimate point of distribution. The IFLS community data showed that the village head and associated staff, along with the BKKBN cadre and the head of neighborhood associations determined which households were eligible for the SSN program, including the food security program. The data further show that only 50 percent of the villages had mechanisms in which a household could have applied to be a program recipient if they felt that they qualified for receiving subsidized rice but were not selected. The long bureaucratic distribution process combined with local and cultural contexts might have restricted some community members, particularly the ones with the lowest socioeconomic status from being involved in determining the food security program's application. Many studies have pointed out the possibility of elite capture in development programs and described community-driven development program efforts to reduce elite capture (Mansuri and Rao 2004, Beard and Dasgupta 2006, Fritzen 2007). This problem appears to have affected the execution of the food security program. Making the program more reflective of people's preferences and involving bottom-up participation are potential methods of improving the design of the food security program as they have benefitted other community-driven development programs (Rao and Ibanez 2005). An inclusive and transparent process of recipient eligibility identification is one of the operational aspects that would help mitigate this problem.

Table 3.9: Ordered Logit Models of Subjective Well-being

	Without lnpce		With lnpce	
	Coefficient	Std. error	Coefficient	Std. error
FS Program Participation(dummy, participate=1)	-0.3563***	0.0578	-0.1645***	0.0592
lnpce			0.5910***	0.0372
Age of HH Head (in years)	0.0072***	0.0017	0.0070***	0.0017
Male HH Head (dummy, male=1)	-0.0253	0.0798	0.1132	0.0804
Education of HH Head (in years)	0.0765***	0.0049	0.0522***	0.0052
Urban (dummy, urban=1)	0.1440***	0.0532	0.0442	0.0538
North Sumatra	-0.3068**	0.1254	0.0014	0.1277
West Sumatra	-0.3433**	0.1422	-0.0786	0.1440
Riau	-0.3480	0.3129	-0.3665	0.3168
South Sumatra	-0.2267	0.1435	0.0808	0.1452
Lampung	-0.2383	0.1490	-0.0026	0.1504
West Java	0.1815*	0.0999	0.3687***	0.1012
Central Java	0.5399***	0.1104	0.7399***	0.1120
Yogyakarta	0.0561	0.1283	0.2345*	0.1294
East Java	0.4126***	0.1076	0.6572***	0.1096
Bali	-0.0620	0.1351	0.1216	0.1358
West Nusa Tenggara	-0.2904**	0.1281	-0.0148	0.1304
South Kalimantan	0.3409**	0.1435	0.6120***	0.1455
South Sulawesi	-0.0622	0.1409	0.2931**	0.1438
Pseudo R-squared	0.0338		0.0502	
LR $\chi^2_{(19)}$	523.49		776.92	
p	0.0000		0.0000	
N	7,178		7,178	

Source: Author calculation based on IFLS data

Note: Standard errors are shown in parentheses, * Denotes statistical significance at 10% level, ** Denotes statistical significance at 5% level, *** Denotes statistical significance at 1% level.

3.8. Conclusion

The Indonesian economic crisis had profound effects on poor households and forced them to adjust their consumption. The food security program has provided highly subsidized rice to poor households. The matching estimators show that the program reached its intended beneficiaries. Households characterized by low quality housing, less education, and residing in rural areas or in Java, were most likely to participate in the food security program. The program's performance suffered from certain flaws, particularly related to the misallocation of benefits to higher income households and geographical biases evident in the program's implementation.

Using propensity score matching, this study revealed that the food security program had positive impacts on selected food and nonfood expenditures. In particular, it was found that the food security program enabled beneficiaries to increase expenditures on higher nutrient food items such as meat, fish, and dairy products. The program also has had positive impacts on health expenditures. Aid-fungibililty was also evident based on increased consumption of adult goods by beneficiary households. The impact of the food security program on adult goods expenditure was even more substantial than its impact on expenditures for meat, fish, and dairy products.

The heterogeneous impacts of the program reveal challenging issues. In the post exposure period, we found that the food security program had a limited impact on the bottom income households. The food security program had only enabled the poorest households to increase their meat and dairy products expenditures, though the treatment effect is very large. The food security program also benefitted nontarget households. Both fly-paper and fungibility effects were evident in the results of this program.

This study also found that being a beneficiary of the food security program was negatively correlated with subjective well-being. Controlling for income, education, and regional characteristics, program recipients tended to feel poorer than nonrecipients. In addition, receiving food security program assistance also lead the households to feel less satisfied with their level of consumption. The program beneficiaries exhibited optimism about their future welfare. This study found that income had a positive and significant effect on subjective well-being. Richer and more educated households reported higher subjective measures relative to poorer and less educated counterparts. Javan residents also felt richer than households in the rest of the country.

To sum up, the food security program supported participants efforts to smoothen their consumption in a period of economic crisis and improved their ability consume nutritious food items. The program had some administration flaws, specifically in the targeting of beneficiary households. In order to improve the program in the future, certain conditions such as requiring food security program beneficiaries to participate in nutrition extension efforts or to send their children to school could be used as incentives to help achieve the desired program impacts. Lastly, further option should be explored particularly specific target the program to woman instead of household which is assumed to induce better impact.

Chapter 4. The Role of Women's Assets and Social Capital on Food and Nonfood Expenditure

4.1. Introduction

Gender considerations must play a role in development and poverty reduction agendas. Gender disparities are the result of social constructions regarding the relationships between men and women (Oakley 1972). In many cases traditional social constructs attach certain stigmas and expectations on women that lead to social inequality based on gender (Tresemer 1975). The 1995 UN Conference in Beijing raised awareness of the need to eliminate gender-based inequality (El-Bushra 2000), which is also one of Millennium Development Goals (Kabeer 2005, Fukuda-Parr 2010). Reducing the gender gap and promoting maternal health are among the main global objectives. Accordingly, a growing amount of literature has explored the role and contribution of women in promoting social welfare and it is recognized that women's preferences and responsibility for decision making within households influence economic outcomes (Doss 2005).

In economics, intra-household relationships have been modeled and examined in a great number of empirical studies. Previously, a household was treated as a single decision making unit (unitary model). The unitary model neglected the bargaining and distribution mechanisms within households and assumed that a household is a pooling box of resources (Chiappori 1997). Current debates on intra-household resource allocation highlight how the distribution of resources within a household affects household welfare. The collective model embraces the concept that individuals within a household have different preferences. This issue is an important consideration for public policy purposes. For instance, if a government wants a social welfare program to target specific individuals based on age or gender rather than entire households, the outcome of the program will depend on how well it is designed to reach those individuals. Without considering the intra-household distributional issues such as resource allocation, policies might not achieve the desired effects. To make policies more effective at reaching the target beneficiaries, understanding the factors that determine resource allocation is important. As has been revealed from collective models, household demand for commodities, nutrition, and health care will vary based on the particular household member responsible for allocating resources. In particular, voluminous studies have found that control of resources by women improved household welfare (Thomas 1994, Thomas et al. 1997, Quisumbing 1997, Quisumbing and Mallucio 2000, Quisumbing and McClafferty 2003, Doss 2004).

In the case of Indonesia, gender issues are associated with a multitude of cultural aspects and institutional contexts. Culture determines the proper conduct or actions in a person's social life. Thus, traditional law and local customs influence living arrangements and patterns of intra-household decision making. Some ethnic groups in Indonesia, such as the Batak in North Sumatra, the Javanese in Java, and the Bugis in South Sulawesi, have patriarchal cultures, whereas the Minangkabau in West Sumatra has a matriarchal culture[28]. Even between the Javanese and Batak cultures, there are many cultural differences among ethnic groups with patriarchal systems. Relatively, Javanese culture is loosely structured and marriage ties are weak (Geertz 1964, Schweizer 1988, Thomas and Frankenberg 2000). Although Javanese culture is patriarchal, women play a key role in the household economy as is reflected by a popular saying, "women are the ministers of home affairs and finance," which affirms the central responsibility of women in the household economy. In contrast, the Batak patriarchal system is widely known for its strong kinship and very hierarchical social structure. In the Batak system of matrimony, the bride moves in with her husband's family after marriage. In terms of matriarchal cultures, the Minangkabau is recognized as one of the largest in the world (Kato 1978). The Minangkabau are a unique case because their matrilineal social system is blended with an Islamic legal framework, however, the matrilineal characteristics are more reflected in daily society practices. In Minangkabau society, husbands continue to belong to the house of their mother and property is inherited through the female line.

In modern Indonesia, traditional laws and customs are less relevant compared to previous decades, due to inter-cultural mixing and intra-ethnic relationships (Schefold 1998)[29]. Modern practices have been assimilated into traditional law and local custom, however, the common conceptualization of womanhood in Indonesia is still strongly rooted in the role of women as mothers or *ibuism*[30] (Suryakusuma 1996). As a result, women are not treated as equals to men in many ways, particularly in terms of opportunities and rights. Gender gaps in terms of education has disadvantaged womens in Indonesian labor market and worsened by the 'reproductive constraint' due to the unequal reproductive obligations between female and male household members (Siegmann; 2003, 2006).

---

28 In terms of land size, Java, Sumatra, and Sulawesi are considered the main islands in Indonesia.
29 For a detailed explanation of this issue, see also van der Kroef (1952) and Geertz (1988).
30 *Ibu* in *Bahasa Indonesia* means "mother".

Some legal frameworks address gender equality, such as Indonesian marriage laws which mention that women and men have equal rights in the family but also that husbands and wives have distinct roles in the family. By law, the husband is the head of the family and the wife plays the role of the "domestic manager" (Robinson and Bessel 2002). To address this dichotomy in the study of intra-household power relations, some scholars have raised the issue of women's agency, because as household agents, women have the capability to respond to and change the circumstances in which they live (Giddens 1984, Saptari 2000).

Using the Indonesian setting with its cultural heterogeneity, this paper examines women's roles in the distribution of household expenditures. To describe the importance of women in the household, two proxies were used: women's shares of household assets and women's social capital. This study contributes to the growing literature of the resource allocation model, particularly in the use of women's social capital as a measure of women's importance in the household.

4.2. Theory and Empirical Specification

The household economics movement (Becker 1973, Michael and Becker 1973) in the 1970s introduced broader recognition of individual behavior in response to incentives (Haddad et al. 1997). This movement also brought new ideas to the economic analysis of nonmarket activities, particularly in terms of the production of goods and services within the household. Alderman et al. (1995) classified household behavior using two models: unitary and collective.

4.1.1. Unitary Model

In the unitary model, all household members share the same preferences, or essentially there is only a single decision maker in each household. In this perspective a household is seen as a set of individuals who act as one entity under a "benevolent dictatorship" (Alderman et al. 1995, Katz 1997). The unitary model assumes that common preferences and all resources within a household such as capital, labor, land, and information are pooled (Haddad et al. 1997). Based on this assumption, Alderman et al. (1995) criticized the model because it does not take into account the processes through which resources are actually distributed within real households. The model is widely criticized for what has been called the difficulty of the individuals' preferences aggregation (Carter and Katz 1997, Haddad et al. 1997, Quisumbing and Mallucio 2000). Unitary models assume that the altruistic leader or benevolent dictator is the representative of the household to ensure pareto-efficient conditions within the household. Nevertheless, a great number of studies of both developed and developing countries show that income is not pooled, even within patriarchal systems (Hayashi 1995, Carter and Katz 1997, Lundberg et al. 1997, Quisumbing 2003).

4.1.2. Collective Model

The collective model addresses the issue of different preferences among household members and is divided into cooperative and noncooperative classifications (Alderman et al. 1995). The efficient cooperative model is based on the concept that household members cannot improve their economic share without detriment to another member. The cooperative model assumes that the benefits to each individual of forming a household outweigh the benefits of remaining single. Some studies suggest that the decision of each member in the cooperative model should not exceed a certain threat point to other members' interests (Sen 1990). Most studies (Alderman et al. 1995, Chiappori 1997) apply Nash equilibrium to the bargaining model. Alderman et al. (1995) stated that the cooperative model can be implemented through enforced behavior in the household. Marital dissolution was proposed as a means of collective decision making, however, McElroy (1997) argued that marital dissolution is not a credible mechanism of enforcement. It was also reported that in forced collective decision making, a noncooperative solution may act as the threat point. In contrast, the noncooperative model of household behavior assumes that each household member cannot be bound and has an enforceable contract within the household, meaning that each individual's actions are conditional on the others. This type of behavior indicates "reciprocal claims" (Carter and Katz 1997).

4.1.3. Theoretical Framework

The theoretical framework behind this study is derived from the standard utility function of each adult household member, i, in a cooperative bargaining model (Doss 2005).

$$U^i = u^i(x_p^i, x_h, q_p^i; Z) \tag{4.1}$$

where:
u is utility
x_p^i is a private purchased consumer good
x_h is a public purchased consumer good
q_p^i is a private non-market consumer good, and

Z is a vector of the demographic variables

Each household member is assumed to maximize their own welfare under household constraint, and each individual's welfare optimization should be pareto-optimal, according to the Nash bargaining problem:

$$\max N = \prod_{i=1}^{I}\{u^i(x_p^i, x_h, q_p^i; Z) - V_0^i(P_x, P_q, w^i, \alpha^i)\} \quad (4.2)$$

Subject to household budget constraint:

$$P_x X + P_q Q = \sum_{i=1}^{I} w^i l^i + \sum_{i=1}^{I} (T^i - l^i) s^i \quad (4.3)$$

where:
X is the vector of purchased goods
Q is the vector of nonpurchased goods
P_x is a set of prices corresponding to X
P_q is a set of prices corresponding to Q
w^i is the market wage of individual i in the household
α^i is a factor that influences the well-being of individual i outside of the household
l^i is the amount of time spent by individual i working
T^i is the total amount of time available from individual i
s^i is the value of labor for home production
V_0^i is the threat point of individual i

This study focuses on obtaining the reduced form of the household expenditure equations in order to examine whether women's roles in the household affect the distribution of a household's expenditures. The reduced form of the equation is as follows:

$$X = f(P_x, P_q, w, \alpha, Z) \quad (4.4)$$

where w and α represent wages and importance of the household members. The reduced form of the equation contains α, which is a set of parameters influencing the threat point of household members. Doss (2005) mentions that α_i could be nonlabor income or transfer, or other variables measuring personal status within the household[31].

---

31 Other variables are detailed in Section 4.4.2.

4.1.4. Empirical Model Specification

To examine women's control over selected food and nonfood expenditure decisions in the demand function, this study expands the method used by Doss (2005) similar to equation (4.4) and thus conceptualizes the function as follows:

$$w_{it} = \beta_0 + \beta_1 A_{fit} + \beta_2 Ed_{fit} + vZ + \varepsilon_{it} \tag{4.5}$$

where:
w_{it} is food and nonfood expenditures,
A_{fit} is the share of women's household assets, nonagricultural land, livestock, savings, and jewelry,
Ed_{fit} is the women's level of education,
Z is a set of household characteristics,
ε_{it} is the error term.

A household's outcome is measured by food and nonfood expenditures. To test the effect of women's control on food and nonfood expenditures, an equation is used. This study focuses on assets as important and quantifiable resources of women. Assets are used instead of labor income in order to avoid the problem of income endogeneity. For women labor income results from joint decision-making in the household. Since household expenditures are affected by other factors, socio-economic variables are included in the model to account for household preferences (Doss 2005). Those variables include the number of household members, the level of education of the household head and their spouse, dummy variables indicating the type of the household (farm or non-farm), the household head's main activity (working or not working), as well as the location (urban or rural). Model (4.5) was applied separately for each type of asset. In addition, the model (4.5) was expanded with the higher order of women's asset share.

To examine the influence of women's social capital on the distribution of household expenditures, similar equations were utilized. The model was used to examine the effect of women's participation in three types of village activities: village meetings, the family welfare movement, and the integrated community health post. Because each type of activity has a different nature of organization and differing objectives their effects may be diverse. Equation (4.5) was estimated using seemingly unrelated regression (Zellner 1962).

4.2. Previous Empirical Studies

According to Quisumbing and Mallucio (2000) and Quisumbing and McClafferty (2003), women's social power in the household is determined by at least four elements: control over resources, influences that can affect the bargaining process, mobilization of interpersonal networks, and the basic attitudinal process. In most economic analyses, resources controlled by women should be exogenous to labor supply, because the decision to participate in the labor market is a joint household decision. Doss (2004), Thomas et al. (1997), and Quisumbing (1997) used assets, whereas Schultz (1990) and Thomas (1990) used nonlabor income to describe women's household status. Another potential measure of resources includes transfer payments (Lundberg et al. 1997). Factors that influence the bargaining process include legal rights such as property ownership, skills, education, and information. These factors are external to women and are more related to institutional aspects. Quisumbing and Mallucio (2003) used education as a measure of bargaining power in the case of four developing countries. In another study, domestic violence was also recognized as a factor that can affect bargaining power in the household (Bhagowalia et al. 2010). Women can also mobilize socially within the community, which is also considered an important factor in household bargaining power. Adato et al. (2000) examined the impact of PROGRESA on intra-household relations. As is generally known, PROGRESA specifically targets household women, hence women's participation in PROGRESA can be seen as empowerment. Not only in consumption aspects, the reallocation of resource also matters in agriculture productivity (von Braun et al. 1994, Udry et al. 1995).

The empowerment of women through participation in organizations and access to social networks is assumed to have positive effects on women's autonomy within the household in at least two complementary channels. First, women's participation in communal organizations enables them to exchange knowledge which might increase their individual capability and influence their household decisions. Second, group-based or community-based activities are often useful tools to empower women[32]. Women's empowerment refers to increasing comprehensive understanding of gender biases among women and awareness of their ability to take control of their own lives. The attitudinal attributes that affect intra-household bargaining power include self-esteem, self-

---

[32] The Grameen Bank is a successful "bank for the poor" initiative that seeks to alleviate poverty through the empowerment of women by providing access to micro-credit (Yunus and Jolis 1998). Amin and Li (1997) mentioned that women's empowerment was becoming one of the top objectives among the activities of various development NGOs.

confidence, and emotional satisfaction. These factors are not independent and are linked to women's endowment. Therefore, a woman's social status and original family status help determine their role in decision making in the household (Williams 1990).

In the case of Indonesia, there have been several empirical studies on issues of intra-household authority. *In situ* research on household behavior in Indonesia was pioneered by Pitt and Rosenzweig (1990), who investigated the effects of morbidity on time allocation within Indonesian households. Illness of household members was considered likely to affect resource allocation within households, particularly the allocation of time. Specifically, the study examined the effects of child mortality on the activities of surviving siblings and mothers. As in many other developing countries, each member of an Indonesian household is assigned a specific principal activity. Pitt and Rosenzweig (1990) revealed a similar pattern of time allocation to those found in many Asian societies. The main activity of the male head of household's was typically in the labour force, while mothers primarily managed care of the household. The principle activity of teenage girls aged 14 to 18 was the in-house care of infants where they were present, whereas boys of the same age group participated in the labour force. The results showed that gender-based differences existed in the division of time between household care, labour, and education. More specifically, educational activities of teenagers decreased when there were higher levels of child morbidity. This effect was even higher for teenage daughters because infant morbidity in the household increased their participation in other household activities. That study also found that the number of sons and daughters in a household significantly affects the distribution of household activities, however, parental characteristics such as education and earnings had no discernable effect on household activity.

Another study conducted by Quisumbing and Mallucio (2003) among the matriarchal Minangkabau, in West Sumatra found that the status of women was reflected by her assets and education at the time of marriage. The type of asset chosen for the analysis was land used for rice production because land is traditionally inherited by women. The study rejected the unitary model in terms of the education difference between husband and wife, but not asset. Whereas assets had less conclusive impacts on expenditures, a woman's land assets had significant effects on the education of her sons. In contrast, a woman's land assets had no impacts on the education of daughters. A similar pattern was found for the effects of a mother's education. Although gender preference was not explicitly evident, a better educational outcome was likely more important to the future wealth of sons compared to daughters, who will directly inherit household assets.

Beegle et al. (2001) also studied household resource management and decision making. That study examined women's authority relative to their husbands' over the use of prenatal and delivery services in Indonesia. Women's authority was described by the proportion of assets controlled by women. The results showed that relative to women without assets, wives with some proportion of assets had relatively more decision-making power on reproductive health choices. In addition, women's authority also varied based on social status and education. If a woman was from a higher social background or more educated than her husband, she was more likely to have greater autonomy in the household. Thomas et al. (1999) examined the effects of women's authority on child health. A woman's status was measured in terms of the assets brought to her marriage. This study showed that the probability that a woman will keep control over some of her income was positively associated with the share of assets that she brought to the marriage. Hence, there is a reasonable basis to use the proportion of assets brought to the marriage by a woman as a reflection of her autonomy within the household. Unlike Thomas (1994), which found similarities between fathers and sons and between mothers and daughters in the US, Brazil, and Ghana, in Indonesia maternal resources were more related to the health of sons than daughters (Thomas et al. 1999). The latter study found that mothers with more resources are more powerful and able to allocate resources towards benefits for their sons. As a result sons had fewer episodes of illness or cough with fever than daughters. In Java and Sumatra, mothers and fathers appear to have distinct preferences, although in other parts of Indonesia the unitary model still appropriate.

This study investigates the relative impact of women's authority on the distribution of household expenditures. More precisely this study emphasizes the relationships of two measures of a women's status; the proportion of household assets and participation in community activities. This study augments the analysis by examining the nonlinearity of a women's share of assets. In a multi-ethnic setting like Indonesia, the results of this study will provide direction for shaping future policy, particularly in terms of individual or household targeting for policy intervention.

4.3. Data and Measures of Women's Power

This section presents the data employed in the study as well as variables used to measure women's authority in the household. The first section describes the measurement of women's status in detail and how the variables were collected from the data. The second and third sections present descriptive statistical results.

4.3.1. Data and Variables

This study analyzed data from a longitudinal dataset provided by the Indonesia Family Life Survey (IFLS). Three rounds of the IFLS (1997, 2000, and 2007) were used for these analyses. Most of the recent literature on intra-household resource allocation has used either men's or women's nonlabor income as a proxy of authority to evaluate whether these measures are associated with household expenditure choices (Thomas 1993, Thomas et al. 1999). To gauge the status of women in the household, asset shares and participation in community activities were used in these analyses. IFLS datasets include information on various types of assets that are associated with family homes and businesses. The data on nonbusiness assets are part of a separate IFLS module. The dataset covers a wide range of assets including; savings, loans, jewelry, household durables, and semi-durables (Thomas et al. 2003, Strauss et al. 2009). These assets were classified into two groups: liquid assets and nonliquid assets. We defined liquid assets as financial assets that may be easily transformed into cash such as livestock, household appliances, savings, and jewelry. Nonliquid assets included the house occupied by each household and land parcels (Haveman 2005, Dercon and Christiansen 2010).

This study uses the concept of social capital from Bourdieu (1977) and Coleman (1988) to measure women's social capital[33]. Those efforts defined social capital as the ability of an actor to gain benefits from participation or membership in social networks or other social organizations. Fortunately, the IFLS dataset provides thorough information on citizen participation in community-based organizations and social development efforts. This information is compiled in a citizen-participation module that includes data on household members aged 15 years and older. Respondents were asked about their knowledge of, and participation in, a list of organizations during the preceding 12 months. Participation in some organizations is limited to women, such as the PKK (*Pemberdayaan Kesejahteraan Keluarga* [Family Welfare Empowerment Movement]) and the POSYANDU (*Pos Pelayanan Terpadu* [Integrated Community Health Post])[34]. The longitudinal nature of the dataset allowed us to ob-

---

33 The precise definition of social capital is debatable. To simplify social capital in a manner consistent with the data, we limited the analysis to women's participation in organized social networks available in the community.

34 Detailed description of each activity is available in Section 4.4.4.

serve long-term characteristics of respondents who have actively participated in community organizations.

The dependent variables examined in this analysis were food and nonfood expenditures. Food expenditures were divided into six groups: staple foods, vegetables and fruit, meat and fish, dairy products, oils, and adult goods. Food expenditure responses were based on one-week recall prior to interviews. Nonfood expenditures consisted of other purchased goods and services such as clothing, medical needs, housing, taxes, and education. All expenditures are presented in terms of budget share of total expenditures along with descriptive statistics in the appendix.

4.3.2. Operational Definition of Other Control

The main independent variable investigated in this analysis was women's role in decision-making[35]. Other control variables included household characteristics such as education, household size, and geographical aspects. Since the unit of this analysis effort was at the household-level, only households including both a husband and wife were included in the analysis. Households described as having female heads were not included in the sample, since they were likely to be single mothers or else situations that would not have contributed to our effort to reveal intra-household power dynamics. The education of both the household head and spouse were measured in years of education. Household size was broken down into the number of household members below 6 years of age, school age children (6-14 years), male and female household members aged 15-59, and all household members aged 60 years and over. Households were described as either rural or urban. The main activity of the household head and income levels were also included in the model.

4.3.3. Women's Asset Ownership

As mentioned earlier the IFLS dataset includes extensive information on both household (nonbusiness holdings) and individual assets. Table 4.1 provides descriptive information on the assets of urban and rural households in the pooled sample. Apart from household furniture, the most frequently owned assets were the residence (87 percent), household appliances (81 percent), jewelry (57 percent), vehicles (49 percent), savings (24 percent), and nonagricultural land (22

---

[35] Detailed measures of women's power is provided in Section 4.4.3 and Section 4.4.4.

percent). Only a small number of households (12 percent) held assets in the form of other houses or buildings, or agricultural land. Rural households were more likely to own their residence, nonagricultural land, and livestock. Urban households were more likely to own other houses or buildings, vehicles, household appliances, savings, receivables, and jewelry. The different types of assets were associated with access to certain markets and information. The limited accessibility of financial institutions in rural areas might explain the low percentage of rural households that reported savings, however, it is also possible that urban versus rural settings also influence the availability of education, activities, and income related to accruing savings. Urban households reported more liquid assets whereas rural households reported more high value nonliquid assets. Existing literature (Frankenberg and Thomas 2003, Thomas et al. 2003) indicate that a greater share of liquid assets facilitate adjusting of consumption.

Table 4.1: Household Asset Ownership (percentage of total sample)

	Urban	**Rural**	**Total**
House	0.80	0.93	0.87
Other house/building	0.16	0.08	0.12
Nonagricultural land	0.19	0.24	0.22
Livestock	0.11	0.23	0.17
Vehicles	0.58	0.42	0.49
Household appliances	0.90	0.73	0.81
Savings	0.33	0.17	0.24
Receivables	0.11	0.09	0.10
Jewelry	0.61	0.53	0.57
Household furniture	0.98	0.98	0.98

Source: Author calculation based on IFLS data

The assets reported were not only those owned by the head of household and the spouse, but also included assets of other household individuals. Table 4.2 reports the distribution of assets within households. Asset ownership was male dominant for every category except for jewelry. The gap of asset shares between men and women in the household was almost 2:1, which clearly indicates male dominancy in asset holding. Comparing rural and urban households, women's asset shares in rural areas were higher than their urban counterparts for residence ownership, nonagricultural land holdings, and livestock. Urban women had relatively higher asset shares of vehicles, household appliances, savings, receivables, jewelry, and household furniture than rural counterparts. The house is often considered the most important household asset, and home ownership by women is considered an asset brought into marriage and may reflect the social status of married women. Ownership by male household heads was reported by 61 percent of households that owned their residence. In both rural and urban areas the house, household appliances, and household furniture were most often considered joint assets. More than a quarter of both rural and urban women reported jewelry assets (33 percent and 28 percent respectively). Reported ownership of receivable assets was particularly low among women.

Table 4.2: Reported Household Asset Shares (in percentages)

	Proportion of Asset Holdings		Female Proportion of Asset Holdings	
	Male	Female	Urban	Rural
House	60.12	39.86	35.64	44.38
Other house/building	7.19	3.03	4.77	2.14
Nonagricultural land	14.20	6.15	5.27	7.52
Livestock	16.46	7.48	4.20	11.05
Vehicles	30.58	11.72	19.03	11.26
Household appliances	50.43	32.21	40.19	28.84
Savings	13.60	6.34	9.56	4.54
Receivables	7.18	2.57	2.56	2.65
Jewelry	20.98	31.98	32.67	27.09
Household furniture	61.53	46.33	46.74	46.12

Source: Author calculation based on IFLS data

4.3.4. Women's Social Capital

According to Bourdieu (1977), social capital is understood as the aspects of social relations that can be transformed into or generate other forms of capital. Grootaert (1999) and Ostrom (1996) described social capital as a metric through which civil society is able to gauge issues that cannot be addressed in the context of either state or market value. Silvey and Elmhirst (2003) added that social capital is important for women, since their participation in a union positively corresponds to a relatively sophisticated knowledge of their rights and entitlements. In this study, social capital is described in terms of women's participation in community organizations or social networks that might provide a social advantage for households such as community meetings, women's associations, and community integrated health posts.

Community meetings are formal engagements at the village-level that serve as a forum to discuss and organize local development and planning activities. In Indonesia anti-poverty development programs such as the Social Safety Net Program, the *Kecamatan* Development Program[36], the Urban Poverty Program, the "Rice for the Poor" program, the conditional cash transfer program, and other programs are discussed in these community meetings. The meetings cover several activities such as program socialization and planning, proposal preparation, funding decisions, and program implementation. Local meetings are attended by several elements of the community such as local legislative bodies, local government staff, and representatives of women's and youth groups.

Women's associations are active at the village-level, particularly the PKK, which is a nationwide women's association in Indonesia that is also represented at the sub-division geopolitical level. The PKK was first established in accordance with the National Development Plan in the late 1960s. During the regime of Soeharto, the second president of Indonesia, the National Development Plan attempted to involve women in social development through formal organizations. As a formal and nationwide organization the PKK is administered by the Ministry of Home and Internal Affairs. The PKK has a long history and began with a positive social mission, although it later became recognized as a government instrument to promote public policies among women (Weringa 1992). Weringa (1992) claimed that the PKK was not intended to empower women, but rather as a tool to promote acceptance among women of their duties as wives and loyal citizens according to the government's criteria and did not take into account the power relations within households. Nonetheless, the PKK is expanding its reach as the largest women's association in Indonesia. Despite the government's vested interests in the PKK, which are debatable, some of its activities are consistent with women's empowerment and the promotion of household

---

[36] A Kecamatan or sub-district is an administrative level below the level of district. Each kecamatan is headed by a Camat and consists of several villages. The Kecamatan Development Program is a community development program supported by The World Bank that addresses social and economic problems in both rural and urban areas (Fang 2006). The program focuses on improving infrastructure in the villages of each kecamatan.

welfare. PKK's activities include a rotating savings and credit project called *arisan*, and informal workshops on family planning, child education, food, and nutrition. Despite criticisms the PKK does benefit women, particularly in terms of acquiring information and knowledge that can enhance household welfare. The PKK also operates "money-go-around" activities that provide additional monetary benefits and may perform as informal savings.

The third women's social activity used in this analysis is participation in POSYANDU, a public health system established in the 1980s that is funded by the national government. POSYANDU offers several primary health services for women and children including: prenatal services, child registration, family planning counseling, and the distribution of supplementary food, vitamins, contraceptives, and information on nutrition and other community health issues. These services are provided on a regular monthly basis in collaboration with local midwives and community health centers. In response to the economic crisis of 1998, the Indonesian government launched a POSYANDU revitalization program. The program was intended to provide incentives for communities to help maintain the welfare of households with children and pregnant women receiving services from POSYANDU, which had declined during the economic crisis. The revitalization program also proposed to improve the skills of POSYANDU cadres. In the last five years, POSYANDU has been expanded to cover health services for the elderly.

Table 4.3: Women's Participation in Community Organizations

	Pooled	**1997**	**2000**	**2007**	**Urban**	**Rural**
Community meeting	0.162 (0.369)	0.195 (0.396)	0.128 (0.334)	0.164 (0.370)	0.196 (0.397)	0.133 (0.340)
PKK	0.160 (0.367)	0.174 (0.379)	0.150 (0.357)	0.156 (0.363)	0.199 (0.399)	0.127 (0.419)
Posyandu	0.223 (0.416)	0.276 (0.447)	0.190 (0.392)	0.202 (0.402)	0.218 (0.413)	0.227 (0.333)

Source: Author calculation based on IFLS data

Note: Standard deviations are shown in parentheses

Table 4.3 presents a breakdown of women's participation in community meetings, PKK, and POSYANDU. Among these three categories women were most likely to participate in POSYANDU activities. Over time women's participation decreased slightly in 2000 and increased again in 2007 for all three groups. There are several underlying reasons for this phenomenon, including the considerable growth of development programs at the local level. Various programs available to communities, such as conditional and unconditional cash transfer efforts and the POSYANDU revitalization program were launched in 2003 and 2004 respectively. These programs might have provided incentives for women to participate more in communal activities, although this explanation remains to be tested. Urban women were more likely to participate in community meetings and the PKK, whereas rural women were a little more likely to participate in POSYANDU. This implies that rural women are optimizing the health services provided by POSYANDU, presumably for children and women, whereas fewer households participated in POSYANDU in urban areas where alternative healthcare facilities are more available relative to rural areas.

4.4. Estimation Results

This section presents the results of the analyses of women's authority over household food and nonfood expenditures. Some of the descriptive statistics for household characteristics are discussed. The household effects of women's asset shares and social capital on food and nonfood expenditures are analyzed in this section.

4.4.1. Characteristics of Households by Asset Type

Table 4.4 reports household characteristics based on asset types. Households with livestock were more likely to be rural with a low level of education (below completion of primary school), and low per-capita expenditures. The average level of education of a household head holding non-agricultural land was limited to having completed primary education. Households with savings had the highest average level of education for both of the household head and their spouse. More than 60 percent of the households with savings were located in urban areas. These facts are most likely linked to the reality that financial institutions are more available in urban areas. Households that reported owning vehicles, jewelry, and household appliances had similar characteristics. Education levels of spouses were higher than households heads in every asset group except for savings. Households with savings had younger heads, whereas households with non-agricultural land tended to have an older household head.

The different characteristics of households reporting certain types of assets might reflect preference and selectivity of asset ownership. Nonagricultural land might have the greatest future value compared to other types of assets. It can be assumed that some of the land owned by these households is not the result of the accumulation of wealth, but rather from inheritance. Accordingly, the high value of assets such as land might not reflect authority status if it was derived from other entity. Of the assets surveyed, around 2 percent of the households mentioned that their house and nonagricultural land were also owned by someone outside of the household.

Table 4.4: Household Characteristics Based on Asset Types*

	Non-Ag land	Livestock	HH Appliances	Vehicles	Savings	Jewelry
Education of HH Head (in years)	7.572 (5.571)	5.513 (4.670)	8.074 (5.436)	8.697 (5.625)	10.376 (5.601)	8.291 (5.594)
Education of Spouse (in years)	8.166 (5.229)	6.790 (4.533)	8.219 (5.189)	8.714 (5.310)	10.260 (5.421)	8.605 (5.283)
Age of HH Head (in years)	50.758 (13.340)	50.266 (13.670)	50.121 (12.970)	49.183 (12.196)	48.610 (12.749)	49.234 (12.944)
HH Size	4.494 (2.016)	4.499 (1.948)	4.541 (1.989)	4.726 (1.869)	4.597 (1.981)	4.571 (1.983)
ln PCE	11.982 (1.035)	11.569 (0.943)	12.234 (0.967)	12.276 (0.988)	12.500 (0.972)	12.210 (0.987)
Urban (dummy, urban = 1)	0.405 (0.491)	0.295 (0.456)	0.517 (0.500)	0.548 (0.498)	0.633 (0.482)	0.501 (0.500)

Source: Author calculation based on IFLS data

Note: Standard deviation are shown in parentheses, * Households with non-agricultural land, households with livestock, households with household appliances, households with vehicles, households with savings, and households with jewelry.

4.4.2. Household Characteristics and Participation in Local Organization by Women

As in the previous section, this section describes household characteristics based on participation of the spouse in local organizations. Beard and Cartmill (2003) and Beard (2007) described women's participation in the social sphere as a kind of social mobilization, implying that women's participation in the public arena is a form of household representation. Furthermore, Beard (2007) found that selectivity exists in community participation, with marital status and education being important determinants of women's participation in local organizations. Because of the burden of domestic responsibilities associated with marriage it would be expected that single women would be more likely to participate in social organizations, however, in the case of Indonesia Beard (2007) found that being married had a positive and significant effect on participation.

From the descriptive statistics of selected household characteristics shown in Table 4.5 it can be seen that for all categories, women who participated in local organizations had higher levels of education than their counterparts who did not participate. Households in which the wife participated in local organizations were also characterized by higher levels of education of the household head compared to nonparticipant households. Specified by the type of organization, women who participated in PKK had the highest average level of education, typically having completed secondary school. Women who participated in POSYANDU had a lower average education level, typically below completion of secondary school. POSYANDU provides health and supplementary feeding services to children, and is mostly accessed by lower income households, which typically also have less access to health and education services. PKK activities focus on enhancing skills and knowledge that help women improve their performance as mothers and members of society, whereas community meetings place greater emphasis on women's participation in local development efforts. Compared to the other types of participation, the community meetings encompass the most socially elite activities. The PKK includes the most strategic activities for women, since it both helps actualize their social capital as well as address their needs for domestic knowledge. In addition, PKK activities also involve economic activities such as micro-credit and savings that offer women additional monetary benefits.

Table 4.5: Household Characteristics According to Women's Participation in Local Activities

	Community Meeting		PKK		Posyandu	
	Yes	No	Yes	No	Yes	No
Education of HH Head (in years)	8.677 (5.576)	7.080 (5.322)	9.459 (5.570)	6.920 (5.261)	7.666 (5.281)	7.261 (5.433)
Education of Spouse (in years)	9.047 (5.353)	7.518 (4.998)	9.481 (5.257)	7.394 (4.977)	8.185 (4.969)	7.666 (5.139)
HH Size	4.674 (1.962)	4.272 (2.020)	4.699 (1.893)	4.268 (2.031)	5.435 (1.952)	5.435 (1.921)
# Under 6 years	0.437 (0.678)	0.441 (0.676)	0.454 (0.668)	0.437 (0.678)	1.059 (0.716)	1.059 (0.548)
# 6 - 14 years	0.884 (0.970)	0.941 (1.023)	0.919 (0.975)	0.934 (1.023)	1.060 (1.021)	1.060 (1.010)
ln PCE	12.254 (1.001)	12.087 (0.978)	12.262 (0.973)	12.086 (0.983)	11.876 (0.956)	11.876 (0.981)
Urban (dummy, urban = 1)	0.555 (0.497)	0.439 (0.496)	0.568 (0.495)	0.436 (0.496)	0.448 (0.497)	0.448 (0.498)

Source: Author calculation based on IFLS data

Note: Standard deviation are shown in parentheses

4.4.3. The Effects of Women's Assets and Social on Household Expenditures

This section presents the results of the analysis of the effects of women's domestic authority as measured by two proxies, their share of household assets and their social capital, on household food and nonfood expenditures. Controlling for household characteristics such as education, household size, and rural versus urban location, the effects of women's assets share on selected food and nonfood expenditures were varied. In general, women's asset shares were positively and significantly associated with expenditures on meat-fish and negatively with expenditures on staple foods. Though less conclusive, women's asset shares had a positive effect on dairy product expenditures. Interestingly, women's asset shares of all types had negative and significant effects on adult goods expenditures such as tobacco and alcohol. Hence, women's asset shares appear to be associated with a women's authority over the household budget with regard to adult goods expenditures. Furthermore, women's asset shares were positively and significantly associated with total nonfood expenditures and also positively associated with education expenditures (Table A4.3 in the Appendix). Overall, wives with a greater asset share appear to have greater domestic authority than those who had fewer household assets. These results support existing empirical evidence indicating the positive effects of women's assets on human capital development through greater consumption of nutrient-rich foods and investment in education (Quisumbing and de la Breire 2000, Doss 2005).

Based on asset type, the effects of women's asset shares on selected food and nonfood expenditures were varied. Ownership of livestock assets had inconclusive effects on expenditures on meat-fish and dairy products. Asset shares of savings and jewelry were positively associated with nonfood expenditures. Table 4.6 shows that liquid assets had a positive and significant association with expenditures on nutrient-rich foods such as vegetables, meat and fish, and dairy products. Nonliquid assets such as homes and nonagricultural land did not have significant effects on expenditures, even though these types of assets are associated with higher social value. Comparing jewelry to savings as a means of storing wealth, jewelry was more accessible for both urban and rural households. Jewelry, normally in the form of gold, was more often indicated among women's assets. In Indonesia the market for jewelry is very active, and even during the financial crisis the price of jewelry remained stable.

It has been claimed that women are more likely to allocate resources on expenditures that improve the human capital outcome of household members, such as for higher nutrient foods, health care, and education (Quisumbing and McClafferty 2006). Expenditures on nutrient-rich food such as meat-fish and dairy products are positively correlated with household member nutritional status, particularly children. Despite the positive association of women's domestic authority to education expenditures, there might be social norms and expectations that govern this pattern. It might also be true that the association of women's assets to household outcomes are related to women's investment in the future. The results of this analysis support previous empirical findings associating women's control over household resource with expenditures on goods that have positive effects on household well-being.

Table 4.6: The Effects of Women's Asset Shares on Selected Nutrient-Rich Foods, Alcohol and Tobacco Goods, and Nonfood Expenditures

	House	Non-Ag Land	Livestock	Savings	Jewelry	Total Asset
Staple Foods	-0.0197	-0.0568***	-0.0075	-0.1093***	-0.1233***	-0.0783***
	(0.0189)	(0.0220)	(0.0472)	(0.0241)	(0.0187)	(0.0183)
Vegetables	0.0078	-0.0039	0.0276	0.0296***	0.0185***	0.0157*
	(0.0091)	(0.0107)	(0.0206)	(0.0116)	(0.0090)	(0.0092)
Meat and Fish	0.0131	-0.0282*	-0.0016	0.0377**	0.0555***	0.0732***
	(0.0139)	(0.0163)	(0.0343)	(0.0177)	(0.0138)	(0.0134)
Dairy Products	-0.0193***	0.0049	0.0183	0.0323***	0.0179***	0.0102
	(0.0071)	(0.0083)	(0.0179)	(0.0093)	(0.0074)	(0.0071)
Alcohol and Tobacco Goods	-0.0478***	-0.0173	-0.0873***	-0.0518***	-0.0387***	-0.0656***
	(0.0130)	(0.0159)	(0.0334)	(0.0175)	(0.0131)	(0.0124)
Nonfood	0.1575***	0.1067***	0.1523***	0.0609	0.0694**	0.1020***
	(0.0306)	(0.0355)	(0.0757)	(0.0385)	(0.0301)	(0.0298)

Source: Author calculation based on IFLS data

Note: Standard deviation are shown in parentheses

The effects of demographic variables such as the number of children under age 5, the number of males and females of working age, the number of elderly, and the level of education of both the household head and their spouse were consistent with the findings of previous research efforts (Quisumbing and Mallucio 2000, Quisumbing and McClafferty 2003, Doss 2004). The details of the results of this analysis are presented in the Appendix in tables A4.2 through A4.11. Holding other variables constant, the budget share of staple foods increased with the number of household members. The number of household members under age 5 had a positive and significant association with the budget share of dairy products, which are one of the main sources of calories and other nutrients that promote physical development. The number of adult household members had the opposite effect on dairy expenditures. The number of adult males in the household had a positive association with the share of adult goods expenditures. The effects of women's education levels were greater than those of household heads for all budget shares. Urban households tended to spend more on dairy products and nonfood expenditures, whereas rural households tended to have larger expenditure shares on staple foods, vegetables, meat and fish, and adult goods.

Social capital in this study was reflected by social networking at the local level in one of three organizations that are common in Indonesia: community meetings, PKK, and POSYANDU. The effect of participation in these organizations on household expenditures is presented in Table 4.7. Controlling for socioeconomic variables such as education, household size, and income, participation by women in any of these social organizations was associated with a lower budget share of staple foods and adult goods expenditures than nonparticipant households. Women's participation in POSYANDU had a positive and significant association with dairy products expenditures, whereas participation in the other categories did not. One of the main POSYANDU services is a supplementary feeding program which provides dairy products such as milk for children. Thus, women who participate in POSYANDU are more likely to have children and therefore spend relatively more on dairy products. The women who participated in community meetings and PKK were more likely to be older and have less children under the age of 5 and correspondingly less dairy product expenditures (Table 4.5). Women's social capital had a negative and significant association with the expenditure share of adult goods. Fostering women's social capital is indeed likely to enhance their domestic authority and reduce adult goods expenditures. Similar to the results of the analysis of the effects of women's asset shares, women' social capital was also positively associated with nonfood expenditures.

Table 4.7: The Effects of Women's Social Capital on Selected Nutrient-Rich Foods, Alcohol and Tobacco Goods, and Nonfood Expenditures

	Village Meeting	PKK	POSYANDU
Staple Foods	-1.3660***	-1.5141***	-0.7658***
	(0.2365)	(0.2328)	(0.2374)
Vegetables	0.5684***	0.4832***	0.0665
	(0.1173)	(0.1156)	(0.1178)
Meat and Fish	-0.3523**	-0.0519	-0.2628
	(0.1694)	(0.1669)	(0.1698)
Dairy Products	0.0559	0.1501*	0.2344***
	(0.0900)	(0.0886)	(0.0902)
Alcohol and Tobacco Goods	-1.0812***	-0.9708***	-0.5653***
	(0.1585)	(0.1562)	(0.1592)
Nonfood Expenditures	2.0424***	1.6969***	1.0108***
	(0.3854)	(0.3798)	(0.3869)

Source: Author calculation based on IFLS data

Note: Standard errors are shown in parentheses, *** Denotes statistical significance at 1% level.

These findings indicate that a woman's social capital is associated with the degree of her control over household expenditures. In addition, a woman's social capital also effects her knowledge of the importance of nutrition. Such knowledge provides an indirect benefit by enhancing the human capital return on investing in healthy and nutrient-rich foods. Participation in community-level women's organizations may provide both tangible benefits such as money in addition to knowledge and information[37]. In terms of monetary benefits, normally money received by women through PKK activities may be spent at her discretion. Furthermore, participating in community organizations is an informal in-

---

[37] Participation in local organizations might also shift time allocations of home maintenance, work, and leisure, as noted by Beard (2007) in the case of consumption smoothing and civil participation in Indonesia.

surance that facilitates the borrowing and sharing of information among members. Social capital creates spillover benefits through improved access to both financial and nonfinancial resources. In the case of Indonesia, a previous study found that participation at the community-level increased the likelihood of receiving government aid during economic crises and the probability of employment of the household head (Perdana 2006).

Participation by women in local activities such as community meetings, the PKK, and POSYANDU translates into social capital that had positive effects on the outcomes of intra-household power relations. More importantly, women's social capital enhances awareness of their role in the development process. Women's participation in the community is also a means of empowerment by helping women to challenge the gender norms embedded in household and kinship hierarchies. In particular, it enables women to be more aware of and promote household welfare. An effective way to promote social welfare is to spread knowledge regarding nutritional issues through women-based organizations.

4.5. Limitations of the Study

In some empirical studies other proxies of women's domestic authority have been used such as the assets brought by women into marriage (Thomas et al. 1999, Quisumbing and Mallucio 2003). This study analyzed women's current assets which implied some limitations. One caveat of these findings is that the current asset shares of the women surveyed might reflect the accumulation of household's assets during marriage and thus be influenced by contributions by husbands. This limitation can be addressed by finding other measures of women's domestic authority, such as women's assets at the time of marriage or a women's inheritance. A second caveat is the behaviour of women's domestic authority, which may or may not be linear and requires further investigation. The relationship between women's domestic authority and household welfare[38] may more closely resemble an inverted U (Anderson and Baland 2002).

---

38 Anderson and Baland (2002) found an inverted-U relationship with woman's bargaining power, as approached by rotating and saving participation. The general wealth of the household is negatively related to women's contribution in rotating saving activity.

4.6. Conclusion

Intra-household resource allocation issues have important implications for public policy design. Consideration of resource distribution and power relations within households are important for determining the outcome of policy interventions, particularly in terms of program targeting. This study examined women's domestic authority over the distribution of household expenditures. Although measures of women's status in the household using non-labour income such as assets has been widely used, this study extended the intra-household power relation by using women's social capital in addition to household asset shares as proxies of women's status in the household. Women's social capital is assumed to have greater pay-offs than income because it also has a multiplier effect in terms of empowerment.

The results show that a women's share of household assets was related to the distribution of household expenditures. Holding other factors constant a women's share of assets had a negative effect on adult goods expenditures regardless of asset type. This supports the claim that a women's asset share reflects her domestic authority over the allocation of household budgets. A women's share of liquid assets such as jewelry and savings had a positive and significant relationship with expenditures on high nutrient foods such as dairy products and meat and fish.

Controlling for education levels, household size, and income, it was found that women's participation in local organizations had negative and significant associations with the budget share of staple foods and adult goods expenditures. Participating in community-based activities is expected to improve women's understanding of household welfare and enable them to allocate the household budget according to their concerns, such as reducing expenditures on entertainment for adult male household members. This finding confirms the importance of women's authority over household expenditures on goods and services that increase the welfare of the household.

Control over resources is an important component of intra-household power relations. It was shown that variables that reflect women's authority in the household were associated with human-capital enhancing expenditures such as dairy products, meat and fish, and nonfood expenditures. Women's social capital is closely related to women's authority within the household and may be developed through appropriate policy to strengthen women's status in intra-household power relations. Hence, promoting control over household resources by women should improve public welfare outcomes.

Chapter 5. Conclusion and Policy Implications

This dissertation includes three major areas of analytic inquiry: an analysis of household food demand in Indonesia, an evaluation of the impacts of the "rice for the poor" program on household consumption, and an examination of the role of women's domestic authority on the distribution of household expenditures. Food consumption is a direct indicator of food security. There is need for comprehensive analyses of how households modify food expenditures in response to changes in prices and income, government intervention, and changes in the status of women in the household. Greater understanding of household consumption will lead to more appropriate food policies and interventions.

The results show that Indonesian households were price and income responsive. Food expenditure patterns also varied across demographic, income, and regional variables. All food groups exhibited positive expenditure elasticity but with differing magnitudes of elasticity depending on food categories. All own price elasticity was negative, showing a negative relationship between prices and quantity demanded. In the pooled sample staple foods, oils, and other foods were necessities, whereas vegetables, meat and fish, dairy products, and adult goods were luxuries. Food demand behavior varied with income. The lowest income households were expenditure elastic for adult goods, and the highest income households were expenditure elastic for dairy products. Concerning nutrient-rich foods such as dairy products and meat and fish, there is a potential to raise low-income households' nutritional status due to expenditure elasticity in these categories.

In terms of the orientation of price versus income policies, the results suggest that income-oriented policies will help households improve food consumption, especially of rich nutrient foods. Income-oriented policies may also be more appropriate as immediate and short-term interventions due to sustainability issues. Income policies may have worrisome unintended effects such as increasing expenditures among the lowest income households on adult goods consumption. This finding reveals a failure of the food security program since support to the lowest income households lead to increased expenditure on adult goods rather than quality foods. Due to the fact that low income households were expenditure elastic for nutrient-rich foods such as dairy products and meat and fish, income policies should be integrated with noneconomic efforts to direct consumption preferences. Larger households tended to spend more on cheaper calories. As low income households were associated with larger household sizes, they confront trade-offs between eating enough and eating well. This study also found that household education and structure were also significantly associated with food demand. Education appeared to improve human capital development as households with higher education levels invested relatively more on nutritious food items.

Regional dimensions had significant effects on food consumption. Java residents and urban households consumed relatively more highly nutritious food items than their counterparts. In choosing the best methods of improving household food consumption, the integration of income and nonincome policies should be considered, particularly education on nutrition. Leveraging regional development is another important issue that should be integrated into food policy. The geographical bias of food security distribution in Indonesia was a result of poor infrastructure outside Java which impeded the expansion of the food security program. Policies that reduce geographical gaps and improve the distribution of income might complement food policy. Inclusive food policy through income policies and policies which improve income distribution might enhance human capital development through increased investment in nutrition and education.

Using matching estimators combined with the difference in difference technique, it appeared that the "rice for the poor" program had accomplished its stated goal. Households characterized by low-quality housing, less education, and location in rural areas and Java, were most likely to participate in the food security program. Mistargeting of aid recipients and geographical imbalances in the application of the program remained problems. Some households in the highest income quintile received benefits of the program even though it was intended to benefit low income households. Reducing regional development imbalances should help reduce distributional and logistical costs of providing food aid. The food security program had positive impacts on expenditures on selected food and nonfood items. In particular, it was found that the food security program has enabled program beneficiaries to increase expenditures on higher nutrient foods such as meat, fish, and dairy products. The program also had a positive impact on health expenditures. Aid-fungibililty was evident due to the fact that extra resources available due to the program resulted in increased adult goods expenditures. The impact of the food security program on adult goods expenditures was even more substantial than impacts on dairy products and meat and fish expenditures.

Despite the positive impacts of the program, the heterogeneous results of the program reveal challenging issues. Mistargeting beneficiaries of a major food security program limited its impacts on the lowest income households. For the higher income households, the food security program increased rice expenditures without observable effects on food and nonfood expenditures. The positive and significant effect on rice expenditures by higher income households implies that higher income households tended to purchase expensive and high quality rice. The effects of the food security program on adult good expenditures is less conclusive for the lowest income households whereas the effect was very significant for the upper income households. Although low income households exhibited increased alcohol and tobacco expenditures as a result of the program, the highest income households contributed serious unintended program effects. Despite evidence of unintended and negative program effects, the food security program did benefit low-income households in nonmonetary aspects.

The program might provide other benefits such as collective action through bottom-up program participation. This study found that being a food security program beneficiary was negatively correlated with subjective well-being. Controlling for income, education, and regional characteristics, program recipients tended to feel poorer than their counterparts. In addition, receiving food security program assistance also lead to lower household satisfaction with their level of consumption. This study found that income had a positive and significant effect on subjective well-being. More educated households also reported higher subjective measures. Involving grass-root initiatives in such a program could help low-income households to elevate their subjective well-being and improve the benefits of the program.

The suitability of women's household asset shares as a proxy of domestic authority in order to determine women's roles in the distribution of household food expenditures is highly relevant to the future direction of food policy. Resource distribution and power relations within households are important considerations for the design of policy intervention, particularly in terms of program targeting. This study confirms previous findings that a women's share of household assets is associated with the distribution of household expenditures. Holding the other variables constant, a women's asset share for all asset types had a negative relationship with adult goods expenditures. This implies that a women's household asset share reflects her domestic authority to control household budget allocations. More liquid women's assets such as jewelry and savings were associated with positive and significant effects on expenditures for higher nutrient foods such as dairy products and meat and fish.

Women's social capital was associated with household expenditure pattern changes that suggest it is an important potential means of improving authority within households. Women who participated in community meetings, the family welfare movement, and integrated health posts likely benefit from greater social prestige. Participation in community activities is likely to have other benefits that empower women, such as expanding social networks, improving awareness of human and gender rights, and enabling self expression at the household and community levels. Participation by women in community meetings, family welfare activities, and community integrated health posts had negative and significant effects on the budget share of staple foods and adult goods (alcohol and tobacco) expenditures. Participating in community-based activities likely augments women's understanding of health and nutrition and may influence them to allocate household budgets in ways that improve household welfare such as increasing expenditures on nutrient-rich food like dairy products and meat and fish.

The analysis of gender roles, particularly when gender-based preferences are reflected by the distribution of household food expenditures, should be integrated in the development of food policy. This study highlights the growing recognition that public welfare efforts that specifically target women are more likely to perform better in terms of household welfare outcomes. Applying conditionality on food program recipients might be another effective policy approach to improve the performance of public assistance efforts. Instead of simply receiving direct food subsidies or income transfers, target households could be required to attend nutritional education courses in order to receive assistance. This would broaden the social benefits of government interventions. Simultaneously, food policies which involve local level participation and accommodate local contexts might provide support not only in terms of monetary value, but also in nonmonetary terms such as stimulating collective action and public empowerment. It should be recognized that providing food subsidies or income transfers to low income households do not necessarily improve nutritional status. Providing micronutrients such as iron, iodine, and vitamins are alternative ways in which the government can support public welfare.

Food policies in Indonesia are still evolving as food issues respond to the complex dynamics and uncertainties of multiple factors, not only economic aspects but also social and political dimensions. Using an example of a food security program that continues to operate in Indonesia, further investigation of program exposure is needed to reveal implications for estimating impact and the sustainability of those impacts. In addition, program impacts could also be evaluated on the basis of whether they contribute to asset accumulation which can have lasting impact on household welfare.

Reference

Abadie, A., and Imbens, G., 2006. On the Failure of the Bootstrap for Matching Estimators. Mimeo, University of California, Berkeley.

Abdulai, A., Jain, D. K., and Sharma, A. K., 1999. Household Food Demand Analysis in India, Journal of Agricultural Economics, 50(2): 316-327.

Abdulai, A., 2002. Household Demand for Food in Switzerland: a quadratic almost ideal demand system, *Swiss Journal of Economics and Statistics*, 138(1): 1-18.

Abebaw, D., Fentie, Y., and Kassa, B., 2010. The Impact of a Food Security Program on Household Food Consumption in Northwestern Ethiopia: a matching estimator approach, *Food Policy*, 35: 286-293.

Adato, M., de la Briere, B., Mindek, D., and Quisumbing, A. R., 2000. *The Impact of PROGRESA on Women's Status and Intra-household Relations*, International Food Policy Research Institute, Washington D. C.

Adato, M., and Hodinott, J., 2009. Conditional Cash Transfer Programs: a "magic bullet"?, in Joachim von Braun, Ruth Vargas Hill, and Rajul Pandya-Lorch (eds.), *The Poorest and Hungry*, International Food Policy Research Institute, Washington, D. C.

Adioetomo, M., Djutaharta, T., and Hendratno, 2005. Cigarette consumption, taxation, and household income: Indonesia case study. World Bank, HNP Discussion Paper No. 26.

Ahmed, A. U., Quisumbing, A. R., Nasreen, M., Hoddinott. J., and Bryan, E., 2009. Comparing Food and Cash Transfers to the Ultra Poor in Bangladesh, Research Monograph No. 163, International Food Policy Research Institute, Washington, D. C.

Akita, T., 2003. Decomposing Regional Income Inequality in China and Indonesia using Two-stage Nested Theil Decomposition Method, *The Annals of Regional Science*, 31(7): 55-77.

Alderman, H. and von Braun, J., 1986. Egypt's food subsidy policy: Lessons and options, *Food Policy*, 11(3): 223-237.

Alderman, H., and Garcia, M., 1993. *Poverty, Household Food Security, and Nutrition in Rural Pakistan*, Research Report 96. International Food Policy Research Institute, Washington, D. C.

Alderman, H., and Garcia, M., 1993. Poverty, Household Food Security, and Nutrition in Rural Pakistan, International Food Policy Research Institute, Research Report 96, International Food Policy Research Institute, Washington D. C.

Alderman, H., Chiappori, P. A., and Haddad, L., 1995. Unitary versus Collective Models of the Household: is it time to shift the burden of proof? *The World Bank Research Observer*, 10(1): 1-19.

Amin, R., and Li, Y., 1997. NGO-Promoted Women's Credit Program, Immunization Coverage, and Child Mortality in Rural Bangladesh, *Women & Health*, 25(1): 71-87.

Anderson, S., and Baland, J., 2002. The Economics of Roscas and Intrahousehold Resource Allocation, *Quarterly Journal of Economics*, 117(3): 963-995.

Ariani, M., 2010. Analisis Konsumsi Pangan Tingkat Masyarakat Mendukung Pencapaian Diversifikasi Pangan, *Gizi Indonesia*, 33(1): 20-28.

Aromolaran, A. B., 2004. Household Income, Women's Income Share and Food Calorie Intake in South Western Nigeria, *Food Policy*, 29: 507-530.

Asian Development Bank, 2007. Key Indicators 2007: Indonesia. Available at: http://www.adb.org/Documents/Books/Key_Indicators/2007/pdf/IND.pdf [Accessed March 12, 2008].

Asian Development Bank, 2008. Key Indicators for Asia and the Pacific 2008: Comparing Poverty across Countries: the role of purchasing power parities. Asian Development Bank, Manila.

Austin, P. C., 2007. A Critical Appraisal of Propensity Score Matching in the Medical Literature between 1996 and 2003, *Statistics in Medicine*, 27: 2037-2049.

Austin, P. C., 2011. An Introduction to Propensity Score Methods for Reducing the Effects of Confounding in Observational Studies, *Multivariate Behavioral Research*, 46(3): 399-424.

Banerjee, A. V., and Duflo, E., 2011. *Poor Economics: A Radical Thinking of the Way to Fight Global Poverty*, PublicAffairs, New York.

Banks, J., Blundell, R., and Lewbel, A., 1997. Quadratic Engel Curves and Consumer Demand, The Review of Economics and Statistics, 79(4): 527-539.

Bappenas, 2006. Rancangan Pangan dan Gizi 2006-2011 – Food and Nutrition Platform 2006-2011. Bappenas, Jakarta.

Barber, S., Adioetomo, M., Ahsan, A., and Setyonaluri, D., 2008. The Tobacco Economics in Indonesia. International Union Against Tuberculosis and Lung Disease, Paris.

Barnett, W. A., and Serletis, A., 2008. Consumer Preferences and Demand Systems, *Journal of Econometrics*, 147: 210-224.

Barten, A. P., 1964. Consumer Demand Functions Under Conditions of Almost Additive Preference, *Econometrica*, 32(1-2): 1-38.

Beard, V. A., 2003. Learning Radical Planning: the power of collective action, *Planning Theory*, 2(1): 13-35.

Beard, V. A., and Dasgupta, A., 2006. Collective Action and Community-driven Development in Rural and Urban Indonesia, *Urban Studies*, 43(9): 1451-1468.

Beard, V. A., and Cartmill, R. S., 2007. Gender, Collective Action and Participatory Development in Indonesia, *International Development Planning Review*, 29(2): 185-213.

Becker, G. S., 1973. A Theory of Marriage: Part I, *Journal of Political Economy*, 81(4): 813-846.

Becker, S., Black, R. E., Brown, K. H., and Nahar, S., 1986. Relations between Socio-economic Status, Morbidity, Food Intake and Growth in Young Children, *Ecology of Food and Nutrition*, 18(4): 251-264.

Beegle, K., Frankenberg, E., and Thomas, D., 2001. *Bargaining Power within Couples and Use of Prenatal and Delivery Care in Indonesia*, CCPR-002-01, California Center for Population Research, University of California, Los Angeles.

Bhagowalia, P., Menon, P., Quisumbing, A. R., and Soundararajan, V., 2010. *Unpacking the Links Between Women's Empowerment and Child Nutrition: evidence using nationally representative data from Bangladesh*, Agricultural & Applied Economics Association 2010 AAEA, CAES, & WAEA Joint Annual Meeting, Denver, July 25-27.

Bhattacharya, J., Currie, J., and Haider, S., 2004. Poverty, Food Insecurity, and Nutritional Outcomes in Children and Adults, *Journal of Health Economics*, 23(4): 839-862.

Blackwood, E., 1997. Women, Land, and Labor: negotiating clientage and kinship in a Minangkabau Peasant Community, *Ethnology*, 36(4): 277-293.

Block, S. A., Kiess, L., Webb, P., Kosen, S., Moench-Pfanner, R., Bloem, M. W., and Timmer, P. C., 2004. Macro Shocks and Micro Outcomes: child nutrition during Indonesia's crisis, *Economics and Human Biology*, 2(1): 21-44.

Blundell, R. W., Pashardes, P., and Weber, G., 1993. What Do We Learn About Consumer Demand Patterns from Micro Data, *American Economic Review*, 83(3): 570-597.

Blundell, R., and Dias, M. C., 2000. Evaluation Methods for Non Experimental Data, *Fiscal Studies*, 21(4): 427-468.

Bopape, L., 2006. Heterogeneity of Household Food Expenditure Patterns in South Africa, Selected Paper prepared for presentation at the American Agricultural Economics Association Annual Meeting, Long Beach, California, July 23-26. Available at: http://ageconsearch.umn.edu/bitstream/21300/1/sp06bo03.pdf [Accessed August 23, 2009].

BULOG, 2010. Raskin Distribution at a Glance, Available at http://www.bulog.co.id/eng/glance_v2.php [Accessed June 6, 2010]

Bouis, H. E., 1995. Comments on Part II methodological Issues, in N. Islam (ed.) *Population and Food in the Early Twenty-First Century: meeting future food demand of an increasing population.* International Food Policy Research Institute: Washington, D. C.

Bouis, H. E., 1999. Economics of Enhanced Micronutrient Density in Food Staples, *Field Crops Research*, 60(1-2): 165-173.

Bourdieu, P., 1977. *Outline of a Theory of Practice*, Cambridge University Press, Cambridge.

Byron, R. P., 1984. On the Flexibility of the Rotterdam Model, European Economic Review, 24(3): 273-283.

Cameron, L., and Worswick, C., 2001. Education Expenditure Responses to Crop Loss in Indonesia: a gender bias. *Economic Development and Cultural Change*, 49(2): 351-363.

Cameron, L., 2009. Can a Public Scholarship Program Successfully Reduce School Drop-Outs in a Time of Economic Crisis? Evidence from Indonesia, *Economics of Education Review*, 28: 308-317.

Carter, M. R., and Katz, E., 1997. Separate Spheres and the Conjugal Contract: understanding the impact of gender-biased development, in L. Haddad, J. Hoddinott, and H. Alderman (eds.), *Intrahousehold Resource Allocation in Developing Countries: models, methods, and policy*, John Hopkins University, London.

Chernichovsky, D., and Meesook, O. A. , 1984. Patterns of Food Consumption and Nutrition in Indonesia, World Bank Staff Working Paper 670, World Bank, Washington, D.C.

Chern, W.S., Ishibashi, K., Taniguchi, K., and Tokoyama, Y., 2003. Analysis of the Food Consumption of Japanese Households, FAO Economic and Social Development Paper 152, Food and Agriculture Organization of the United Nations, Rome.

Chiappori, P. A., 1997. Introducing Household Production in Collective Models of Labor Supply, *Journal of Political Economy*, 105(1): 191-209.

Chung, C. F., 2001. Modelling Demand System with Demographic Effects Based on the Modifying Function Approach, Economic Letters, 73: 269-274.

Christensen, L. R., Jorgenson, D. W., and Lau, L. J., 1975. Transcendental Logarithmic Utility Functions, *The American Economic Review*, 65(3): 367-383.

Clark, A. E., and Senik, C., 2011. Will GDP Growth Increase Subjective Happiness in Developing Countries? in M. Aglietta, S. Alkire, F. Bourguignon,

A. E. Clark, A. Deaton, and C. Senik (eds.), *Measure for Measure: How Well Do We Measure Development?*, Proceedings of the 8th AFD-EUDN Conference 2010, European Development Research Network and Agence Francaise de Development.

Coleman, J. S., 1988. Social Capital in the Creation of Human Capital, *American Journal of Sociology*, 94: 95-121.

Cummins, R. A., 2000. Personal Income and Subjective Well-being: a review, *Journal of Happiness Studies*, 1: 133-158.

Deaton, A., and Muellbauer, J., 1980a. *Economics and Consumer Behavior*, Cambridge University Press, Cambridge.

Deaton, A., and Muellbauer, J., 1980b. An Almost Ideal Demand System, *American Economic Review* 70(3): 312-336.

Deaton, A., 1990. Price Elasticity from Survey Data: an extension for Indonesian results, Journal of Econometrics, 44(3): 281-309.

Deaton, A., 1997. The Analysis of Household Surveys: A Microeconomic Approach to Development Policy. John Hopkins University Press, Baltimore.

Deaton, A. and Zaidi, S., 2002. Guidelines for constructing consumption aggregates for welfare analysis. *LSMS Working Paper* 135, World Bank, Washington D. C.

Deaton, A., 2011. Measuring Development: Different Data, Different Conclusion?, in M. Aglietta, S. Alkire, F. Bourguignon, A. E. Clark, A. Deaton, and C. Senik (eds.), *Measure for Measure: How Well Do We Measure Development?*, Proceedings of the 8th AFD-EUDN Conference 2010, European Development Research Network and Agence Francaise de Development.

Dercon, S., and Christiansen, L., 2010. Consumption Risk, Technology Adoption and Poverty Traps: evidence from Ethiopia, *Journal of Development Economics*, 96(2): 159-173.

Diener, E., and Biswas-Diener, R., 2002. Will Money Increase Subjective Well-being? *Social Indicators Research*, 57: 119-169.

Dixon, J. A., 1982. Food Consumption Patterns and Related Demand Parameters in Indonesia: a review of available evidence. International Food Policy Research Institute, Washington.

Doss, C., 2005. The Effects of Intrahousehold Property Ownership on Expenditure Patterns in Ghana, *Journal of African Economies*, 15(1): 149-180.

Easterlin, R., 1974. Does Economic Growth Improve the Human Lot?, in P. A. David and W. B. Melvin (eds.), *Nations and Households in Economic Growth*, Stanford University Press, Palo Alto.

Easterlin, R., 1995. Will Raising the Incomes of All Increase the Happiness of All?, *Journal of Economic Behavior and Organization*, 27: 35-47.

Ecker, O., and Qaim, M., 2008. Income and Price Elasticities of Food Demand and Nutrient Consumption in Malawi, Selected Paper prepared for presentation at the American Agricultural Economics Association Annual Meeting, Orlando, Available at http://ageconsearch.umn.edu/bitstream/6349/2/451037.pdf [Accessed August 23, 2009]

El-Bushra, J., 2000. Rethinking Gender and Development Practice for the Twenty-First Century, *Gender and Development*, 8(1): 55-62.

Erwidodo, Molyneaux, J., and Pribadi, N., 2002. Household food demand: An almost ideal. Demand Systems (AIDS), Working Paper.

Fabiosa, J. F., Jensen, H., and Yan, D., 2005. Household Welfare Cost of the Indonesian Macroeconomic Crisis, Selected Paper prepared for presentation at the American Agricultural Economics Association Annual Meeting, Rhode Island, 24-27 July. Available at http://ageconsearch.umn.edu/bitstream/19311/1/sp05fa01.pdf [Accessed March 21, 2009]

Fan, S., Wailes, E. J., and Cramer, G. L., 1995. Household Demand in Rural China: a two-stage LES-AIDS model, *American Journal of Agricultural Economics*, 54-62.

Fang, K., 2006. Designing and Implementing a Community-Driven Development Program in Indonesia, *Development in Practice*, 16(1): 74-79.

FAO, 1983. *World Food Security: a reappraisal of the concepts and approaches*. Director General's Report. Rome.

FAO, 2003. Trade Reform and Food Security: conceptualizing the linkages, Food and Agriculture Organization of the United Nations, Rome. Availabe at: ftp://ftp.fao.org/docrep/fao/005/y4671e/y4671e00.pdf [Accessed February 28, 2012]

Frankenberg, E., Thomas, D., and Beegle, K., 1999. The Real Cost of Indonesia's Economic Crisis: preliminary findings of the Indonesia Family Life Surveys, DRU-2064-NIA/NICHD. RAND Corporation, Santa Monica.

Frankenberg, E., Smith, J. P., and Thomas, D., 2003. Economic Shocks, Wealth, and Welfare, *Journal of Human Resources*, 38(2): 280-321.

Frey, B. S., and Stutzer, A., 2000. Happiness, Economy, and Institutions, *Economic Journal*, 110(466): 918-938.

Fritzen, S. A., 2007. Can the Design of Community-driven Development Reduce the Risk of Elite Capture? Evidence from Indonesia, *World Development*, 35(8): 1359-1375.

Fuglie, K. O., 2004. Challenging Bennett's Law: the new economics of starchy staples in Asia, Food Policy, 29: 187-202

Fukuda-Parr, S., 2010. Reducing Inequality – The Missing MDG: a content review of PRSPs and Bilateral Donor Policy Statements, *IDS Bulletin*, 41(1): 26-35.

Garcia, M., 1990. Resource Allocation and Household Welfare: a study of the impact of personal income on food consumption, nutrition, and health in the Philippines, Dissertation, Institute of Social Studies, The Hague.

Garcia, M., 1991. Impact of Female Sources of Income on Food Demand among Rural Households in the Pihippines, *Quarterly Journal of International Agriculture*, 30(2): 109-124.

Garett, J., and Ruel, M., 1999. Are Determinants of Rural and Urban Food Security and Nutritional Status Different? Some Insights from Mozambique, *World Development*, 27(11): 1955-1975.

Geertz, C., 1984. Culture and Social Change: the Indonesian case, *Man*, 19(4): 511-532

Geertz, C., 1988. *Work and Lives: the anthropologist as author*, Stanford University Press, Stanford.

Giddens, A., 1984. *The Construction of Society*, University of California Press, Berkeley.

Giles, J., and Satriawan, E., 2010. Protecting Child Nutritional Status in the Aftermath of a Financial Crisis, The World Bank Policy Research Working Paper No. 5471. The World Bank, Washington, D. C.

Gilligan, D. O., and Hoddinott, J., 2007. Is There Persistence in the Impact of Emergency Food Aid? Evidence on Consumption, Food Security, and Assets in Rural Ethiopia, *American Journal of Agricultural Economics*, 89(2): 225-242.

Gould, B. W., and Villareal, H. J., 2006. An Assessment of the Current Structure of Food Demand in Urban China, *Agricultural Economics*, 34: 1-16.

Grootaert, C., 1999. Social capital, Household Welfare, and Poverty in Indonesia, *World Bank Policy Research Working Paper* No. 2148, World Bank, Washington D. C.

Haddad, L., Hoddinott, J., and Alderman, H., 1997. *Intrahousehold Resource Allocation in Developing Countries*, John Hopkins University Press, London.

Haddad, L., 1999. The Earned Income by Women: impacts on Welfare Outcomes, *Agricultural Economics*, 20(2): 135-141.

Hartmanshenn, T., Egle, K., Georges, M., Kessels, K., Manga, A., von Rauch, A., and Wiesenhuetter, J. M., 2002. Integration of Food and Nutrition Security in Poverty Reduction Strategy: a case study of Ethiopia, Mozambique, Rwanda, and Uganda. SLE, Berlin.

Hastuti, 2008. The Effectiveness of the Raskin Program, Social Monitoring and Early Response Unit (SMERU), Research Report, Available at http://www.smeru.or.id/report/research/raskin2007/raskin2007_eng.pdf [Accessed March 23, 2008]

Hayashi, F., 1995. Is the Japanese Extended Family Altruistically Linked? A test Based on Engel Curve, *NBER Working Paper Series*, WP Number 5033, National Bureau of Economic Research, Cambridge.

Haveman, R., and Wolff, E. N., 2005. The Concept and Measurement of Asset Poverty: levels, trends, and composition for the U. S., 1983-2001, *Journal of Economic Inequality*, 2(2): 145-169.

Hill, H., 1992. Regional Development in a Boom and Bust Petroleum Economy: Indonesia since 1970, Economic Development and Cultural Change, 40(2): 351-379.

Hill, H., 2000. The Indonesian Economy, Cambridge University Press, Cambridge.

Hines, J. R., and Thaleer, R. H., 1995. Anomalies: The Fly-paper Effect, *Journal of Economic Perspectives*, 9(4): 217-226.

Heckman, J. J., Lochner, L. J., and Todd, P. E., 2006. Eranings Functions, Rates of Return and Treatment Effects: the Mincer equation and beyond, In E. A. Hanushek, S. Machin and L. Woessmann (eds.) in Handbook of the Economics of Education, North-Holland, Amsterdam.

Hoddinott, J., and Haddad, L., 1995. Does Female Income Share Influence Household Expenditure Patterns?, *Oxford Bulletin of Economics and Statistics*, 57(1): 77-96.

Hodinott, J., and Yohanes, Y., 2002. Dietary Diversity as a Food Security Indicator, *FCND DP* No. 136, International Food Policy Research Institute, Washington, D. C.

Hoddinott, J., and Skoufias, E., 2004. The Impact of PROGRESA on Food Consumption, *Economic Development and Cultural Change*, 53(1): 37-61.

Indonesian Bureau of Statistics, 2009. Statistical Year Book of Indonesia 2009. Indonesian Bureau of Statistics, Jakarta.

Islam, M., and Hoddinot, J., 2009. Evidence of Intra-household Fly-paper Effects from a Nutrition Intervention in Rural Guatemala, *Economic Development and Cultural Change*, 57(2): 215-238.

Jallan, J., and Ravallion, M., 2003. Does Piped Water Reduce Diarrhea for Children in Rural India?, *Journal of Econometrics*, 112: 153-173.

Jensen, H., and Manrique, J., 1998. Demand for Food Commodities by Income Groups in Indonesia, Applied Economics, 30(4): 491-501.

Jensen, R. T., and Miller, N. H., 2002. Giffen Behavior in China: evidence from the China Health and Nutrition Survey, Faculty Research Working Paper

RWP-02-014, John F. Kennedy School of Government, Harvard University.

Jensen, R. T., and Miller, N. H., 2008. Giffen Behavior and Subsistence Consumption, *American Economic Review*, 98(4): 1553-1577.

Johar, M., 2009. The Impact of the Indonesian Health Card program: a matching estimator approach, *Journal of Health Economics*, 28: 35-53.

Jones, G., and Hagul, P., 2001. Schooling in Indonesia: crisis related and longer term issues, *Bulletin of Indonesian Economic Studies*, 37(2): 207-232.

Kabeer, N., 1991. Gender Dimensions of Rural Poverty: analysis from Bangladesh, *Journal of Peasant Studies*, 18(2): 241-261.

Kabeer, N., 2005. Gender Equality and Women's Empowerment: a critical analysis of the third millennium development goal 1, *Gender and Development*, 13(1): 13-24.

Kahneman, D., and Krueger, A. B., 2006. Developments in the Measurement of Subjective Well-being, *Journal of Economic Perspectives*, 20(1): 3-24.

Kakwani, N., 1977. On the Estimation of Engel Elasticities from Grouped Observation with Application to Indonesian Data, Journal of Econometrics, 6: 1-19.

Kato, T., 1978. Change and Continuity in the Minangkabau Matrilineal System, *Indonesia*, 25: 1-16.

Katz, E., 1997. The Intra-household Economics of Voice and Exit, *Feminist Economics*, 3(3): 25-46.

Khandker, S. R., Koolwal, G. B., and Samad, H. A., 2009. *Handbook of Impact Evaluation: a quantitative methods and practices*. The World Bank, Washington D. C.

Kochar, A., 2005. Can Targeted Food Programs Improve Nutrition? An empirical analysis of India's Public Distribution System, *Economic Development and Cultural Change*, 54(1): 203-235.

Kompas, 2009. Uang BLT Habis buat Merokok – The Cash Transfer is Spent Out for Cigarette, http://bisniskeuangan.kompas.com/read/2009/02/26/19191949/Uang.BLT. Habis.buat.Merokok [Accessed April 25, 2010].

Krugman, P., 1998. What Happened to Asia? MIT, Cambridge. Available at: http://web.mit.edu/krugman/www/DISINTER.html [Accessed December 20, 2010].

Lalluka, T., Laaksonen, M., Rahkonen, O., Roos, E., and Lehelma, E., 2006. Multiple Socio-economic Circumstances and Healthy Food Habits, *European Journal of Clinical Nutrition*, 61: 701-710.

Lechner, M., 2002. Program Heterogeneity and Propensity Score Matching: an application to the evaluation of active labor market policies, *Review of Economics and Statistics*, 84(2): 205-220.

Levy, P. S., and Lemeshow, S., 1999. *Sampling of Populations: methods and applications*, Wiley-Interscience Publication, Massachusetts.

Lundberg, S., Pollak, R., and Wales, T., 1997. Do Husbands and Wives Pool Their Resources? Evidence from UK Child Benefit, *Journal of Human Resources*, 32: 463-480.

Mansuri, G., and Rao, V., 2004. Community-based and Driven Development: a critical review, *The World Bank Research Observer*, 19(1): 1-39.

Maxwell, S., 1990. Food Security in Developing Countries: issues and options for the 1990s, *IDS Bulletin*, 21(3): 2-13.

Maxwell, S., 1996. Food Security: a post-modern perspective, *Food Policy*, 21(1): 155-170.

McElroy, M. B., 1997. The Policy Implications of Family Bargaining and Marriage Market, in L. Haddad, J. Hoddinott, and H. Alderman (eds.), *Intrahousehold Resource Allocation in Developing Countries: models, methods, and policy*, John Hopkins University, London.

Michalek, J., and Keyzer, M.A., 1992. Estimation of a two-stage LES-AIDS consumer demand system for eight EC countries, *European review of Agricultural Economics*, 19(2): 137-163.

Ministry of Agriculture, 2007. Sustainable Food Security Development in Indonesia: Policies and Its Implementation, Available at: http://www.unescap.org/LDCCU/Meetings/HighLevel-RPD-food-fuel-crisis/Paper-Presentations/C2-FoodSecurity/ASuryana-DOA-Indonesia-FoodSecurity.pdf [Accessed March 28, 2009].

Mittal, S., 2006. Structural Shift in Demand for Food: projections for 2020, Working Paper No. 184, Indian Council for Research on International Economic Relations, India.

Moffitt, R., 1991. Program Evaluation with Non Experimental Data, *Evaluation Review*, 15(3): 291-314.

Molina, J. A., 1994. Food Demand in Spain: an application of the almost ideal demand system, Journal of Agricultural Economics, 45(2): 252-258.

Moro, D., and Sckokai, P., 2000. Heterogeneous Preferences in Household Food Consumption in Italy, European Review of Agricultural Economics, 27(3): 305-323.

Mukherjee, N., 2006. Voices of the Poor: making the services work for the poor in Indonesia, The World Bank, Washington, D. C.

Nayga, M. R., 1996. Wife's Labor Force Participation and Family Expenditure for Prepared Food, Food Prepared at Home and Food Away from Home, Agricultural and Resource Economic Review, 179-186.

Ninno, C., and Dorosh, P. A., 2002. In-kind Transfers and Household Food Consumption: implications for targeted food programs in Bangladesh, FCND Discussion Paper No. 134. International Food Policy Research Institute, Washington, D. C.

Nordhaus, W. D., and Tobin, J., 1973. Is Growth Obsolete?, in M. Moss (ed.), *The Measurement of Economic and Social Performance*, National Bureau of Economic Research, New York.

Oakley, A., 1972. *Gender, Sex and Society*, Maurice Temple Smith, London.

Olken, B. A., Nabiu, M., Toyamah, N., and Perwira, D., 2001. Sharing Wealth: how villages decide to distribute OPK Rice, SMERU Working Paper. SMERU Research Institute, Jakarta.

Olken, B. A., 2001. Corruption and the Costs of Redistribution: micro evidence from Indonesia, *Journal of Public Economics*, 90: 853-870.

Oswald, A., and Powdthavee, N., 2005. Does Happiness Adapt? A Longitudinal Study of Disability with Implications for Economics and Judges, Mimeo, University of Warwick, September.

Ostrom, E., 1996. Crossing the Great Divide: coproduction, synergy, and development, *World Development*, 24(6): 1073-1087.

Pack H., and Pack, J. R., 1990. Is Foreign Aid Fungible? The Case of Indonesia. *Economic Journal*, 100(399): 188-194.

Perdana, A. A., 2006. Better Together or Not? Community Participation, Consumption Smoothing and Household Head Employment in Indonesia, *Development Economics Working Paper* Number 777, East Asian Bureau Economic Research.

Piggot, R. R., Parton, K. A., Treadgold, E. M., and Hutabarat, B., 1993. Food Price Policy in Indonesia. Watson Ferguson & Co, Brisbane.

Pincus, J., and Ramli, R., 1998. Indonesia: from showcase to basket case, *Cambridge Journal of Economics*, 22: 723-734.

Pinstrup-Andersen, P. and Alderman, H., 1988. The Effectiveness of Consumer-Oriented Food Subsidies in Reaching Rationing and Income Transfer Goals, in P. Pinstrup-Andersen (ed.), *Food Subsidies in Developing Countries: Costs, Benefits and Policy Options*, The John Hopkins University Press, Baltimore and London.

Pitt, M. M., and Rosenzweig, M, R., 1990. Estimating the Intrahousehold Incidence of Illness: child health and gender-inequality in the allocation of time, *International Economic* Review, 31(4): 969-989.

Pitt, M. M., and Rosenzweig, M. R., 1985. Health and Nutrient Consumption Across and Within Farm Household, *The Review of Economics and Statistics*, 67(2): 212-223.

Pitt, M. M., and Rosenzweig, M. R., 1986. Agricultural Prices, Food Consumption, and Health and Productivity of Farmers, in I. Singh, L. Squire, and J. Strauss (eds.), *Agricultural Household Models: extensions, applications, and policy*, The World Bank, Washington D. C.

Pitt, M. M., Rosenzweig, M. R., Hassan, M. N., 1990. Productivity, Health and Inequality in the Intra-household Distribution of Food in Low-Income Countries, *American Economic Review*, 80(5): 1139-1156.

Pollak, R. A., and Wales. T. J., 1992. Demand System Specification and Estimation, Oxford University Press, New York.

Powdthavee, N., 2009. How Important is Rank to Individual Perception of Economic Standing? A within-community analysis, *Journal of Economic Inequality*, 7: 225-248.

Psacharopoulos, G., and Patrinos, H., 2004. Returns to Investment in Education: a further update, Education Economics, 12(2): 111-134.

Quisumbing, A. R., 1997. Better Rich, or Better There? Grandparent Wealth, Coresidence, and Intrahousehold Allocation, *FCND DP* Number 23, International Food Policy Research Institute, Washington D. C.

Quisumbing, A. R., and de la Briere, B., 2000. Women's Assets and Intrahousehold Allocation in Rural Bangladesh: Testing Measures of Bargaining Power, FCND DP Number 86, International Food Policy Research Institute, Washington D. C.

Quisumbing, A. R., and Mallucio, J. A., 2000. Intrahousehold Allocation and Gender Relations: new empirical evidence from four developing countries, FCND DP Number 84, International Food Policy Research Institute, Washington D. C.

Quisumbing, A. R., and Otsuka, K., 2001. Land Inheritance and Schooling in Matrilineal Societies: evidence from Sumatra, *World Development*, 29(1): 2093-2110.

Quisumbing, A. R., 2003. Food Aid and Child Nutrition in Rural Ethiopia, *World Development*, 31(7): 1309-1324.

Quisumbing, A. R., and Mallucio, J. A., 2003. Resources at Marriage and Intrahousehold Allocation: evidence from Bangladesh, Ethiopia, Indonesia, and South Africa, *Oxford Bulletin of Economics and Statistics*, 65(3): 0305-9049.

Quisumbing, A. R., and McClafferty, B., 2006. *Food Security in Practice: using gender research in development*. International Food Policy Research Institute, Washington, D. C.

RAND, 2010. IFLS4 Public Release, Available at http://www.rand.org/labor/FLS/IFLS.html [Accessed December 22, 2010]

Rao, V., and Ibanez, A. M., 2005. The Social Impacts of Social Funds in Jamaica: a "participatory econometric" analysis of targeting, collective action, and participation in community-driven development, *Journal of Development Studies*, 41(5): 788-838.

Ravallion, M., 1990. Income Effects on Undernutrition. *Economic Development and Cultural Change*, 38(3), 489-515.

Rivera, J. A., Sotres-Alvarez, D., Habicht, J., Shamah, T., and Villalpando, S., 2004. Impact of Mexican Program for Education, Health, and Nutrition (Progresa) on Rates of Growth and Anemia in Infants and Young Children: a randomized effectiveness study, *Journal of American Medical Association*, 291(21): 2563-2570.

Robinson, K., and Bessel, S., 2002. Women *in Indonesia: gender, equity and development*, Institute of Southeast Asian Studies, Singapore.

Rodgers, B. L., 1986. Design and Implementation Considerations for Consumer-Oriented Food Subsidies, in P. Pinstrup-Andersen (ed.), *Consumer-Oriented Food Subsidies: Benefits, Costs, and Policy Options*, The John Hopkins University Press, Baltimore and London.

Rosegrant, M. W., Paisner, M. S., Meijer, S., and Witcover, J., 2001. *Global Food Projections to 2020: emerging trends and alternative futures*, International Food Policy Research Institute, Washington, D. C.

Rosenbaum, P. R., 2002. *Observational Studies*. Springer-Verlag, New York and Berlin.

Rubin, D. B., and Thomas, N., 1996. Matching using estimated propensity scores: relating theory to practice, *Biometrics*, 52: 249-264.

Ruel, M., Levine, C., Armar-Klemesu, M., and Maxwell, D., 1999. Good Care Practices Can Mitigate the Negative Effects of Poverty and Low Maternal Schooling on Children's Nutritional Status: evidence from Accra, World Development, 27(11): 1993-2009.

Ruiz-Arranz, M., Davis, B., Handa, S., Stampini, M., and Winters, P., 2006. Program Conditionality and Food Security: the impact of PROGRESA and PROCAMPO transfers in rural Mexico, *Economia*, 7(2): 249-278.

Rusastra, I. W., Napitupulu, T. A., and Bourgeois, R., 2008. The Impact of Support for Imports in Food Security in Indonesia, Bogor: UNESCAP-CAPSA.

Salim, Z., 2010. Food Security Policies in Maritime Southeast Asia: the case of Indonesia, Series on Trade and Food Security Policy Report No. 1, International Institute for Sustainable Development. Available at:

http://www.iisd.org/tkn/pdf/food_security_policies_indonesia.pdf [Accessed January 4, 2012].

Sadoulet, E., and de Janvry, A., 1995. Quantitative Development Policy Analysis, The John Hopkins University Press, Baltimore and London.

Sadoulet, E., de Janvry, A., and Davis, B., 2001. Cash Transfer Programs with Income Multipliers: PROCAMPO in Mexico, *World Development*, 29(6): 1043-1056.

Saptari, R., 2000. Women, Family and Household: tensions in culture and practice, in J. Koenig, M. Nolten, J. Rodenburg, and R. Saptari (eds.), *Women and Households in Indonesia*, Curzon Press, Richmond.

Schmidt, M. K., Muslimatun, S., West, C. E., Schultink, W., Gross, R., and Hautwast, J. G. A. J., 2002. Nutritional Status and Linear Growth of Indonesian Infants in West Java are Determined More by Prenatal Environment than Postnatal Factors, Journal of Nutrition, 132: 2202-2207.

Schwarz, A., 2000. A Nation in Waiting: Indonesia's Search for Stability, Westview Press, Boulder.

Schefold, R., 1998. *The domestication of culture: nation building and ethnic diversity in Indonesia*, KITLV, Leiden.

Schultz, T. P., 1990. Testing the Neoclassical Model of Family Labor Supply and Fertility, *Journal of Human Resources*, 25(4): 599-634.

Schweizer, T., 1988. Detecting Positions in Networks: a formal analysis of loose social structure in Rural Java, *American Anthropologist*, 90(4): 944-951.

Sen, A., 1981. *Poverty and Famine: an Essay on Entitlement and Deprivation*, Oxford University Press, New York.

Sen, A., 1990. Gender and Cooperative Conflicts, in I. Tinker (ed.), *Persistent Inequalities: Women and World Development*, Oxford University Press, New York.

Senauer, B., Garcia, M., and Jacinto, E., 1988. Determinants of the Intrahousehold Allocation of Food in the Rural Philippines, *American Journal of Agricultural Economics*, 70(1): 170-180.

Siamwalla, A., and Valdes, S., 1980. Food Insecurity in Developing Countries, *Food Policy*, 5(4): 258-272.

Sidik, M., 2004. Indonesia Rice Policy in View of Trade Liberalization, Proceedings of the FAO Rice Conference 2004: rice in global market, Available at http://www.fao.org/rice2004/en/pdf/sidik.pdf [Accessed November 13, 2010]

Siegmann, K. A., 2003. Gender Employment and Equity - Effects of Foreign Direct Investment in Rural Indonesia, unpublished Ph. D. thesis, Bonn.

Siegmann, K. A., 2006. Globalization, Gender, and Equity - Effects of Foreign Direct Investment on Labour Markets in Rural Indonesia, *Intervention Journal of Economics*, 3(1): 113-130.

Silvey, R., and Elmhirst, R., 2003. Engendering Social Capital: Women Workers and Rural-Urban Networks in Indonesia's Crisis, *World Development*, 31(5): 865-879.

Simpson, G., 1998. World Bank Memo Depicts Diverted Funds, Corruption in Jakarta. Wall Street Journal, August 19.

Skoufias, E., 2003. Is the Calorie-Income Elasticity Sensitive to Price Changes? Evidence from Indonesia, World Development, 31(7): 1291-1307.

Smith, G. D., and Brunner, E., 1997. Socio-economic Differentials in Health: the role of nutrition, *Proceedings of the Nutrition Society*, 56: 75-90.

Smith, J. A., and Todd, P. E., 2005. Does Matching Overcome LaLonde's Critique of Non Experimental Estimators?, *Journal of Econometrics*, 125: 305-353.

Solomon, J., 1998. Poor Indonesians are facing hunger as crisis mounts, Asian Wall Street Journal, July 10.

St-Onge, M., Keller, K. L., Heymsfield, S. B., 2003. Changes in Childhood Food Consumption Patterns: a cause for concern in light of increasing body weights, American Journal of Clinical Nutrition, 78(6): 1068-1073.

Stiglitz, J., 1998. Sound Finance and Sustainable Development in Asia, The World Bank, Washington, D. C. Available at: http://web.worldbank.org/WBSITE/EXTERNAL/NEWS/0,,contentMDK: 20025728~menuPK:3325365~pagePK:34370~piPK:42770~theSitePK:46 07,00.html [Accessed December 20, 2010]

Strauss, J., Beegle, K., Dwiyanto, A., Herawati, Y., Pattinasarany, D., Satriawan, E., Sikoki, E., Sukamdi, and Witoelar, F., 2004. *Indonesian Living Standard: before and after the financial crisis*, RAND Corporation, Santa Monica.

Strauss, J., Witoelar. F., Sikoki, B., and Wattie, A. M., 2009. The Fourth Wave of Indonesian Family Life Survey: Overview and Field Report Volume 1, WR-675/1-NIA/NICHD, RAND Corporation, Washington D. C.

Stevenson, B., and Wolfers, J., 2008. Economic Growth and Subjective Wellbeing: reassessing the Easterlin paradox, NBER Working Papers 14282, National Bureau of Economic Research, New York.

Stutzer, A., and Frey, B. S., 2010. Recent Advances in the Economics of Individual Subjective Well-being, *Social Research: An International Quaterly*, 77(2): 679-714.

Stone, R., 1954. Linear Expenditure Systems and Demand Analysis: an application to the pattern of British demand, The Economic Journal, 6(225): 511-527.

Suara Media, 2010. Pengguna Rokok Mayoritas Orang Miskin – Smokers are Mostly the Poor, http://www.suaramedia.com/berita-nasional/19121-lm3-heran-pengguna-rokok-mayoritas-orang-miskin.html

Soekirman, 2011. Taking the Indonesian Nutrition History to Leap into Betterment of the Future Generation: development of the Indonesian Nutrition Guidelines, *Asia Pacific Journal of Clinical Nutrition*, 20(3): 447-451.

Sumarto, S., Suryahadi, A., and Widyanti, W., 2002. Designs and Implementation of Indonesian Social Safety Net Programs, *The Developing Economies*, XL(1): 3-31.

Sumarto, S., 2006. Social Safety Net: Indonesia, Policy Brief 6, Overseas Development Institute London. Available at: http://www.odi.org.uk/resources/download/1071.pdf [Accessed March 12, 2008].

Sumarto, S., Suryahadi, A., and Widyanti, W., 2005. Assessing the Impact of Indonesian Social Safety Net Programs on Welfare and Poverty Dynamics, *European Journal of Development Research*, 17: 155-177.

Suryahadi, A., and Sumarto, S., 2003. Evolution of Poverty during the Crisis in Indonesia. *Asian Economic Journal*, 17(3): 221-241.

Suryakusuma, J., 1996. The State and Sexuality in New Order Indonesia, in L. J. Sears (ed.), *Fantasizing the Feminine in Indonesia*, Duke University Press, Durham.

Suyanto, S., Khususiyah, N., and Leimona, B., 2007. Poverty and Environmental Services: case study in Way Besai Watershed, Lampung Province, Indonesia, *Ecology and Society*, 12(2): 13.

Tabor, S. R., Dillon, H. S., and Sawit, M., 1999. *Understanding the 1988 food crisis: supply, demand or policy failure?* In International Seminar on Agricultural Sector During the Turbulence of Economic Crisis: Lessons and Future Directions Proceeding. 17-18 February, Center for Agro-Socioeconomic Research: Bogor.

Tabor, S. R., and Sawit, M. H., 2001. Social Protection via Rice: the OPK Rice subsidy program in Indonesia, *The Developing Economies*, XXXIX(3): 267-294.

Tabor, S. R., and Sawit, M. H., 2005. RASKIN: A Macro-Program Assessment, Available at http://www.bulog.co.id/old_website/data/doc/20070321RASKIN_Executive_Summary_for_Distribution.pdf. [Accessed February 27, 2009].

Taylor, R. J., Chatters, L. M., Hardison, C. B., and Riley, A., 2001. Informal Social Support Networks and Subjective Well-being among African Americans, *Journal of Black Psychology*, 27(4): 439-463.
Thoenes, S., 1998. Indonesia: the offshore borrowing trap, Financial Times, January 12.
Thomas, D., and Frankenberg, E., 2001. Measuring Power, FCND DP Number 113, International Food Policy Research Institute, Washington D. C.
Thomas, D., and Frankenberg, E., 2004. *Household Responses to Financial Crisis in Indonesia: longitudinal evidence on poverty, resources, and well-being*, University of Chicago Press, Chicago.
Thomas, D., 1990. Intra-household Resource Allocation: an inferential approach, *Journal of Human Resources*, 25(4): 635-664.
Thomas, D., 1997. Incomes, Expenditures, and Health Outcomes: evidence on intra-household resource allocation, in L. Haddad, J. Hoddinott, and H. Alderman (eds.), *Intrahousehold Resource Allocation in Developing Countries: models, methods, and policy*, John Hopkins University, London.
Thomas, D., 1994. Like Father, Like Son; Like Mother, Like Daughter: Parental Resource and Child Health, *Journal of Human Resources*, 29(4): 950-988.
Thomas, D., 1993. The Distribution of Income and Expenditure within the Household, *Annales d'Économie et de Statistique*, (29): 109-135.
Thomas, D., Contreras, D., and Frankenberg, E., 1999. Distribution of Power within the Household and Child Health, Available at http://www.rand.org/labor/FLS/IFLS/distpow.pdf, [Accessed March 28, 2008].
Timmer, P. C., and Alderman, H., 1979. Estimating Consumption Parameters for Food Policy Analysis, American Journal of Agricultural Economics, 61(5): 982-987.
Timmer, P. C., Falcon, W. P., and Pearson, S. R., 1983. Food Policy Analysis, The John Hopkins University Press, Baltimore and London.
Timmer, P. C., 1997. Farmers and Markets: the political economy of new paradigms, American Journal of Agricultural Economics, 79(2): 621-627.
Timmer, P. C., 2000. The Macro Dimensions of Food Security: economic growth, equitable distribution, and food price stability, Food Policy, 25: 283-295.
Timmer, P. C., 2003. Food Security and Rice Price Policy in Indonesia: the economics and politics of the Food Price Dilemma, in T. W. Mew, D. S. Brar, S. Peng, D. Dawe and B. Hardy (eds), *Rice Science: Innovations and Impact for Livelihood*, Proceedings of the International Rice Research Conference, 16-19 September 2002, Beijing, International Rice Research In-

stitute, Chinese Academy of Engineering, and Chinese Academy of Agricultural Sciences.

Timmer, P. C., 2004. Food Security in Indonesia: current challenge and the long-run outlook, Center for Global Development, Working Paper 48.

Tresemer, D., 1975. Assumptions Made about Gender Roles, *Sociological Inquiry*, 45(2-3): 308-339.

Turell, G., Hewitt, B., Patterson, C., and Oldenburg, B., 2002. Measuring Socio-economic Position in Dietary Research: is choice of socio-economic indicator important?, *Public Health Nutrition*, 6(2): 191-200.

Udry, C., Hoddinott, J., and Alderman, H., 1995. Gender Differentials in Farm Productivity: implications for household efficiency and agricultural policy, *Food Policy*, 20(5): 407-423.

UN General Assembly, 1948. Unversal Declaration of Human Rights, 10 December 1948, 217 A (III), Available at: http://www.unhcr.org/refworld/docid/3ae6b3712c.html. [Accessed 4 January 2012]

van der Kroef, 1952. Society and Culture in Indonesia, *The American Journal of Sociology*, 58(1): 11-24.

von Braun, J., and de Haen, H., 1983. The effects of food price and subsidy policies on Egyptian agriculture. International Food Policy Research Institute, Washington, D.C.

von Braun, J., 1988. Food Subsidies in Egypt: implications for the agricultural sector, in P. Pinstrup-Andersen (ed.), *Food Subsidies in Developing Countries: Costs, Benefits and Policy Options*, The John Hopkins University Press, Baltimore and London.

von Braun, J., Bouis, H., Kumar, S., and Pandya-Lorch, R., 1992. *Improving Food Security of The Poor: Concept, Policy, and Programs*, International Food Policy Research Institute, Washington, D. C.

von Braun, J., Bohm, K. B., and Puetz, D., 1994. Nutritional Effects of Commercialization of a Woman's Crop: irrigated rice in the Gambia, in J. von Braun and E. Kennedy (eds.), *Agricultural Commercialization, Economic Development, and Nutrition*, The John Hopkins University Press, Baltimore and London.

von Braun, J., Hill, R. V., and Pandya-Lorch, R., 2009. The Poorest and the Hungry: a synthesis of analyses and actions in J. von Braun, R. V. Hill, and R. Pandya-Lorch (eds.), The Poorest and Hungry, International Food Policy Research Institute, Washington, D. C.

Walker, P., Rhubart-Berg, P., McKenzie, S., Kelling, K., and Lawrence, R. S., 2005. Public Health Implications of Meat Production and Consumption, Public Health Nutrition, 8(4): 348-356.

Weringa, S., 1992. IBU or the Beast: gender interests in two Indonesian Women's Organizations, *Feminist Review*, 41: 98-113.

Widodo, T., 2006. Demand Estimation and Household's Welfare Measurement: Case Studies on Japan and Indonesia, Available at http://harp.lib.hiroshima-u.ac.jp/bitstream/harp/1956/1/keizai2006290205.pdf [Accessed March 21, 2009]

Williams, L. B., 1990. *Development, Demography, and Family Decision Making: the status of women in rural Java*, Westview Press, Boulder.

Winkelmann, R., 2005. Subjective Well-being and the Family: results from an ordered probit model with multiple random effects, *Empirical Economics*, 30: 749-761.

Witoelar, F., Rukumnuaykit, P., and Strauss, J., 2005. Smoking Behaviour among Youth in Developing Countries: case of Indonesia, Selected Paper prepared for presentation at the Population Association of America, Available at http://paa2006.princeton.edu/download.aspx?submissionId=60756 [Accessed March 21, 2009]

World Bank, 1993. *The East Asian Miracle: economic growth and public policy*. Word Bank/Oxford University Press, Oxford.World Bank, 2000. Curbing the Tobacco Epidemic in Indonesia, *East and Asia Pacific Watching Brief*, Vol 6, The World Bank, Washington D. C.

Yanovitzky, I., Zanutto, E., and Hornik, R., 2005. Estimating Causal Effects of Publich Health Education Campaigns Using Propensity Score Methodology, *Evaluation and Program Planning*, 28: 209-220.Yen, S. T., 1992. Working Wives and Food Away from Home: The Box-Cox Double Hurdle Model, *American Journal of Agricultural Economics*, 75(4): 884-895.

Yunus, M., and Jolis, A., 1998. *Banker to the Poor: micro-lending and the battle against world poverty*, Aurum Press, London.

Zellner, A., 1962. An Efficient Method of Estimating Seemingly Unrelated Regression and Tests for Aggregation Bias, *Journal of the American Statistical Association*, 57: 348-368.

Appendix

Table A2.1: Prices across Surveys

Prices	1997	2000	2007	Rural	Urban
Price Staple Foods	855.985	1,681.486	4,483.462	2,142.357	2,307.84
Price Vegetables and Fruits	967.3651	1,895.693	2,843.784	1,688.67	1,982.849
Price Meat and Fish	6,166.837	13,569.08	24,854.95	13,623.71	14,743.73
Price Dairy Products	8,533.196	20,216.5	43,140.3	22,402.81	23,010.38
Price Oils	2,516.182	3,604.371	3,604.371	5,480.272	5,707.244
Price Alcohol and Tobacco Goods	1,247.451	2,999.591	7,171.426	3,531.972	3,668.039
Price Snacks and Dried Foods	1,711.632	4,898.3	14,769.02	6,507.332	6,884.621

Source: Author calculation based on IFLS data

Note: Prices are in rupiahs per kg

Table A2.2: Parameter Estimates for QUAIDS Model (Pooled Sample)

Variables	Equation	Coefficient	Std. Error
Constant	α_1	0.2726	0.0125
	α_2	0.0906	0.0050
	α_3	0.1993	0.0110
	α_4	0.0456	0.0058
	α_5	0.0524	0.0040
	α_6	0.0266	0.0073
	α_7	0.1319	0.0062
	α_8	0.1810	0.0074
Expenditure	β_1	-0.0610	0.0022
	β_2	0.0047	0.0012
	β_3	0.0263	0.0015
	β_4	0.0154	0.0008
	β_5	-0.0043	0.0006
	β_6	0.0013	0.0015
	β_7	0.0286	0.0021
	β_8	-0.0110	0.0012
Prices	γ_{11}	0.0416	0.0077
	γ_{12}	-0.0199	0.0026
	γ_{13}	-0.0064	0.0046
	γ_{14}	-0.0123	0.0027
	γ_{15}	0.0046	0.0021
	γ_{16}	-0.0054	0.0039
	γ_{17}	-0.0096	0.0031
	γ_{18}	0.0075	0.0035
	γ_{21}	-0.0199	0.0026
	γ_{22}	0.0070	0.0017
	γ_{23}	0.0207	0.0020
	γ_{24}	0.0012	0.0012
	γ_{25}	-0.0030	0.0008
	γ_{26}	-0.0087	0.0017
	γ_{27}	-0.0078	0.0014
	γ_{28}	0.0105	0.0016
	γ_{31}	-0.0064	0.0046
	γ_{32}	0.0207	0.0020

γ_{33}	0.0043	0.0056
γ_{34}	-0.0023	0.0024
γ_{35}	-0.0078	0.0019
γ_{35}	0.0101	0.0031
γ_{37}	-0.0052	0.0021
γ_{38}	-0.0135	0.0035
γ_{41}	-0.0123	0.0027
γ_{42}	0.0012	0.0012
γ_{43}	-0.0023	0.0024
γ_{44}	0.0020	0.0020
γ_{44}	-0.0010	0.0011
γ_{45}	0.0039	0.0018
γ_{46}	0.0024	0.0012
γ_{47}	0.0061	0.0018
γ_{48}	0.0046	0.0021
γ_{51}	-0.0030	0.0008
γ_{52}	-0.0078	0.0019
γ_{53}	-0.0010	0.0011
γ_{54}	0.0113	0.0013
γ_{55}	-0.0007	0.0013
γ_{56}	0.0004	0.0008
γ_{57}	-0.0039	0.0014
γ_{58}	-0.0054	0.0039
γ_{61}	-0.0087	0.0017
γ_{62}	0.0101	0.0031
γ_{63}	0.0039	0.0018
γ_{64}	-0.0007	0.0013
γ_{65}	0.0050	0.0037
γ_{66}	0.0076	0.0020
γ_{67}	-0.0118	0.0024
γ_{68}	-0.0096	0.0031
γ_{71}	-0.0078	0.0014
γ_{72}	-0.0052	0.0021
γ_{73}	0.0024	0.0012
γ_{74}	0.0004	0.0008
γ_{75}	0.0076	0.0020
γ_{76}	0.0125	0.0027
γ_{77}	-0.0004	0.0016
γ_{78}	0.0075	0.0035
γ_{81}	0.0105	0.0016

	γ_{82}	-0.0135	0.0035
	γ_{83}	0.0061	0.0018
	γ_{84}	-0.0039	0.0014
	γ_{85}	-0.0118	0.0024
	γ_{86}	-0.0004	0.0016
	γ_{87}	0.0055	0.0034
	γ_{88}	-0.0047	0.0015
Expenditure-squared	λ_1	-0.0021	0.0008
	λ_2	0.0018	0.0010
	λ_3	-0.0011	0.0006
	λ_4	0.0010	0.0004
	λ_5	-0.0072	0.0010
	λ_6	0.0089	0.0014
	λ_7	0.0033	0.0008
	λ_8	0.2726	0.0125

Source: Author calculation based on IFLS data

Note: 1 = staple foods, 2 = vegetables and fruit, 3 = meat and fish, 4 = dairy products, 5 = oils, 6 = alcohol and tobacco goods, 7 = snacks and dried foods, 8 = other foods

Table A2.3: Marshallian Own and Cross-Price Elasticity Estimates

Food Groups	Staple	Vege and Fruit	Meat and Fish	Dairy	Oils	Alcohol and Tobacco Goods	Snack-Dried Food	Other
Staple	-0.7706	-0.0541	0.0196	-0.0394	0.0302	-0.0073	-0.0050	0.0702
	(0.0324)	(0.0108)	(0.0194)	(0.0113)	(0.0088)	(0.0162)	(0.0127)	(0.0149)
Vege and Fruit	-0.1889	-0.9580	0.1736	0.0079	-0.0286	-0.0807	-0.0767	0.0843
	(0.0229)	(0.0160)	(0.0177)	(0.0103)	(0.0072)	(0.0155)	(0.0127)	(0.0142)
Meat and Fish	-0.0711	0.0652	-1.0032	-0.0205	-0.0521	-0.0604	-0.0517	-0.1025
	(0.0270)	(0.0138)	(0.0331)	(0.0140)	(0.0108)	(0.0102)	(0.0120)	(0.0204)
Dairy	-0.3002	-0.0928	-0.0998	-0.9771	-0.0316	0.0536	0.0010	0.0656
	(0.0506)	(0.0277)	(0.0450)	(0.0367)	(0.0201)	(0.0344)	(0.0222)	(0.0346)
Oils	0.1301	-0.0248	-0.1560	-0.0162	-0.7367	-0.0089	0.0260	-0.0721
	(0.0483)	(0.0204)	(0.0425)	(0.0245)	(0.0292)	(0.0294)	(0.0186)	(0.0332)
Alcohol and Tobacco Goods	-0.0801	-0.1295	0.1083	0.0430	-0.0114	-0.9451	0.0817	-0.1508
	(0.0463)	(0.0216)	(0.0368)	(0.0218)	(0.0153)	(0.0438)	(0.0235)	(0.0283)
Snack-Dried Food	-0.1012	-0.1137	-0.0660	0.0082	-0.0042	0.0421	-0.9374	-0.0277
	(0.0212)	(0.0138)	(0.0143)	(0.0081)	(0.0056)	(0.0135)	(0.0181)	(0.0113)
Other	0.0701	0.1030	-0.0736	0.0448	-0.0223	-0.0729	0.0099	-0.9495
	(0.0237)	(0.0125)	(0.0233)	(0.0122)	(0.0097)	(0.0158)	(0.0108)	(0.0230)

Source: Author calculation based on IFLS data

Note: Standard errors are shown in parentheses

Table A2.4: Hicksian Own and Cross Price Elasticity Estimates

Food Groups	Staple	Vege and Fruit	Meat and Fish	Dairy	Oils	Alcohol and Tobacco Goods	Snack-Dried Food	Other
Staple	-0.5899	0.0312	0.1489	0.0009	0.0633	0.0562	0.1057	0.1836
	(0.0324)	(0.0108)	(0.0193)	(0.0112)	(0.0088)	(0.0162)	(0.0128)	(0.0149)
Vege and Fruit	0.0628	-0.8391	0.3535	0.0641	0.0175	0.0076	0.0776	0.2422
	(0.0228)	(0.0158)	(0.0176)	(0.0103)	(0.0072)	(0.0155)	(0.0128)	(0.0141)
Meat and Fish	0.2031	0.1947	-0.8071	0.0406	-0.0019	0.1454	0.1163	0.0695
	(0.0269)	(0.0137)	(0.0330)	(0.0140)	(0.0108)	(0.0179)	(0.0120)	(0.0204)
Dairy	0.0110	0.0542	0.1227	-0.9077	0.0254	0.1629	0.1918	0.2608
	(0.0504)	(0.0275)	(0.0448)	(0.0367)	(0.0201)	(0.0343)	(0.0223)	(0.0345)
Oils	0.3422	0.0754	-0.0044	0.0312	-0.6978	0.0656	0.1560	0.0610
	(0.0482)	(0.0202)	(0.0423)	(0.0245)	(0.0292)	(0.0294)	(0.0187)	(0.0331)
Alcohol and Tobacco Goods	0.1747	-0.0091	0.2905	0.0998	0.0352	-0.8556	0.2379	0.0091
	(0.0461)	(0.0212)	(0.0365)	(0.0218)	(0.0153)	(0.0438)	(0.0236)	(0.0282)
Snack-Dried Food	0.1757	0.0171	0.1320	0.0699	0.0465	0.1393	-0.7678	0.1459
	(0.0209)	(0.0134)	(0.0140)	(0.0081)	(0.0056)	(0.0135)	(0.0183)	(0.0111)
Other	0.2883	0.2061	0.0824	0.0934	0.0177	0.0037	0.1437	-0.8126
	(0.0236)	(0.0124)	(0.0232)	(0.0122)	(0.0097)	(0.0158)	(0.0108)	(0.0229)

Source: Author calculation based on IFLS data

Note: Standard errors are shown in parentheses

Table A2.5: Expenditure Elasticity Estimates of Food-Producing and Non-Food-Producing Households

Food Groups	Non-Food-Producing	Food-Producing
Staple	0.7590	0.7576
	(0.0171)	(0.0096)
Vegetables and Fruit	1.0388	1.0552
	(0.0184)	(0.0111)
Meat and Fish	1.0950	1.1601
	(0.0146)	(0.0096)
Dairy	1.2628	1.3192
	(0.0253)	(0.0176)
Oils	0.9027	0.8728
	(0.0219)	(0.0139)
Adult Goods	1.0343	1.0759
	(0.0306)	(0.0188)
Snack and Dried Food	1.1728	1.1626
	(0.0232)	(0.0145)
Other	0.9297	0.9104
	(0.0133)	(0.0082)

Source: Author calculation based on IFLS data

Note: Standard errors are shown in parentheses

Table A2.6: Own Price Elasticity Estimates of Food-Producing and Non-Food-Producing Households

Food Groups	Marshallian Non-Food-Producing	Marshallian Food-Producing	Hicksian Non-Food-Producing	Hicksian Food-Producing
Staple	-0.7134	-0.8955	-0.5490	-0.7082
	(0.0693)	(0.0371)	(0.0692)	(0.0370)
Vegetables and Fruit	-0.9173	-0.9556	-0.7989	-0.8368
	(0.0333)	(0.0179)	(0.0329)	(0.0179)
Meat and Fish	-0.9464	-1.0209	-0.7557	-0.8240
	(0.0604)	(0.0393)	(0.0602)	(0.0391)
Dairy	-1.0569	-0.9461	-0.9820	-0.8789
	(0.0687)	(0.0446)	(0.0687)	(0.0446)
Oils	-0.8309	-0.7172	-0.7919	-0.6792
	(0.0557)	(0.0361)	(0.0557)	(0.0361)
Adult Goods	-1.0148	-0.9068	-0.9241	-0.8172
	(0.0911)	(0.0494)	(0.0911)	(0.0494)
Snack and Dried Food	-0.9331	-0.9463	-0.7484	-0.7815
	(0.0337)	(0.0214)	(0.0341)	(0.0215)
Other	-0.9392	-0.9510	-0.8019	-0.8135
	(0.0442)	(0.0262)	(0.0440)	(0.0262)

Source: Author calculation based on IFLS data

Note: Standard errors are shown in parentheses

Table A2.7: Parameter Estimates for QUAIDS model (Poorest Households)

Variables	Equation	Coefficient	Std. Error
Constant	α_1	0.2115	0.0631
	α_2	0.0650	0.0262
	α_3	0.2254	0.0451
	α_4	0.0426	0.0171
	α_5	0.0003	0.0177
	α_6	0.0573	0.0297
	α_7	0.1513	0.0432
	α_8	0.2466	0.0379
Expenditure	β_1	-0.0884	0.0574
	β_2	-0.0137	0.0254
	β_3	0.0184	0.0299
	β_4	0.0098	0.0115
	β_5	-0.0420	0.0126
	β_6	0.1083	0.0258
	β_7	0.0373	0.0484
	β_8	-0.0298	0.0315
Prices	γ_{11}	0.0243	0.0358
	γ_{12}	-0.0192	0.0113
	γ_{13}	0.0323	0.0177
	γ_{14}	-0.0129	0.0074
	γ_{15}	-0.0011	0.0089
	γ_{16}	-0.0184	0.0151
	γ_{17}	-0.0039	0.0145
	γ_{18}	-0.0012	0.0167
	γ_{21}	-0.0192	0.0113
	γ_{22}	-0.0073	0.0067
	γ_{23}	0.0252	0.0072
	γ_{24}	0.0033	0.0030
	γ_{25}	-0.0045	0.0034
	γ_{26}	-0.0072	0.0063
	γ_{27}	-0.0016	0.0059
	γ_{28}	0.0114	0.0071
	γ_{31}	0.0323	0.0177
	γ_{32}	0.0252	0.0072

γ_{33}	-0.0181	0.0205
γ_{34}	-0.0037	0.0067
γ_{35}	-0.0001	0.0073
γ_{35}	0.0282	0.0104
γ_{37}	-0.0176	0.0075
γ_{38}	-0.0462	0.0139
γ_{41}	-0.0129	0.0074
γ_{42}	0.0033	0.0030
γ_{43}	-0.0037	0.0067
γ_{44}	-0.0055	0.0043
γ_{44}	0.0067	0.0033
γ_{45}	0.0049	0.0045
γ_{46}	0.0007	0.0031
γ_{47}	0.0064	0.0055
γ_{48}	-0.0011	0.0089
γ_{51}	-0.0045	0.0034
γ_{52}	-0.0001	0.0073
γ_{53}	0.0067	0.0033
γ_{54}	0.0124	0.0052
γ_{55}	-0.0084	0.0049
γ_{56}	-0.0006	0.0038
γ_{57}	-0.0045	0.0061
γ_{58}	-0.0184	0.0151
γ_{61}	-0.0072	0.0063
γ_{62}	0.0282	0.0104
γ_{63}	0.0049	0.0045
γ_{64}	-0.0084	0.0049
γ_{65}	-0.0049	0.0117
γ_{66}	0.0063	0.0078
γ_{67}	-0.0005	0.0095
γ_{68}	-0.0039	0.0145
γ_{71}	-0.0016	0.0059
γ_{72}	-0.0176	0.0075
γ_{73}	0.0007	0.0031
γ_{74}	-0.0006	0.0038
γ_{75}	0.0063	0.0078
γ_{76}	0.0285	0.0124
γ_{77}	-0.0118	0.0078
γ_{78}	-0.0012	0.0167
γ_{81}	0.0114	0.0071

	γ_{82}	-0.0462	0.0139
	γ_{83}	0.0064	0.0055
	γ_{84}	-0.0045	0.0061
	γ_{85}	-0.0005	0.0095
	γ_{86}	-0.0118	0.0078
	γ_{87}	0.0464	0.0155
	γ_{88}	-0.0347	0.0184
Expenditure-squared	λ_1	-0.0050	0.0078
	λ_2	0.0050	0.0092
	λ_3	0.0011	0.0035
	λ_4	-0.0117	0.0038
	λ_5	0.0325	0.0080
	λ_6	0.0181	0.0149
	λ_7	-0.0054	0.0096
	λ_8	0.2115	0.0631

Source: Author calculation based on IFLS data

Note: 1 = staple foods, 2 = vegetables and fruit, 3 = meat and fish, 4 = dairy products, 5 = oils, 6 = alcohol and tobacco goods, 7 = snacks and dried foods, 8 = other foods

Table A2.8: Marshallian Own and Cross-Price Elasticity Estimates of the Poorest Households

Food Groups	Staple	Vege and Fruit	Meat and Fish	Dairy	Oils	Alcohol and Tobacco Goods	Snack-Dried Food	Other
Staple	-0.9473	-0.0641	0.1013	-0.0383	-0.0126	-0.0678	-0.0061	-0.0125
	(0.1081)	(0.0344)	(0.0554)	(0.0229)	(0.0269)	(0.0476)	(0.0419)	(0.0518)
Vege and Fruit	-0.1920	-1.0703	0.2446	0.0324	-0.0474	-0.0586	-0.0117	0.1070
	(0.1103)	(0.0654)	(0.0703)	(0.0293)	(0.0323)	(0.0571)	(0.0552)	(0.0696)
Meat and Fish	0.2344	0.1731	-1.1402	-0.0286	0.0017	-0.0651	-0.1367	-0.3422
	(0.1294)	(0.0536)	(0.1510)	(0.0495)	(0.0530)	(0.0498)	(0.0538)	(0.1018)
Dairy	-0.5949	0.0392	-0.2008	-1.2391	0.2777	0.1606	-0.0153	0.2264
	(0.3098)	(0.1446)	(0.2825)	(0.1786)	(0.1382)	(0.1843)	(0.1234)	(0.2293)
Oils	-0.0121	-0.0213	0.0408	0.1399	-0.7757	-0.0878	0.0348	-0.0664
	(0.1673)	(0.0868)	(0.1385)	(0.0636)	(0.0981)	(0.0917)	(0.0634)	(0.1164)
Alcohol and Tobacco Goods	-0.2983	-0.2327	0.3988	0.0608	-0.1042	-1.2450	0.0135	-0.0339
	(0.2416)	(0.1323)	(0.1724)	(0.0748)	(0.0811)	(0.1868)	(0.1094)	(0.1583)
Snack-Dried Food	0.0159	0.0227	-0.1317	0.0057	0.0094	0.0300	-0.7680	-0.0718
	(0.1148)	(0.0646)	(0.0619)	(0.0241)	(0.0279)	(0.0523)	(0.0954)	(0.0644)
Other	0.0081	0.0937	-0.2455	0.0398	-0.0259	0.0141	-0.0519	-0.7258
	(0.0944)	(0.0498)	(0.0784)	(0.0308)	(0.0339)	(0.0516)	(0.0421)	(0.0874)

Source: Author calculation based on IFLS data

Note: Standard errors are shown in parentheses

Table A2.9: Hicksian Own and Cross Price Elasticity Estimates of the Poorest Households

Food Groups	Staple	Vege and Fruit	Meat and Fish	Dairy	Oils	Alcohol and Tobacco Goods	Snack-Dried Food	Other
Staple	-0.6194 (0.1074)	0.0416 (0.0346)	0.2399 (0.0544)	-0.0140 (0.0228)	0.0402 (0.0266)	-0.0080 (0.0482)	0.1200 (0.0420)	0.1673 (0.0512)
Vege and Fruit	0.1300 (0.1075)	-0.9666 (0.0643)	0.3807 (0.0694)	0.0563 (0.0292)	0.0045 (0.0320)	0.0001 (0.0570)	0.1122 (0.0555)	0.2836 (0.0679)
Meat and Fish	0.5690 (0.1286)	0.2808 (0.0525)	-0.9988 (0.1505)	-0.0038 (0.0494)	0.0557 (0.0528)	0.2317 (0.0798)	-0.0080 (0.0541)	-0.1587 (0.1012)
Dairy	-0.1814 (0.3076)	0.1724 (0.1426)	-0.0260 (0.2817)	-1.2085 (0.1783)	0.3443 (0.1379)	0.2361 (0.1841)	0.1438 (0.1243)	0.4532 (0.2275)
Oils	0.2451 (0.1650)	0.0616 (0.0863)	0.1494 (0.1385)	0.1590 (0.0635)	-0.7343 (0.0980)	-0.0409 (0.0915)	0.1337 (0.0638)	0.0746 (0.1149)
Alcohol and Tobacco Goods	0.1400 (0.2365)	-0.0915 (0.1303)	0.5841 (0.1722)	0.0933 (0.0748)	-0.0336 (0.0807)	-1.1651 (0.1863)	0.1821 (0.1098)	0.2065 (0.1550)
Snack-Dried Food	0.3096 (0.1093)	0.1173 (0.0597)	-0.0076 (0.0596)	0.0275 (0.0240)	0.0567 (0.0269)	0.0836 (0.0524)	-0.6550 (0.0956)	0.0893 (0.0607)
Other	0.3033 (0.0932)	0.1887 (0.0491)	-0.1207 (0.0779)	0.0617 (0.0307)	0.0217 (0.0337)	0.0680 (0.0515)	0.0616 (0.0423)	-0.5639 (0.0867)

Source: Author calculation based on IFLS data

Note: Standard errors are shown in parentheses

Table A2.10: Demographic Characteristics

Food Groups	HH Size	Urban	Male HH Head	HH Head Educ	Java
Staple	0.0137 (0.0007)	-0.0477 (0.0027)	-0.0009 (0.0033)	-0.0050 (0.0003)	-0.0184 (0.0028)
Vege and Fruit	-0.0018 (0.0004)	0.0068 (0.0014)	-0.0084 (0.0018)	0.0004 (0.0002)	0.0045 (0.0015)
Meat and Fish	-0.0011 (0.0005)	-0.0033 (0.0018)	-0.0078 (0.0023)	0.0016 (0.0002)	-0.0143 (0.0020)
Dairy Products	-0.0008 (0.0003)	0.0122 (0.0010)	-0.0093 (0.0013)	0.0020 (0.0001)	0.0030 (0.0011)
Oils	0.0002 (0.0002)	-0.0039 (0.0007)	-0.0016 (0.0008)	0.0000 (0.0001)	-0.0021 (0.0007)
Alcohol and Tobacco Goods	0.0017 (0.0004)	-0.0015 (0.0018)	0.0419 (0.0022)	-0.0012 (0.0002)	-0.0087 (0.0019)
Snack-Dried Food	-0.0106 (0.0006)	0.0443 (0.0025)	-0.0211 (0.0031)	0.0036 (0.0003)	0.0422 (0.0026)

Source: Author calculation based on IFLS data

Note: Standard errors are shown in parentheses

Figure A3.1: Average Rice Distribution of the Food Security Program (in kg) per Household by Province

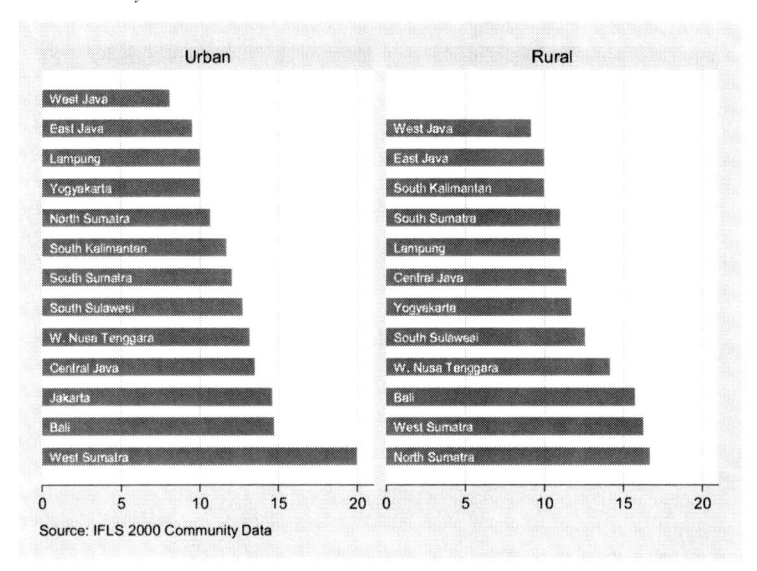

Source: IFLS 2000 Community Data

Figure A3.2: Estimated Propensity Score

Source: Author calculation based on IFLS data

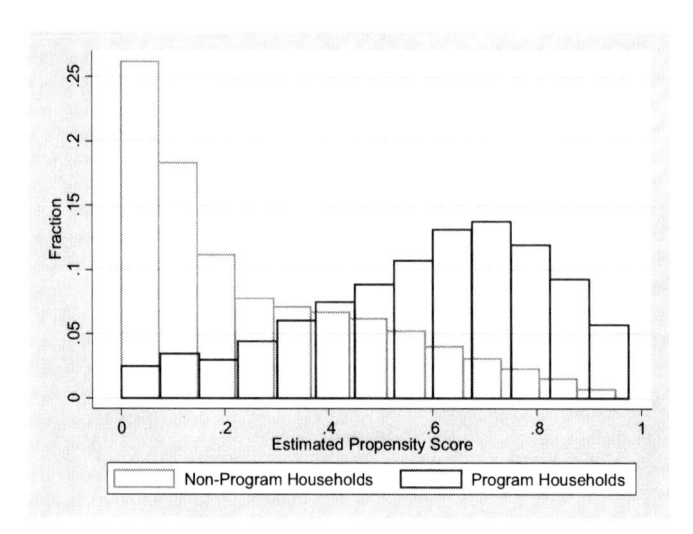

Figure A3.3: Estimated Propensity Score without Health Card Program in the Participation Model

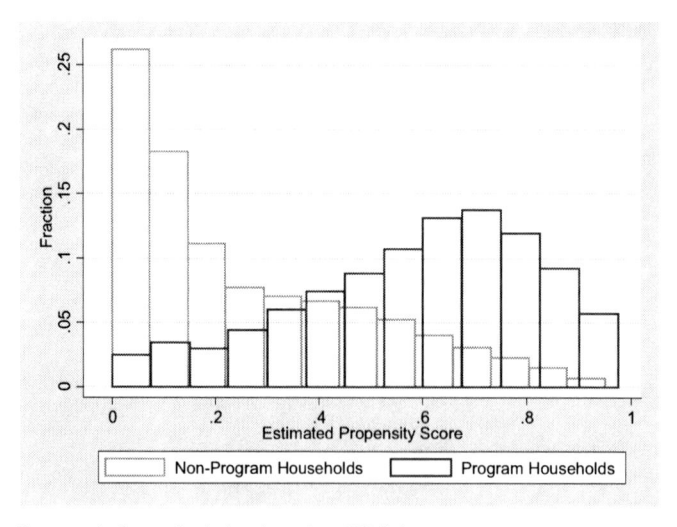

Source: Author calculation based on IFLS data

Figure A3.4: Distribution of Food Expenditure Change between Health Card Program Participants and Nonparticipants

Source: Author calculation based on IFLS data

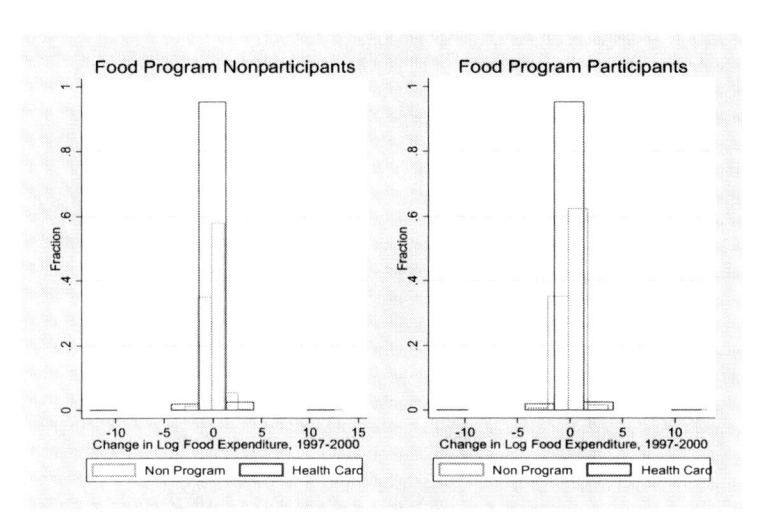

Figure A3.5: Distribution of Non-Food-Expenditure Change between Health Card Program Participants and Nonparticipants

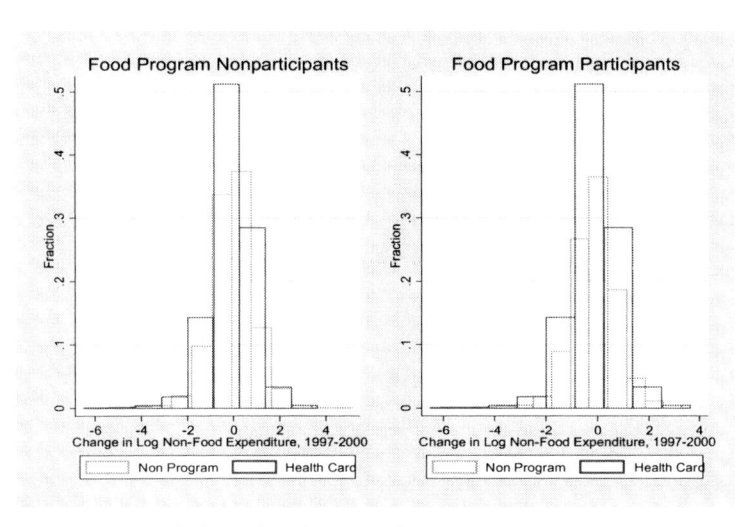

Source: Author calculation based on IFLS data

Table A3.1: Summary Statistics of Household Characteristics in the Post Exposure Year

	Recipient Mean	Recipient Std. Deviation	Control Mean	Control Std. Deviation
Household Head's Characteristics				
Age of household head (in years)	50.268	14.173	48.867	13.760
Education (in years)	6.621	4.616	9.754	5.667
Work (dummy, working=1)	0.807	0.395	0.784	0.412
Male household head (dummy, male=1)	0.790	0.408	0.838	0.368
Household characteristics				
Under 6 years	0.500	1.025	0.501	1.068
6 - 14 years	0.997	1.025	0.988	1.068
15 - 59 years (male)	1.707	1.199	1.853	1.372
15 - 59 years (female)	1.762	1.115	2.001	1.392
60 years and over (male)	0.231	0.425	0.205	0.408
60 years and over (female)	0.299	0.480	0.252	0.459
HH size	4.326	1.944	4.469	2.049
Ln PCE	11.823	0.629	12.272	0.776
Ln Asset	15.920	1.520	16.495	2.008
Fridge	0.032	0.175	0.215	0.411
Health Card	0.305	0.461	0.139	0.346
Urban	0.348	0.477	0.516	0.500
Java	0.755	0.430	0.497	0.500
Housing characteristics				
Owner	0.902	0.297	0.815	0.388
Ceramic floor	0.083	0.083	0.206	0.405
Tiles floor	0.216	0.412	0.217	0.412
Dirt Floor	0.244	0.430	0.066	0.249
Bamboo wall	0.179	0.384	0.069	0.253
Brick wall	0.594	0.491	0.658	0.475
Piped water	0.167	0.373	0.315	0.464
Community Remoteness				
Nearest bus stop in the village (dummy, yes=1)	0.304	0.460	0.362	0.481
District capital in the village (dummy, yes=1)	0.008	0.091	0.022	0.148

Average Prices at Village Level

Rice price (per kg)	1,926.159	240.442	1,969.743	334.355
Chicken price (per kg)	11,325.980	1,822.767	11,561.680	2,609.748
N	2,729		4,449	

Source: Author calculation based on IFLS data

Note: Prices are in Indonesian rupiahs

Table A3.2: Results of the Matching Estimator

	Coefficient	Std. Error
Household Head's Characteristics		
Age of household head (in years)	-0.0055**	0.0027
Education (in years)	-0.0369**	0.0054
Work (dummy, working=1)	-0.0263	0.0681
Gender (dummy, male=1)	-0.0632	0.0774
Household characteristics		
Under 6 years	0.0132	0.0367
6 - 14 years	0.0384	0.0246
15 - 59 years (male)	0.0543***	0.0217
15 - 59 years (female)	0.0275	0.0225
60 years and over (male)	0.0657	0.0820
60 years and over (female)	0.1162*	0.0587
Income category	-0.2355***	0.0378
Health Card	0.3466***	0.0605
Urban (dummy)	-0.1199*	0.0651
Java	0.3848***	0.1240
Housing characteristics		
Ceramic floor	-0.3584***	0.0724
Dirt Floor	0.2610***	0.0808
Bamboo wall	0.0657	0.0878
Community Remoteness and Village Economy		
Nearest bus stop in the village (dummy, yes=1)	-0.1259**	0.0538
District capital in the village (dummy, yes=1)	-0.1966	0.1835
Rice price (per kg)	0.0006***	0.0001
Chicken price (per kg)	0.0000	0.0000
Community Average Per Capita	-0.3718***	0.0837
Provincial Dummy		
North Sumatra	-0.9669***	0.1576
West Sumatra	-0.7845***	0.1538
Lampung	1.1732***	0.1218
West Java	0.3862***	0.1076
Central Java	1.0718***	0.1136
Yogyakarta	0.7227***	0.1208
East Java	0.6555***	0.1128
Bali	-0.3853***	0.1464

West Nusa Tenggara	0.7404***	0.1120
N	7178	
Pseudo R-squared	0.2594	

Source: Author calculation based on IFLS data

Note: ** Denotes statistical significance at 10% level, ** Denotes statistical significance at 5% level, *** Denotes statistical significance at 1% level.*

Table A3.3: Perception on Subjective Well-being (percentages)

	1 (poorest)	2	3	4	5	6 (richest)
All						
1 year ago	5.79	25.45	48.69	17.37	2.39	0.31
today	5.26	23.07	55.05	15.31	1.02	0.3
1 year later	3.69	17.73	46.24	26.15	5.39	0.8
Raskin Recipient						
1 year ago	7.49	30.75	45.91	13.91	1.87	0.37
today	6.97	27.52	52	12	1.03	0.48
1 year later	4.92	21.54	46.28	21.69	4.48	1.1
Non-Raskin Recipient						
1 year ago	4.87	22.59	50.36	19.24	2.67	0.28
today	4.33	20.67	56.69	17.1	1.01	0.2
1 year later	3.03	15.68	46.22	28.56	5.88	0.63

Source: Author calculation based on IFLS data

Table A3.4: Perception on Selected Quality of Life (percentages)

	Recipient			Non Recipient		
	Less than Adequate	Adequate	More than Adequate	Less than Adequate	Adequate	More than Adequate
General living standard	21.36	66.94	11.71	15.95	68.11	15.93
Food Consumption	12.66	74.75	12.59	9.96	72.37	17.68
Children's living standard	17.12	73.07	9.8	12.48	74	13.51
Children's Food Consumption	10	78.89	11.11	8.61	76.43	14.96

Source: Author calculation based on IFLS data

Table A3.5: Ordered Logit Models of Food Consumption Perception

	Without lnpce		With lnpce	
	Coefficient	Std. error	Coefficient	Std. error
FS Program Participation (dummy, participate=1)	-0.2890***	0.0686	-0.1338	0.0704
lnpce			0.4746	0.0426
Age of HH Head (in years)	-0.0012	0.0020	-0.0016	0.0020
Male HH Head (dummy, male=1)	-0.0242	0.0937	0.0924	0.0943
Education of HH Head (in years)	0.0676***	0.0058	0.0480	0.0061
Urban (dummy, urban=1)	0.0850	0.0623	0.0022	0.0630
North Sumatra	-0.2668*	0.1485	-0.0425	0.1506
West Sumatra	-0.1044	0.1707	0.0891	0.1720
Riau	1.0462***	0.3553	1.0396	0.3583
South Sumatra	1.8747***	0.1682	2.1542	0.1714
Lampung	0.5448***	0.1824	0.7526	0.1843
West Java	0.4798***	0.1211	0.6332	0.1220
Central Java	1.5063***	0.1316	1.6922	0.1334
Yogyakarta	0.9029***	0.1502	1.0662	0.1516
East Java	0.5867***	0.1288	0.7856	0.1304
Bali	2.0312***	0.1530	2.2040	0.1548
West Nusa Tenggara	0.8007***	0.1592	1.0421	0.1618
South Kalimantan	1.2534***	0.1733	1.4759	0.1755
South Sulawesi	0.1337	0.1733	0.4203	0.1754
Pseudo R-squared	0.0690		0.0820	
LR $\chi^2_{(19)}$	694.76		824.44	
p	0.0000		0.0000	
N	7,178		7,178	

Source: Author calculation based on IFLS data

Note: Standard errors are shown in parentheses, * Denotes statistical significance at 10% level, ** Denotes statistical significance at 5% level, *** Denotes statistical significance at 1% level.

Table A3.6: Ordered Logit Models of Children Food Consumption Perception

	Without lnpce		With lnpce	
	Coefficient	Std. error	Coefficient	Std. error
FS Program Participation(dummy, participate=1)	-0.2989***	0.0947	-0.1057	0.0970
lnpce			0.7464***	0.0662
Age of HH Head (in years)	-0.0156***	0.0042	-0.0178***	0.0043
Male HH Head (dummy, male=1)	0.3271	0.2218	0.4115*	0.2205
Education of HH Head (in years)	0.0783***	0.0080	0.0482***	0.0085
Urban (dummy, urban=1)	0.1843**	0.0877	0.0839	0.0892
North Sumatra	-0.0856	0.2210	0.2961	0.2252
West Sumatra	-0.3443	0.2463	-0.0590	0.2479
Riau	-0.0032	0.6085	0.0545	0.6071
South Sumatra	0.5591**	0.2528	0.8692***	0.2554
Lampung	0.6350***	0.2464	0.9269***	0.2500
West Java	0.5933***	0.1817	0.8490***	0.1839
Central Java	1.7091***	0.1970	2.0047***	0.2011
Yogyakarta	0.7594***	0.2439	0.9592***	0.2456
East Java	0.6033***	0.1941	0.9227***	0.1977
Bali	1.7913***	0.2223	2.1094***	0.2271
West Nusa Tenggara	1.0849***	0.2218	1.4665***	0.2271
South Kalimantan	0.9320***	0.2486	1.2971***	0.2527
South Sulawesi	-0.0394	0.2429	0.3821	0.2456
Pseudo R-squared	0.0747		0.0999	
LR $\chi^2_{(19)}$	381.84		509.87	
P	0.0000		0.0000	
N	7,178		7,178	

Source: Author calculation based on IFLS data

Note: *Standard errors are shown in parentheses, * Denotes statistical significance at 10% level, ** Denotes statistical significance at 5% level, *** Denotes statistical significance at 1% level.*

Table A4.1: Household Expenditures Based on Women's Social Capital

	Community Meeting Yes	Community Meeting No	PKK Yes	PKK No	Posyandu Yes	Posyandu No
Staple Foods	11.8644	14.9306	11.4699	14.9970	14.1728	14.5093
	(9.6913)	(11.5959)	(9.5391)	(11.5949)	(10.5509)	(11.5887)
Vegetables	6.4917	6.2737	6.4427	6.2836	6.4278	6.2748
	(4.9795)	(4.8554)	(4.8772)	(4.8758)	(4.5957)	(4.9538)
Meat and Fish	9.4345	9.8598	9.6791	9.8121	9.8514	9.7735
	(6.5642)	(7.0716)	(6.5046)	(7.0826)	(6.5442)	(7.1179)
Dairy Products	3.3343	2.8937	3.4695	2.8692	3.6239	2.7751
	(3.6548)	(3.6169)	(3.7203)	(3.6007)	(4.3420)	(3.3688)
Alcohol and Tobacco Goods	4.1229	5.2879	4.1365	5.2820	5.2921	5.0436
	(5.5034)	(6.6598)	(5.5380)	(6.6522)	(6.1839)	(6.5882)
Nonfood Expenditures	46.2447	41.2476	46.4272	41.2269	41.4700	42.2262
	(17.5704)	(17.1814)	(17.5660)	(17.1751)	(16.6440)	(17.5357)

Source: Author calculation based on IFLS data

Note: Standard deviation are shown in parentheses

Table A4.2: The Effects of Women's Assets on Budget Share of Vegetables, Meat and Fish, Dairy Products, and Alcohol and Tobacco Goods Expenditures

	Vegetables	Dairy Products	Meat and Fish	Alcohol and Tobacco Goods
Farm Household (dummy, farm = 1)	0.2783*** (0.1062)	-0.0769 (0.0819)	0.5304*** (0.1548)	-0.4911*** (0.1430)
Urban Household (dummy, urban = 1)	-0.2632** (0.1060)	0.1872** (0.0817)	-0.8183*** (0.1545)	-0.4795*** (0.1428)
Age of HH Head (in years)	-0.0059 (0.0053)	0.0079* (0.0041)	0.0118 (0.0078)	-0.0606*** (0.0072)
Educ of HH Head (in years)	-0.0121 (0.0117)	0.0397*** (0.0090)	0.0432** (0.0171)	-0.0878*** (0.0158)
Educ of Spouse (in years)	-0.0110 (0.0119)	0.0593*** (0.0091)	-0.0327* (0.0173)	-0.0841*** (0.0160)
HH Head Employment (dummy, working = 1)	0.2324* (0.1399)	0.0689 (0.1079)	-0.3274 (0.2040)	0.3897*** (0.1885)
Under 6 years	0.0377 (0.0648)	0.6698*** (0.0500)	0.2238** (0.0945)	0.1845** (0.0873)
6 - 14 years	-0.0768* (0.0447)	-0.1934*** (0.0345)	0.1220* (0.0652)	-0.1447** (0.0603)
15 - 59 years (male)	-0.0049 (0.0392)	-0.0909*** (0.0302)	0.0473 (0.0572)	0.3929*** (0.0528)
15 - 59 years (female)	-0.0049 (0.0412)	-0.0823*** (0.0317)	0.0195 (0.0600)	-0.2152*** (0.0554)
60 years and over (male)	0.3707*** (0.1423)	0.0159 (0.1097)	0.2992 (0.2075)	0.2668 (0.1917)
60 years and over (female)	-0.0387 (0.1119)	-0.0169 (0.0863)	-0.0559 (0.1631)	-0.2199 (0.1507)
Ln Expenditure	-0.5587*** (0.0723)	0.2140*** (0.0558)	-0.1422 (0.1055)*	-0.6744*** (0.0974)
Dummy 2000	-0.1169 (0.1131)	0.2993*** (0.0872)	0.2982 (0.1649)	1.4848*** (0.1523)
Dummy 2007	-1.3505*** (0.1248)	-0.0864 (0.0962)	-1.2013*** (0.1819)	2.1907*** (0.1680)
Share of Asset	0.0157* (0.0092)	0.0102 (0.0071)	0.0732*** (0.0134)	-0.0656*** (0.0124)
Constant	14.6900***	-1.1617	10.5703***	18.7770***

	(0.9732)	(0.7503)	(1.4188)	(1.3108)
R-square	0.0417	0.0470	0.0198	0.0595
F	30.44	34.51	14.17	44.26
P	0.0000	0.0000	0.0000	0.0000
N	11221	11221	11221	11221

Source: Author calculation based on IFLS data

Note: *Standard errors are shown in parentheses, * Denotes statistical significance at 10% level, ** Denotes statistical significance at 5% level, *** Denotes statistical significance at 1% level.*

Table A4.3: The Effects of Women's Assets on Budget Share of Education, Medical, and Non-food Expenditures

	Medical	Education	Nonfood
Farm Household	-0.1482	0.2248	-2.2499***
(dummy, farm = 1)	(0.1137)	(0.2638)	(0.3447)
Urban Household	-0.1233	0.7812***	4.1432***
(dummy, urban = 1)	(0.1139)	(0.2642)	(0.3452)
Age of HH Head (in years)	0.0163***	0.0935***	0.0392**
	(0.0057)	(0.0133)	(0.0174)
Educ of HH Head (in years)	0.0094	0.2382***	0.1164***
	(0.0123)	(0.0284)	(0.0371)
Educ of Spouse (in years)	0.0109	0.1452***	0.2695***
	(0.0127)	(0.0295)	(0.0385)
HH Head Employment	-0.9458***	2.1861***	-1.4128***
(dummy, working = 1)	(0.1504)	(0.3488)	(0.4557)
Under 6 years	0.2281***	-2.2806***	-2.1881***
	(0.0695)	(0.1611)	(0.2105)
6 - 14 years	-0.2553***	1.1725***	-0.4778***
	(0.0480)	(0.1113)	(0.1455)
15 - 59 years (male)	-0.1180***	0.3377***	-0.8109***
	(0.0412)	(0.0955)	(0.1248)
15 - 59 years (female)	-0.1018***	0.5267***	0.0661***
	(0.0433)	(0.1005)	(0.1313)
60 years and over (male)	0.2924**	-3.9309***	-2.0063***
	(0.1526)	(0.3540)	(0.4625)
60 years and over (female)	0.1680	-0.4567	-0.0432
	(0.1198)	(0.2779)	(0.3631)
Ln Expenditure	0.6132***	-0.1841	7.6216***
	(0.0754)	(0.1749)	(0.2285)
Dummy 2000	0.0327	-0.6825***	-2.6676***
	(0.1216)	(0.2821)	(0.3670)
Dummy 2007	-0.2581*	-0.4984	-4.0926***
	(0.1342)	(0.3112)	(0.4048)
Share of Assets	-0.0164	0.0494***	0.0478***
	(0.0097)	(0.0225)	(0.0294)
Constant	-6.5737***	-0.4391	-67.9058***
	(1.0466)	(2.4279)	(3.1580)

R-square	0.0237	0.0804	0.2391
F	16.99	61.24	220.06
P	0.0000	0.0000	0.0000
N	11221	11221	11221

Source: Author calculation based on IFLS data

Note: *Standard errors are shown in parentheses, * Denotes statistical significance at 10% level, ** Denotes statistical significance at 5% level, *** Denotes statistical significance at 1% level.*

Table A4.4: The Effects of Women's Shares of Savings on Budget Share of Vegetables, Dairy Products, Alcohol and Tobacco Goods, and Nonfood Expenditures

	Vegetables	Dairy Products	Alcohol and Tobacco Goods	Nonfood
Farm Household (dummy, farm = 1)	0.3144** (0.1294)	-0.0640 (0.1031)	-0.2721 (0.1951)	-2.8151*** (0.4287)
Urban Household (dummy, urban = 1)	-0.5263*** (0.1303)	0.1910* (0.1038)	-0.2791 (0.1964)	2.8649*** (0.4316)
Age of HH Head (in years)	0.0013 (0.0065)	0.0048 (0.0052)	-0.0644*** (0.0098)	0.0201 (0.0215)
Educ of HH Head (in years)	-0.0138 (0.0136)	0.0313*** (0.0109)	-0.0822*** (0.0206)	0.1525*** (0.0452)
Educ of Spouse (in years)	-0.0127 (0.0144)	0.0562*** (0.0114)	-0.0973*** (0.0216)	0.2708*** (0.0476)
HH Head Employment (dummy, working = 1)	0.3550** (0.1717)	0.0681 (0.1368)	0.5147** (0.2588)	-0.8741 (0.5688)
Under 6 years	-0.0914 (0.0816)	0.5994*** (0.0650)	0.1697 (0.1231)	-2.1999*** (0.2705)
6 - 14 years	-0.0795 (0.0556)	-0.2167*** (0.0443)	-0.2560*** (0.0838)	-0.4743*** (0.1841)
15 - 59 years (male)	-0.0636 (0.0438)	-0.0873** (0.0349)	0.3928*** (0.0660)	-0.4348*** (0.1451)
15 - 59 years (female)	0.0059 (0.0462)	-0.0530 (0.0368)	-0.1725** (0.0697)	0.3353** (0.1532)
60 years and over (male)	0.3693** (0.1646)	0.0834 (0.1312)	0.2714 (0.2483)	-1.1473** (0.5455)
60 years and over (female)	0.0720 (0.1313)	-0.0168 (0.1047)	-0.3899** (0.1980)	0.4620 (0.4352)
Dummy Year 2000	-0.1499 (0.2673)	0.2783 (0.2130)	1.2604*** (0.4031)	-2.5310*** (0.8858)
Dummy Year 2007	-1.3886*** (0.2742)	-0.0694 (0.2185)	1.7940*** (0.4135)	-3.5870*** (0.9086)
Ln Expenditure	-0.5827*** (0.0921)	0.1805** (0.0734)	-0.5363 (0.1389)	7.5523*** (0.3053)
Share of Shavings	0.0296** (0.0116)	0.0323*** (0.0093)	-0.0518*** (0.0175)	0.0609 (0.0385)

Constant	14.9593***	-0.3941	16.3625***	-63.0166
	(1.2741)	(1.0153)	(1.9211)	(4.2218)
R-square	0.0557	0.0473	0.0519	0.2397
F	24.77	20.84	22.97	132.36
P	0.0000	0.0000	0.0000	0.0000
N	9634	9634	9634	9634

Source: Author calculation based on IFLS data

Note: *Standard errors are shown in parentheses, * Denotes statistical significance at 10% level, ** Denotes statistical significance at 5% level, *** Denotes statistical significance at 1% level.*

Table A4.5: The Effects of Women's Shares of Jewelry on Budget Share of Vegetables, Dairy Products, Alcohol and Tobacco Goods, and Nonfood Expenditures

	Vegetables	Dairy Products	Alcohol and Tobacco Goods	Nonfood
Farm Household	0.3352***	-0.1208	-0.3218*	-2.4039***
(dummy, farm = 1)	(0.1236)	(0.1012)	(0.1795)	(0.4133)
Urban Household	-0.2529***	0.0618	-0.3723**	3.1193***
(dummy, urban = 1)	(0.1245)	(0.1019)	(0.1809)	(0.4163)
Age of HH Head (in	-0.0017	0.0098*	-0.0580***	0.0185
years)	(0.0063)	(0.0052)	(0.0092)	(0.0211)
Educ of HH Head (in	-0.0083	0.0403***	-0.0911***	0.1610***
years)	(0.0134)	(0.0109)	(0.0194)	(0.0447)
Educ of Spouse (in years)	-0.0121	0.0576***	-0.0780***	0.2355***
	(0.0137)	(0.0112)	(0.0200)	(0.0460)
HH Head Employment	0.4158**	0.0212	0.4814**	-1.1352**
(dummy, working = 1)	(0.1664)	(0.1362)	(0.2417)	(0.5564)
Under 6 years	-0.0301	0.6988***	0.1438	-2.4775***
	(0.0796)	(0.0651)	(0.1155)	(0.2660)
6 - 14 years	-0.0062	-0.1889***	-0.1560**	-0.5919***
	(0.0533)	(0.0436)	(0.0774)	(0.1782)
15 - 59 years (male)	-0.0325	-0.0569	0.4057***	-0.5229***
	(0.0441)	(0.0361)	(0.0641)	(0.1475)
15 - 59 years (female)	-0.0156	-0.1100***	-0.1776***	0.3837**
	(0.0464)	(0.0380)	(0.0674)	(0.1552)
60 years and over (male)	0.3264**	0.0957	0.2842	-1.4621***
	(0.1621)	(0.1327)	(0.2355)	(0.5420)
60 years and over (female)	0.0739	-0.0980	-0.2074	0.5351
	(0.1276)	(0.1044)	(0.1853)	(0.4265)
Dummy Year 2000	-0.1332	0.3042**	1.3317***	-2.4391***
	(0.1552)	(0.1270)	(0.2254)	(0.5188)
Dummy Year 2007	-1.2862***	-0.0442	1.9219***	-3.8484***
	(0.1673)	(0.1369)	(0.2429)	(0.5592)
Ln Expenditure	-0.5726***	0.1664**	-0.6982***	7.9131***
	(0.0877)	(0.0717)	(0.1273)	(0.2931)
Share of Jewelry	0.0185**	0.0179**	-0.0387***	0.0694**
	(0.0090)	(0.0074)	(0.0131)	(0.0301)

Constant	14.4765***	-0.4686	18.1604***	-67.5996***
	(1.1792)	(0.9649)	(1.7126)	(3.9426)
R-square	0.0459	0.0446	0.0561	0.2409
F	22.19	21.51	27.43	146.36
P	0.0000	0.0000	0.0000	0.0000
N	8956	8956	8956	8956

Source: Author calculation based on IFLS data

Note: Standard errors are shown in parentheses, * Denotes statistical significance at 10% level, ** Denotes statistical significance at 5% level, *** Denotes statistical significance at 1% level.

Table A4.6: The Effects of Women's Shares of Nonagricultural Land on Budget Share of Vegetables, Dairy Products, Alcohol and Tobacco Goods, and Nonfood Expenditures

	Vegetables	Dairy Products	Alcohol and Tobacco Goods	Nonfood
Farm Household (dummy, farm = 1)	0.2206* (0.1230)	-0.1337 (0.0951)	-0.3735** (0.1820)	-2.0070*** (0.4072)
Urban Household (dummy, urban = 1)	-0.4465*** (0.1250)	0.1141 (0.0967)	-0.3409* (0.1850)	3.5821*** (0.4137)
Age of HH Head (in years)	-0.0015 (0.0063)	0.0064 (0.0048)	-0.0470*** (0.0093)	0.0104 (0.0207)
Educ of HH Head (in years)	-0.0159 (0.0130)	0.0384*** (0.0101)	-0.1098*** (0.0192)	0.1827*** (0.0431)
Educ of Spouse (in years)	-0.0092 (0.0137)	0.0505*** (0.0106)	-0.0848*** (0.0203)	0.2690*** (0.0453)
HH Head Employment (dummy, working = 1)	0.3518** (0.1622)	-0.0117 (0.1255)	0.6014** (0.2401)	-1.3934*** (0.5370)
Under 6 years	-0.0209 (0.0774)	0.6499*** (0.0599)	0.2280** (0.1145)	-2.3842*** (0.2562)
6 - 14 years	-0.0652 (0.0527)	-0.1863*** (0.0407)	-0.1592** (0.0780)	-0.5463*** (0.1744)
15 - 59 years (male)	-0.0469 (0.0419)	-0.0783** (0.0324)	0.4266*** (0.0621)	-0.4985*** (0.1388)
15 - 59 years (female)	-0.0065 (0.0441)	-0.0648* (0.0341)	-0.2193*** (0.0653)	0.3070** (0.1461)
60 years and over (male)	0.3881** (0.1583)	0.0217 (0.1224)	0.1813 (0.2343)	-1.2872** (0.5240)
60 years and over (female)	0.0856 (0.1251)	-0.0713 (0.0968)	-0.1696 (0.1852)	0.2029 (0.4142)
Dummy Year 2000	-0.3402 (0.2263)	0.2937* (0.1750)	1.1760*** (0.3349)	0.0132 (0.7490)
Dummy Year 2007	-1.5493*** (0.2373)	-0.0254 (0.1835)	1.6855*** (0.3511)	-1.0981 (0.7854)
Ln Expenditure	-0.5788*** (0.0865)	0.1740*** (0.0669)	-0.6015*** (0.1280)	7.8275*** 80.2864)
Share of Non-Ag Land	-0.0039	0.0049	-0.0173	0.1067***

	(0.0107)	(0.0083)	(0.0159)	(0.0355)
Constant	16.5180***	-0.2719	16.4297	-68.7989
	(0.8003)	(0.9171)	(1.7549)	(3.9253)
R-square	0.0536	0.0445	0.0499	0.2489
F	26.66	21.90	24.73	155.93
P	0.0000	0.0000	0.0000	0.0000
N	10231	10231	10231	10231

Source: Author calculation based on IFLS data
Note: Standard errors are shown in parentheses, * Denotes statistical significance at 10% level, ** Denotes statistical significance at 5% level, *** Denotes statistical significance at 1% level.

Table A4.7: The Effects of Women's Shares of Livestock on Budget Share of Vegetables, Dairy Products, Alcohol and Tobacco Goods, and Nonfood Expenditures

	Vegetables	Dairy Products	Alcohol and Tobacco Goods	Nonfood
Farm Household	0.2051	-0.0646	-0.7794***	-1.8310***
(dummy, farm = 1)	(0.1458)	(0.1266)	(0.2361)	(0.5352)
Urban Household	-0.2305	0.1573	-0.4581*	3.6078***
(dummy, urban = 1)	(0.1500)	(0.1303)	(0.2429)	(0.5505)
Age of HH Head (in	0.0108	0.0079	-0.0703***	0.0257
years)	(0.0073)	(0.0064)	(0.0119)	(0.0269)
Educ of HH Head (in	0.0004	0.0394***	-0.1026***	0.1689***
years)	(0.0156)	(0.0135)	(0.0252)	(0.0571)
Educ of Spouse (in years)	-0.0152	0.0517***	-0.1055***	0.2869***
	(0.0161)	(0.0140)	(0.0261)	(0.0592)
HH Head Employment	0.3941**	-0.1109	0.2798	0.1069
(dummy, working = 1)	(0.1984)	(0.1723)	(0.3213)	(0.7282)
Under 6 years	-0.1462	0.7510***	0.2411	-2.4596***
	(0.0951)	(0.0826)	(0.1539)	(0.3489)
6 - 14 years	-0.0689	-0.2427***	-0.1662	-0.3371
	(0.0638)	(0.0554)	(0.1033)	(0.1937)
15 - 59 years (male)	0.0148	-0.0997**	0.4121***	-1.0399***
	(0.0485)	(0.0421)	(0.0786)	(0.2343)
15 - 59 years (female)	0.0150	-0.0497	-0.1600*	0.4704**
	(0.0511)	(0.0443)	(0.0827)	(0.1874)
60 years and over (male)	0.0459	-0.0539	0.1874	-1.0841
	(0.1802)	(0.1565)	(0.2918)	(0.6614)
60 years and over (female)	-0.0417	0.1354	-0.1774	0.5712
	(0.1450)	(0.1259)	(0.2348)	(0.5323)
Dummy Year 2000	-0.3439	0.5946	2.2785***	-3.0991*
	(0.4543)	(0.3945)	(0.7356)	(1.6674)
Dummy Year 2007	-1.4356***	-0.0735	1.4449***	-0.9909
	(0.2658)	(0.2308)	(0.4303)	(0.9755)
Ln Expenditure	-0.7374***	0.3588***	-0.3942**	7.4766***
	(0.1037)	(0.0901)	(0.1680)	(0.3808)
Share of Livestock	0.0276	0.0183	-0.0873***	0.1523*

	(0.0206)	(0.0179)	(0.0334)	(0.0757)
Constant	16.4386***	-2.9387**	15.4293***	-66.5786***
	(1.4171)	(1.2306)	(2.2945)	(5.2014)
R	0.0768	0.0561	0.0571	0.2367
F	22.15	15.81	16.12	82.56
P	0.0000	0.0000	0.0000	0.0000
N	6730	6730	6730	6730

Source: Author calculation based on IFLS data

Note: Standard errors are shown in parentheses, * Denotes statistical significance at 10% level, ** Denotes statistical significance at 5% level, *** Denotes statistical significance at 1% level.

Table A4.8: The Effects of Women's Shares of the House on Budget Share of Vegetables, Dairy Products, Alcohol and Tobacco Goods, and Nonfood Expenditures

	Vegetables	Dairy Products	Alcohol and Tobacco Goods	Nonfood
Farm Household (dummy, farm = 1)	0.0078** (0.0091)	-0.0131 (0.0973)	-0.3021* (0.1774)	-2.7699*** (0.4176)
Urban Household (dummy, urban = 1)	-0.2157* (0.1258)	0.0790 (0.0981)	-0.2952* (0.1788)	3.4447*** (0.4210)
Age of HH Head (in years)	0.0009 (0.0067)	0.0103** (0.0052)	-0.0587*** (0.0095)	0.0043 (0.0223)
Educ of HH Head (in years)	-0.0203 (0.0136)	0.0397*** (0.0106)	-0.0961*** (0.0194)	0.1609*** (0.0456)
Educ of Spouse (in years)	-0.0077 (0.0140)	0.0635*** (0.0109)	-0.0948*** (0.0199)	0.3055*** (0.0469)
HH Head Employment (dummy, working = 1)	0.3256** (0.1669)	0.1227 (0.1301)	-0.0961* (0.0194)	-1.7308*** (0.5584)
Under 6 years	0.0714 (0.0783)	0.6445*** (0.0610)	0.2148* (0.1113)	-2.5649*** (0.2619)
6 - 14 years	-0.0218 (0.0538)	-0.1802*** (0.0419)	-0.2419*** (0.0764)	-0.4145*** (0.1799)
15 - 59 years (male)	-0.0128 (0.0442)	-0.0877** (0.0345)	0.3740*** (0.0629)	-0.5485*** (0.1481)
15 - 59 years (female)	-0.0439 (0.0479)	-0.0772** (0.0373)	-0.1917*** (0.0680)	0.3073* (0.1601)
60 years and over (male)	0.2635 (0.1728)	-0.0113 (0.1347)	0.2462 (0.2457)	-1.2875** (0.5783)
60 years and over (female)	0.0266 (0.1391)	-0.0001 (0.1085)	-0.0377 (0.1978)	-0.2724 (0.4655)
Dummy Year 2000	0.0194 (0.1390)	0.3770*** (0.1084)	1.3049*** (0.1976)	-2.1798*** (0.4650)
Dummy Year 2007	-1.2033*** (0.1496)	0.0671 (0.1167)	2.0456*** (0.2127)	-3.2249*** (0.5008)
Ln Expenditure	-0.5342*** (0.0857)	0.2480*** (0.0668)	-0.6416*** (0.1218)	7.5826*** (0.2868)
Share of House	0.0078 (0.0091)	-0.0193*** (0.0071)	-0.0478*** (0.0130)	0.1575*** (0.0306)

Constant	13.8399***	-1.5142*	18.0028***	-64.2240***
	(1.1704)	(0.9126)	(1.6639)	(3.9165)
R	0.0444	0.0482	0.0562	0.2409
F	21.87	23.83	28.01	149.32
P	0.0000	0.0000	0.0000	0.0000
N	8229	8229	8229	8229

Source: Author calculation based on IFLS data

Note: *Standard errors are shown in parentheses, * Denotes statistical significance at 10% level, ** Denotes statistical significance at 5% level, *** Denotes statistical significance at 1% level.*

Table A4.9: The Effects of Women's Participation in Community Meetings on Budget Share of Vegetables, Dairy Products, Alcohol and Tobacco Goods, and Nonfood Expenditures

	Vegetables	Dairy Products	Alcohol and Tobacco Goods	Nonfood
Farm Household (dummy, farm = 1)	0.2229 (0.1092)	-0.0836 (0.0838)	-0.2566* (0.1476)	-2.7582*** (0.3588)
Urban Household (dummy, urban = 1)	-0.1885* (0.1103)	0.1741** (0.0846)	-0.5927*** (0.1490)	3.7674*** (0.3624)
Age of HH Head (in years)	-0.0072 (0.0055)	0.0076* (0.0042)	-0.0673*** (0.0075)	0.0654*** (0.0182)
Educ of HH Head (in years)	-0.0030 (0.0120)	0.0471*** (0.0092)	-0.0695*** (0.0163)	0.1114*** (0.0396)
Educ of Spouse (in years)	-0.0180 (0.0123)	0.0619*** (0.0094)	-0.1048*** (0.0163)	0.3404*** (0.0403)
HH Head Employment (dummy, working = 1)	0.1761 (0.1490)	0.0161 (0.1143)	0.3103 (0.2013)	-0.9528* (0.4895)
Under 6 years	0.0917 (0.0679)	0.6612*** (0.0521)	0.0855 (0.0917)	-2.0012*** (0.2230)
6 - 14 years	-0.0370 (0.0463)	-0.1793*** (0.0356)	-0.2191*** (0.0626)	-0.2555* (0.1523)
15 - 59 years (male)	-0.0930** (0.0405)	-0.0950*** (0.0311)	0.4985*** (0.0548)	-0.9576*** (0.1332)
15 - 59 years (female)	-0.0381 (0.0427)	-0.0700** (0.0328)	-0.1056* (0.0577)	-0.0225 (0.3812)
60 years and over (male)	0.3411** (0.1465)	0.0176 (0.1124)	0.5130*** (0.1979)	-2.7116*** (0.4814)
60 years and over (female)	-0.1154 (0.1160)	-0.0576 (0.0890)	0.1979 (0.1568)	-0.2010 (0.3812)
Ln Expenditure	-0.7023*** (0.0610)	0.1390*** (0.0468)	-0.0245 (0.0824)	4.9820*** (0.2005)
Village Meeting	0.5684*** (0.1173)	0.0559 (0.0900)	-1.0812*** (0.1585)	2.0424*** (0.3854)
Constant	16.2416*** (0.7985)	0.1412 (0.6126)	10.1299*** (1.0790)	-27.9433*** (2.6238)

R-square	0.0337	0.0459	0.0423	0.1951
F	26.13	36.04	33.05	181.57
P	0.0000	0.0000	0.0000	0.0000
N	10503	10503	10503	10503

Source: Author calculation based on IFLS data

Note: *Standard errors are shown in parentheses, * Denotes statistical significance at 10% level, ** Denotes statistical significance at 5% level, *** Denotes statistical significance at 1% level.*

Table A4.10: The Effects of Women's Participation in the PKK on Budget Share of Vegetables, Dairy Products, Alcohol and Tobacco Goods, and Nonfood Expenditures

	Vegetables	Dairy Products	Alcohol and Tobacco Goods	Nonfood
Farm Household	0.2376**	-0.0847	-0.2833***	-2.7045***
(dummy, farm = 1)	(0.1091)	(0.0837)	(0.1475)	(0.3587)
Urban Household	-0.1823	0.1712**	0.0779***	3.7912***
(dummy, urban = 1)	(0.1103)	(0.0846)	(0.0918)	(0.3624)
Age of HH Head (in	-0.0065	0.0075*	-0.0684***	0.0678***
years)	(0.0055)	(0.0042)	(0.0075)	(0.0182)
Educ of HH Head (in	-0.0056	0.0462***	-0.0642***	0.1023***
years)	(0.0121)	(0.0093)	(0.0163)	(0.0397)
Educ of Spouse (in years)	-0.0173	0.0611***	-0.1055***	0.3429***
	(0.0123)	(0.0094)	(0.0166)	(0.0403)
HH Head Employment	0.1848	0.0147	0.2950	-0.9209*
(dummy, working = 1)	(0.1490)	(0.1143)	(0.2013)	(0.4896)
Under 6 years	0.0952	0.6631***	0.0779	-1.9889***
	(0.0679)	(0.0521)	(0.0918)	(0.2231)
6 - 14 years	-0.0404	-0.1790***	-0.2130***	-0.2679*
	(0.0463)	(0.0355)	(0.0626)	(0.1523)
15 - 59 years (male)	-0.0953**	-0.0950***	0.5028***	-0.9661***
	(0.0405)	(0.0311)	(0.0548)	(0.1332)
15 - 59 years (female)	-0.0312	-0.0691**	-0.1188**	0.0021
	(0.0427)	(0.0328)	(0.0577)	(0.1404)
60 years and over (male)	0.3414**	0.0209	0.5108***	-2.7118***
	(0.1465)	(0.1124)	(0.1980)	(0.4816)
60 years and over (female)	-0.1222	-0.0592	-0.0178	-0.2252
	(0.1161)	(0.0890)	(0.1568)	(0.3814)
Ln Expenditure	-0.6972***	0.1391***	-0.0339	5.0003***
	(0.0610)	(0.0468)	(0.0824)	(0.2005)
PKK	0.4832***	0.1501*	-0.9708***	1.6969
	(0.1156)	(0.0886)	(0.1562)	(0.3798)
Constant	16.1477***	0.1385	10.3053***	-28.2832***
	(0.7984)	(0.6123)	(1.0789)	(2.6236)
R-square	0.0331	0.0461	0.0415	0.1945

F	25.68	36.22	32.46	180.85
P	0.0000	0.0000	0.0000	0.0000
N	10503	10503	10503	10503

Source: Author calculation based on IFLS data
Note: Standard errors are shown in parentheses, * Denotes statistical significance at 10% level, ** Denotes statistical significance at 5% level, *** Denotes statistical significance at 1% level.

Table A4.11: The Effects of Women's Participation in POSYANDU on Budget Share of Vegetables, Dairy Products, Alcohol and Tobacco Goods, and Nonfood Expenditures

	Vegetables	Dairy Products	Alcohol and Tobacco Goods	Nonfood
Farm Household	0.2481**	-0.0859	-0.2953**	-2.6840***
(dummy, farm = 1)	(0.1092)	(0.0837)	(0.1477)	(0.3588)
Urban Household	-0.1653	0.1776**	-0.6393***	3.8552***
(dummy, urban = 1)	(0.1103)	(0.0845)	(0.1491)	(0.3624)
Age of HH Head (in	-0.0056	0.0083**	-0.0714***	0.0729***
years)	(0.0055)	(0.0042)	(0.0075)	(0.0182)
Educ of HH Head (in	-0.0024	0.0473***	-0.0710***	0.1142***
years)	(0.0121)	(0.0092)	(0.0163)	(0.0396)
Educ of Spouse (in years)	-0.0137	0.0617***	-0.1117***	0.3537***
	(0.0122)	(0.0094)	(0.0166)	(0.0402)
HH Head Employment	0.1953	0.0166	0.2766	-0.8889*
(dummy, working = 1)	(0.1491)	(0.1142)	(0.2015)	(0.4898)
Under 6 years	0.0689	0.5937***	0.2545**	-2.3041***
	(0.0758)	(0.0581)	(0.1025)	(0.2492)
6 - 14 years	-0.0422	-0.1762***	-0.2162***	-0.2619*
	(0.0464)	(0.0356)	(0.0627)	(0.1525)
15 - 59 years (male)	-0.0967**	-0.0949***	0.5044***	-0.9689***
	(0.0406)	(0.0311)	(0.0549)	(0.1333)
15 - 59 years (female)	-0.0324	-0.0687**	-0.1180**	0.0007
	(0.0428)	(0.0328)	(0.0578)	(0.1405)
60 years and over (male)	0.3259**	0.0153	0.5438***	-2.7695***
	(0.1466)	(0.1123)	(0.1982)	(0.4817)
60 years and over (female)	-0.1188	-0.0618	-0.0173	-0.2265
	(0.1162)	(0.0890)	(0.1570)	(0.3816)
Ln Expenditure	-0.6946***	0.1419***	-0.0432	5.0168***
	(0.0611)	(0.0468)	(0.0826)	(0.2006)
POSYANDU	0.0665	0.2344***	-0.5653***	1.0108***
	(0.1178)	(0.0902)	(0.1592)	(0.3869)
Constant	16.0929***	0.0434	10.5731***	-28.7597
	(0.8002)	(0.6130)	(1.0817)	(2.6289)
R-square	0.0316	0.0465	0.0392	0.1935

F	24.42	36.51	30.53	179.69
P	0.0000	0.0000	0.0000	0.0000
N	10503	10503	10503	10503

Source: Author calculation based on IFLS data

Note: *Standard errors are shown in parentheses, * Denotes statistical significance at 10% level, ** Denotes statistical significance at 5% level, *** Denotes statistical significance at 1% level.*

Development Economics and Policy

Series edited by Franz Heidhues, Joachim von Braun and Manfred Zeller

Band 1 Andrea Fadani: Agricultural Price Policy and Export and Food Production in Cameroon. A Farming Systems Analysis of Pricing Policies. The Case of Coffee-Based Farming Systems. 1999.

Band 2 Heike Michelsen: Auswirkungen der Währungsunion auf den Strukturanpassungsprozeß der Länder der afrikanischen Franc-Zone. 1995.

Band 3 Stephan Bea: Direktinvestitionen in Entwicklungsländern. Auswirkungen von Stabilisierungsmaßnahmen und Strukturreformen in Mexiko. 1995.

Band 4 Franz Heidhues / François Kamajou: Agricultural Policy Analysis – Proceedings of an International Seminar, held at the University of Dschang, Cameroon on May 26 and 27 1994, funded by the European Union under the Science and Technology Program (STD). 1996.

Band 5 Elke M. Förster: Protection or Liberalization? A Policy Analysis of the Korean Beef Sector. 1996.

Band 6 Gertrud Schrieder: The Role of Rural Finance for Food Security of the Poor in Cameroon. 1996.

Band 7 Nestor R. Ahoyo Adjovi: Economie des Systèmes de Production intégrant la Culture de Riz au Sud du Bénin: Potentialités, Contraintes et Perspectives. 1996.

Band 8 Jenny Müller: Income Distribution in the Agricultural Sector of Thailand. Empirical Analysis and Policy Options. 1996.

Band 9 Michael Brüntrup: Agricultural Price Policy and its Impact on Production, Income, Employment and the Adoption of Innovations. A Farming Systems Based Analysis of Cotton Policy in Northern Benin. 1997.

Band 10 Justin Bomda: Déterminants de l'Epargne et du Crédit, et leurs Implications pour le Développement du Système Financier Rural au Cameroun. 1998.

Band 11 John M. Msuya: Nutrition Improvement Projects in Tanzania: Implementation, Determinants of Performance, and Policy Implications. 1998.

Band 12 Andreas Neef: Auswirkungen von Bodenrechtswandel auf Ressourcennutzung und wirtschaftliches Verhalten von Kleinbauern in Niger und Benin. 1999.

Band 13 Susanna Wolf (ed.): The Future of EU-ACP Relations. 1999.

Band 14 Franz Heidhues / Gertrud Schrieder (eds.): Romania – Rural Finance in Transition Economies. 2000.

Band 15 Katinka Weinberger: Women's Participation. An Economic Analysis in Rural Chad and Pakistan. 2000.

Band 16 Christof Batzlen: Migration and Economic Development. Remittances and Investments in South Asia: A Case Study of Pakistan. 2000.

Band 17 Matin Qaim: Potential Impacts of Crop Biotechnology in Developing Countries. 2000.

Band 18 Jean Senahoun: Programmes d'ajustement structurel, sécurité alimentaire et durabilité agricole. Une approche d'analyse intégrée, appliquée au Bénin. 2001.

Band 19 Torsten Feldbrügge: Economics of Emergency Relief Management in Developing Countries. With Case Studies on Food Relief in Angola and Mozambique. 2001.

Band 20 Claudia Ringler: Optimal Allocation and Use of Water Resources in the Mekong River Basin: Multi-Country and Intersectoral Analyses. 2001.

Band 21   Arnim Kuhn: Handelskosten und regionale (Des-)Integration. Russlands Agrarmärkte in der Transformation. 2001.

Band 22   Ortrun Anne Gronski: Stock Markets and Economic Growth. Evidence from South Africa. 2001.

Band 23   Patrick Webb / Katinka Weinberger (eds.): Women Farmers. Enhancing Rights, Recognition and Productivity. 2001.

Band 24   Mingzhi Sheng: Lebensmittelkonsum und -konsumtrends in China. Eine empirische Analyse auf der Basis ökonometrischer Nachfragemodelle. 2002.

Band 25   Maria Iskandarani: Economics of Household Water Security in Jordan. 2002.

Band 26   Romeo Bertolini: Telecommunication Services in Sub-Saharan Africa. An Analysis of Access and Use in the Southern Volta Region in Ghana. 2002.

Band 27   Dietrich Müller-Falcke: Use and Impact of Information and Communication Technologies in Developing Countries' Small Businesses. Evidence from Indian Small Scale Industry. 2002.

Band 28   Wolfram Erhardt: Financial Markets for Small Enterprises in Urban and Rural Northern Thailand. Empirical Analysis on the Demand for and Supply of Financial Services, with Particular Emphasis on the Determinants of Credit Access and Borrower Transaction Costs. 2002.

Band 29   Wensheng Wang: The Impact of Information and Communication Technologies on Farm Households in China. 2002.

Band 30   Shyamal K. Chowdhury: Institutional and Welfare Aspects of the Provision and Use of Information and Communication Technologies in the Rural Areas of Bangladesh and Peru. 2002.

Band 31   Annette Luibrand: Transition in Vietnam. Impact of the Rural Reform Process on an Ethnic Minority. 2002.

Band 32   Felix Ankomah Asante: Economic Analysis of Decentralisation in Rural Ghana. 2003.

Band 33   Chodechai Suwanaporn: Determinants of Bank Lending in Thailand: An Empirical Examination for the Years 1992 to 1996. 2003.

Band 34   Abay Asfaw: Costs of Illness, Demand for Medical Care, and the Prospect of Community Health Insurance Schemes in the Rural Areas of Ethiopia. 2003.

Band 35   Gi-Soon Song: The Impact of Information and Communication Technologies (ICTs) on Rural Households. A Holistic Approach Applied to the Case of Lao People's Democratic Re- public. 2003.

Band 36   Daniela Lohlein: An Economic Analysis of Public Good Provision in Rural Russia. The Case of Education and Health Care. 2003.

Band 37   Johannes Woelcke. Bio-Economics of Sustainable Land Management in Uganda. 2003.

Band 38   Susanne M. Ziemek: The Economics of Volunteer Labor Supply. An Application to Countries of a Different Development Level. 2003.

Band 39   Doris Wiesmann: An International Nutrition Index. Concept and Analyses of Food Insecurity and Undernutrition at Country Levels. 2004.

Band 40   Isaac Osei-Akoto: The Economics of Rural Health Insurance. The Effects of Formal and Informal Risk-Sharing Schemes in Ghana. 2004.

Band 41   Yuansheng Jiang: Health Insurance Demand and Health Risk Management in Rural China. 2004.

Band 42 Roukayatou Zimmermann: Biotechnology and Value-added Traits in Food Crops: Relevance for Developing Countries and Economic Analyses. 2004.

Band 43 F. Markus Kaiser: Incentives in Community-based Health Insurance Schemes. 2004.

Band 44 Thomas Herzfeld: *Corruption begets Corruption.* Zur Dynamik und Persistenz der Korruption. 2004.

Band 45 Edilegnaw Wale Zegeye: The Economics of On-Farm Conservation of Crop Diversity in Ethiopia: Incentives, Attribute Preferences and Opportunity Costs of Maintaining Local Varieties of Crops. 2004.

Band 46 Adama Konseiga: Regional Integration Beyond the Traditional Trade Benefits: Labor Mobility contribution. The Case of Burkina Faso and Côte d'Ivoire. 2005.

Band 47 Beyene Tadesse Ferenji: The Impact of Policy Reform and Institutional Transformation on Agricultural Performance. An Economic Study of Ethiopian Agriculture. 2005.

Band 48 Sabine Daude: Agricultural Trade Liberalization in the WTO and Its Poverty Implications. A Study of Rural Households in Northern Vietnam. 2005.

Band 49 Kadir Osman Gyasi: Determinants of Success of Collective Action on Local Commons. An Empirical Analysis of Community-Based Irrigation Management in Northern Ghana. 2005.

Band 50 Borbala E. Balint: Determinants of Commercial Orientation and Sustainability of Agricultural Production of the Individual Farms in Romania. 2006.

Band 51 Pamela Marinda: Effects of Gender Inequality in Resource Ownership and Access on Household Welfare and Food Security in Kenya. A Case Study of West Pokot District. 2006.

Band 52 Charles Palmer: The Outcomes and their Determinants from Community-Company Contracting over Forest Use in Post-Decentralization Indonesia. 2006.

Band 53 Hardwick Tchale: Agricultural Policy and Soil Fertility Management in the Maize-based Smallholder Farming System in Malawi. 2006.

Band 54 John Kedi Mduma: Rural Off-Farm Employment and its Effects on Adoption of Labor Intensive Soil Conserving Measures in Tanzania. 2006.

Band 55 Mareike Meyn: The Impact of EU Free Trade Agreements on Economic Development and Regional Integration in Southern Africa. The Example of EU-SACU Trade Relations. 2006.

Band 56 Clemens Breisinger: Modelling Infrastructure Investments, Growth and Poverty Impact. A Two-Region Computable General Equilibrium Perspective on Vietnam. 2006.

Band 57 Meike Wollni: Coping with the Coffee Crisis. An Analysis of the Production and Marketing Performance of Coffee Farmers in Costa Rica. 2007.

Band 58 Franklin Simtowe: Performance and Impact of Microfinance. Evidence from Joint Liability Lending Programs in Malawi. 2008.

Band 59 Xiangping Jia: Credit Rationing and Institutional Constraint. Evidence from Rural China. 2008.

Band 60 Holger Seebens: The Economics of Gender and the Household in Developing Countries. 2009.

Band 61 Stephan Piotrowski: Land Property Rights and Natural Resource Use. An Analysis of Household Behavior in Rural China. 2009.

Band 62 Sebastian M. Scholz: Rural Development through Carbon Finance. Forestry Projects under the Clean Development Mechanism of the Kyoto Protocol. Assessing Smallholder Participation by Structural Equation Modeling. 2009.

Band 63 Jakob Rupert Friederichsen: Opening Up Knowledge Production through Participatory Research? Agricultural Research for Vietnam's Northern Uplands. 2009.

Band 64 Olivier Ecker: Economics of Micronutrient Malnutrition. The Demand for Nutrients in Sub-Saharan Africa. 2009.

Band 65 Julia Johannsen: Operational Assessment of Monetary Poverty by Proxy Means Tests. 2009

Band 66 Ephraim Nkonya / Nicolas Gerber / Philipp Baumgartner / Joachim von Braun / Alessandro De Pinto / Valerie Graw / Edward Kato / Julia Kloos / Teresa Walter: The Economics of Land Degradation. Toward an Integrated Global Assessment. 2011.

Band 67 S. Idriss Nazaire Houssou: Operational Poverty Targeting by Proxy Means Tests. 2013.

Band 68 Abdul Salam Lodhi: Education, Child Labor and Human Capital Formation in Selected Urban and Rural Settings of Pakistan. 2013.

Band 69 Evita Hanie Pangaribowo: Household Food Consumption, Women´s Asset and Food Policy in Indonesia. 2013.

www.peterlang.de